# ELEMENTAL
# SHAMAN

———◀〇▶———

One Man's Journey
into the Heart of Humanity,
Spirituality & Ecology

Rob Daly

## About the Author

Adventurer and explorer Omar W. Rosales writes extensively on the topic of shamanism. He combines adventure travel with spirituality as he searches the world for spiritual masters in order to convey their messages to humanity. A student of William R. Fowler and Arthur Demarest, Rosales holds an honors degree in anthropology from Vanderbilt University and a law degree from the University of Texas School of Law. A former captain in the Marine Corps, Rosales is an experienced hiker and expedition leader. For photos and other information about the journeys in *Elemental Shaman*, please visit www.elementalshaman.com.

# ELEMENTAL SHAMAN

One Man's Journey
into the Heart of Humanity,
Spirituality & Ecology

## OMAR W. ROSALES

LLEWELLYN PUBLICATIONS
Woodbury, Minnesota

FIRST EDITION
First Printing, 2009

Book design by Rebecca Zins
Cover photo © Pouech/Nonstock/Jupiter Images
Cover design by Lisa Novak
Interior part page map from *The Century Dictionary and Cyclopedia*,
vol. X (1904: The Century Co., New York)
Interior chapter opener roadway photo and part page compass photo
from Comstock Images' *Concepts for Advertising* CD-ROM

Llewellyn is a registered trademark of Llewellyn Worldwide, Ltd.

Library of Congress Cataloging-in-Publication Data
Rosales, Omar W., 1975-
  Elemental shaman : one man's journey into the heart of humanity,
spirituality & ecology / Omar W. Rosales.
    p.    cm.
  ISBN 978-0-7387-1501-8
  1. Shamanism. 2. Shamans. I. Title.
  BF1611.R64 2009
  201´.44—dc22

                              2008050856

Llewellyn Publications
A Division of Llewellyn Worldwide, Ltd.
2143 Wooddale Drive, Dept. 978-0-7387-1501-8
Woodbury, Minnesota 55125-2989, U.S.A.

www.llewellyn.com

Printed in the United States of America

For the woman of my dreams,
the "operator" for keeping me out of trouble,
and the spirit guides.
VTTIVA

# CONTENTS

# Acknowledgments

FIRST AND FOREMOST, I would like to acknowledge and thank the saints, the power of prayer, ancestors, and the gods of good luck, fortune, and chance that have assisted me in this unique journey. Deep spiritual reverence and thanks to His Holiness the 14th Dalai Lama and Quan Yin, who have shifted worldwide consciousness to a deeper, more loving level.

I would like to thank many friends and family for their support. A big thanks goes out to "Dr. Karma"—Dr. Carmen Harra, Ph.D., whose exceptional insight, leadership, and love helped make this dream a reality. Other spiritual friends include Deborah Young, Stacey Anne Wolf, and Sue Hubbard. Special thanks to my first copyeditor, the esteemed Julie Steigerwaldt, for believing in an unknown author and helping me tame my writing. Thanks to Nancy Peske for reading the first version and picking out a winner. Kudos to my wonderful editor at Llewellyn, Carrie Obry.

Thanks to the three wise men of Vanderbilt: William R. Fowler, Arthur Demarest, and Edward Fischer, with a special thanks to Dr. Fowler for being my mentor and smartly allowing me to lose myself in the field of Archaeoreligion. Two professors at the University of Texas School of Law, capable scholars and good human beings: Ernest Young and Loftus Carson III. With another round of thanks to Alen Christenson of BYU who helped me with guides in Guatemala. Also to Sakten Tours in Seattle/Thimphu for arranging my last-minute visas and journey to Bhutan.

"Team Austin"—the outfitters at REI and Whole Earth Provisions—for hiking equipment, boots, food, clothing, and maps. Josh and Sarah at Progress Coffee for allowing me to hijack a table and work for hours on end. Special thanks to Michelle for listening to my dreams while cutting hair and not thinking I was crazy. Whole Foods for snacks and the people of Austin for making it such a great city. And a big thanks to Dr. Rocky Salinas, M.D., for help with last-minute shots and meds. Last, but not least, Jose Santiago "Jim" Solis, a kind mentor and exceptional friend.

Acknowledgments to Michael Harner, who opened up the field of shamanism to Western hearts. As well as to John Edward, James Van Praagh, and Sylvia Brown, who have made spirituality once again mainstream. With two Quetzal chirps to the great Martin Prechtel—Nicolas says he's watching over you.

Thanks to Mom and Dad, who raised me and were patient as I informed them of last-minute (literally) trips to Central America and Asia. My dog, Anya, whose gentle snoring kept me company as I typed long hours into the night. And my brother Andrew, the "Kokopelli" who cheered me up and believed in my wild quests.

With a special thanks to Tabitha Chapman, Marianne Hunter, and Brittany Hunter, the Hermione G., Alice C., and Buffy S. of the web. And, of course, to Professor Robert A. F. Thurman of Columbia University for his tireless efforts and last-minute help with Bhutan.

Deep gratitude to the Earth Mother and Father Sky, the four directions, brother Sage, and Native American guides who assisted and protected me in Arizona.

To the woman of my dreams, who fascinates me with her kindness, warmth, and spirit: I hope to meet you one day so that I may once again hold your hand.

And, finally, to the readers: I profusely thank each and every one of you. For the last four years, this book has been my obsession, joy, and sacred quest. I hope you enjoy it.

OWR
*August 2008*
AUSTIN, TEXAS

# Introduction

IT WAS LATE afternoon when the call came in. My mom's words were erratic. Her voice was shaking, and her panic seemed to convey a deeper, hidden truth.

"The weirdest thing happened to me at school," she began. She had been working at an elementary school for a few years. Every semester was easier as she gained a grasp of her job and her goals, but this year was different. Troubles seemed to follow her around, and she was bothered by feelings of unease. One person in particular gave her feelings of dread. In fact, every incident of lost classroom keys, fighting students, and malfunctioning computer equipment was connected to this employee. To make matters worse, whenever my mother would interact with this person, she would get headaches, slight nausea, and a sense of unease.

Something was wrong, but she could never put her finger on it. The interactions were always fleeting but never solidly bad—until one day.

After work one afternoon, she approached her car with hesitation. Something felt wrong. Suspicion turned to fear when she looked at the ground: a fine, ashen powder was sprinkled around her car, commingling with drops of crimson blood. As she crossed the threshold and opened the door, a shudder went through her body, and she knew something was terribly wrong. The next day, she became very ill. Nausea and headaches followed, as did more problems at school, and she stayed at home, ill, for days.

After she finished retelling the story, my mind began to review the incident. The scene played again in my thoughts, over and over. The parking lot. Her car circled by ashen powder and drops of blood. It was a barrier of some sort or perhaps a warning. I was puzzled and couldn't get it out of my mind. My background is in archaeology and ancient religion. I've spent years studying lost civilizations and their artifacts. From the red and green paintings on the pyramids of Teotihuacan to Etruscan pottery depicting kings with raven beards, my time and passion have been devoted to solving these mysteries. And these cultures are mysterious, as all that remain are fragments—bits and pieces of greatness lost to the passage of time.

I have also spent many years studying shamanism. Shamanism predates all religion on the planet and represents the limitless expanse of human potential emerging from the mysterious depths of the human mind. Over thirty thousand years ago, shamans were living in caves in the south of France, drawing figures that were half-human, half-bison. And the figures! They were shown flying amongst the stars. In ice excavations in Norway, human beings of forty thousand years ago were found intact, deep in frozen slumber. On their bodies, animal furs offered protection from the cold. In their stomachs, meat was being digested. And in their sacred pouches, held close to their hearts, were small carved figures of antelope and pieces of crystal. From the priests of Ra, who were determined to make the Pharaoh live forever, to Aboriginal elders, who led their tribes on walkabouts to find sacred springs, the practice of shamanism is the one unifying force in all of human history.

In the mystic forest of the arcane, a tree stands, pointing one branch to the heavens and another toward the earth. This cosmic tree, or shamanic tree, links ages of wisdom to the totality of human experience. Practiced for more than fifty thousand years, shamanism is the set of beliefs and rituals that are used by indigenous cultures to create change in the world. Combining aspects of archaeology and cultural anthropology, shamanism provides us a window into the past. The shamans are the lifeblood of this tree, resurrecting long-dead rituals, spirit songs, and metaphysical beliefs.

The basics of shamanism always remain the same from culture to culture: a belief in ritual and ritualized beliefs. It is the energy of these beliefs that propels consciousness. It is the ritual that gives structure and order to these energized beliefs. To shamans, there is no separation between the world of spirit and the realm of the flesh. To these mystics, gods and deities are as real as ice cream and baseball. Shamans have the ability to enter altered states of consciousness and journey into non-ordinary, or non-linear, reality.

Shamans are not like you and me. By meditating and changing their brain waves at will, they have the ability to walk between worlds and harness energy fields to create lasting physical effects in people and things. With the ability to navigate otherworldly realms, shamans act as intermediaries, or psychopomps, between the worlds of spirit and flesh. And shamans are different from one another, just as all cultures have different means to heal the sick, connect with divinity, communicate over long distances, and predict the future. But shamans do have one thing in common: the ability to effectuate change at the infinitesimally small yet potent quantum level.

ANCIENT RELIGION IS my background, but could I use my skills to find out what happened to my mother? Would I be able to piece together the puzzles and find a cure? I wanted to follow the trail and understand how—and more importantly why—my mother became sick. What was the significance of the powder? Whose blood was on the ground? And why was my mother suffering with an inexplicable illness for weeks on end? Was this real, and could there actually be a supernatural cause?

I had an idea where to start: I knew that the ash was important. Recalling the classes I took on shamanism and native cultures, I began the hunt in earnest. I remembered bits and pieces—the Amazonian tribes who consumed the powerful ayahuasca, and the lonely shamans of Siberia who would spend days in solitude near the permafrost and snow velds with only nature spirits as their guides. In native cultures such as these, fire is used to purify. Fire is powerful because it radiates heat, gives energy, and transforms objects. Fire, along with sunlight, is used to balance energy and cleanse objects. The heat burns off impurities, spiritual or otherwise, bringing the substance back to a zero-state of creation. In Lakota ceremonies, sacred spaces are created with fires of sweetgrass and sage. The Zoroastrians regard flame as holy. Cathedrals and Buddhist temples are cleansed by the burning of incense. In Norse legends, fires are chariots that carry great warriors to Valhalla. And in Abrahamic tradition, God, in the form of fire, spoke to Moses on Mount Sinai. For traditional cultures, fire is not the problem. The problem is ash.

Any time an object is burned, ash remains. Ash is symbolic of the transformation taking place, the spiritual and chemical change that alters the fundamental nature of an object. As solid becomes gas, radiates heat, and emits light, the form changes once more back into a solid—and in those resulting flakes, something always remains. Something has to remain. Perhaps you need a microscope to find it, but it's still there, like pieces of a crop left behind in a field after the harvest. While these pieces may be infinitesimally small, they still exist. So what may seem a process to purify something, to cleanse something, may actually inadvertently separate and concentrate parts of the object that was to be destroyed. These potent pieces always remain in the ash.

Not all cultures are hesitant to handle ash. In Vedic fire ceremonies, or pujas, offerings are made to Hindu gods and burned in sacred flame to present gifts to the deities. Believers are blessed when the resulting ash is placed on their third eye chakra. In Catholicism, on Ash Wednesday, priests bless the faithful with the ash from palms burned during Palm Sunday. The sanctified ash has healing and purifying properties. But there is one shamanic tradition that is especially careful with the handling of ash. This tradition is Toltec shamanism.

Curanderismo is the name for Toltec folk healing and shamanism. Derived from post-conquest Catholic faith and remnants of Aztec deity worship, Toltec shamanism blends different belief systems to create a new and dynamic tradition. The word *curanderismo* means "the healing of others." The Toltec practitioner, or curandero, uses medicinal herbs, along with prayers to God and saints, to heal the sick and perform other miraculous and inexplicable phenomena. The plants and herbs used by the curandero are those found readily around the Southwest region of the United States.

Toltec shamanism could be likened to a type of farm medicine. The shaman (who can be male or female) gathers and combines readily available ingredients such as limes, chiles, eggs, basil, and garlic, and then prays as the patient eats these plants or drinks their essence in the form of teas. The curandero also fills the role of community sage.

An interesting aspect of the Toltec healer as a type of shaman is their mild-manneredness in relation to the rest of the community. The curandero is neither a superstar nor a messiah. He does not wear an elaborate feather tunic, nor does he have piercings, nor does he paint his face with ochre. On the contrary, you will find that most curanderos are quite ordinary, wearing short-sleeved shirts, jeans, and talking in a normal speaking voice. An adept curandero doesn't need to rely on appearance or costume to convey power. In fact, just the opposite is true: mild-manneredness is a disguise that the most gifted curanderos use to hide in plain sight.

The most important rule of a Toltec shaman is to use powers only to help—never to inflict pain, disease, or suffering. And these shamans are very careful with ash. Anything that falls into a fire must be thrown away. Anything that touches ash must be disposed of. And after an object is eaten by the tongues of flame, the remaining ash is considered dangerous and unholy.

If it was ash and blood that was sprinkled around my mother's car, and my mother became ill after crossing the barrier, then the ash had something to do with it. The sickness would be supernatural, and to combat the effects of a supernatural attack, we would need a supernatural cure.

To my mind, there was only one kind of person who best knew about these types of attacks. I needed to find a shaman skilled in the handling of ash and blood. I needed a healer whose traditions began on the slopes of stone pyramids and moonlit valleys. I needed to find a Toltec shaman. I needed a curandero.

So where does one look—in the Yellow Pages under the heading "supernatural healer"? Call 411 and ask for the number to a learned sage? Or call that far-off aunt who seems to know everything about everyone? About a week later, I had the answer.

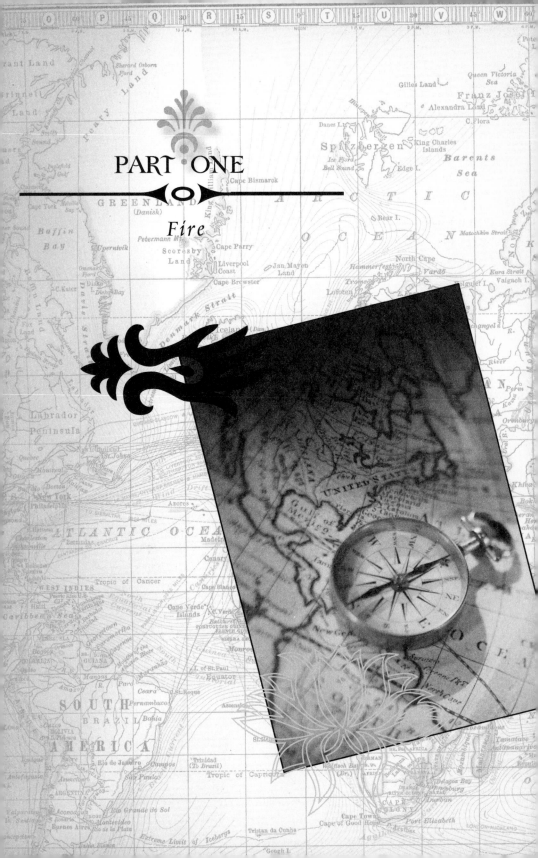

# PART ONE

## *Fire*

# CHAPTER 1
## Curandero: Toltec Shaman

———◦———

IN THE BORDER region of the United States and Mexico, there once lived an enigmatic man—a teacher, healer, and savant—and he is the first shaman I ever visited.

I was at home one night watching a National Geographic special that was part of an anthropology series on indigenous medicine, profiling different countries, including Haiti, Mexico, and Peru. The segment I saw featured a Toltec shaman, or curandero, and how he performed various cleansing rituals to rid people of maladies, suffering, and illness. What was unique about the segment wasn't so much the curandero—it was how he was dispersing and neutralizing the disease affecting his patients: he destroyed evil creations with fire. The special showed him in a high-desert environment with oddly shaped mounds of earth. The shaman was reaching into these mounds, pulling out evil conjurings, and setting them ablaze. Grotesque creations of blood and wax filled the jars and bottles in his hands, with animal entrails, cow tongues, and worse things still inside.

After removing all sorts of glamoury, the shaman began to douse the rancorous mound with gasoline. He then lit a match and tossed it toward the miserable earth. Quickly, the dancing flames devoured the concoctions of fear, hate, envy, and greed, and the wax figures melted away. Untold liquids bubbled, broiled, and evaporated as the Mason jars turned black and shattered. Slips of weathered paper turned brown-black, then crumpled up into nothingness. Dark prayers and darker hopes were destroyed.

Fire purifies, and Toltec shamanism is no different. By placing objects into a flame, vengeful energy is released, the holding vessel is destroyed, and supernatural energy is neutralized. What was once created to inflict pain and bring disease is no more. After the fire, all that was left was ash—on the ground, next to the mound, and lifted into the air by the wind. Ash was everywhere, and it was potent and unclean.

The shaman was not alone. He was accompanied by a professor from a local university, and the professor was overwhelmed. After this burning, he was felled to his knees as quick as a lightning bolt, overcome by the concentrated release of so much psychic energy. But the shaman was fine. He fought the evil and destroyed it with a holy flame. This was the shaman I wanted to meet.

After seeing the episode, my head buzzed with questions. Could I find this shaman? What types of tools did he use? Would his healing powers help my mother? I immediately tried to locate the shaman. In hindsight, it was a bit brash. I thought, "My mom is sick, there's ash around her car, someone may be hurting her, so let's go see a shaman. In fact, let's go see the shaman from the National Geographic special." It seems ridiculous now, but it didn't at the time. After coming up empty trying to find the Toltec shaman online, I did the next best thing: I found the professor. Several phone calls and explanations later, he gave up his secret: the name and location of the shaman. I now had a plan.

WITHIN A WEEK, I was at my mother's home. Using the information gleaned from the professor, I tracked down the healer and arranged for a visit. My mother was still sick, experiencing tremendous headaches and nausea. She was apprehensive about the journey. She had read the books by Shirley MacLaine, Rosemary Althea, and John Edward, but she wasn't exactly a New Ager. Still, I convinced her to keep an open mind and that the Toltec shaman was our best bet for a cure, or at least for a new perspective.

The next morning, after a several-hour drive through backroads, one-stop-sign towns, and hanging stoplights, we arrived at the shaman's ranch. The milieu was ethereal, like stepping into a dream. The colors were soothing, the air a bit hazy, and softness filled the space. I was overwhelmed by the sense of something lost, an effervescent innocence stolen by the skirmishes of adulthood. These feelings of nostalgia were veiled yet all too familiar—summers of baseball, hot popcorn, children laughing, sun shining.

Moments after we stepped out of the car, a man appeared. With whitish hair, standing six feet tall, and in a white robe with a single wooden cross like an amulet around his neck, the man approached us and said, "Hello, Omar. I've been expecting you."

About five other people were standing in the yard. The shaman guided us around the side of his house to a carport that had been converted into a type of a ceremonial space. We were greeted by whitecaps amidst a sea of concrete: white chairs were arranged next to white tables adorned by white tablecloths underneath a white carport with white string banners. A breeze ruffled this ocean of purity as the healer leaned down and placed a handful of incense in a small cast-iron cup. A charcoal tablet had already been lit, and soon the smoke from the incense rose and enveloped him.

When shamans burn incense, it's not the type of stick incense one usually buys at the store. The shaman will light charcoal tablets about the size of a silver dollar and then place a particular resin, root, or substance on the tablet. As the resin or root comes from the actual item to be burned, the incense is pure. For example, a shaman burns sandalwood, instead of sandalwood in stick incense form, or amber resin, instead of amber extract from stick incense. By burning pure compounds, the shaman is burning concentrated ingredients, not excess or unnecessary filler, such as glue or oils that are added during manufacture. As the shaman's tablet continued to burn, I could make out distinct smells of frankincense and balsam.

The healer asked us to sit down, and we all eagerly gathered around him as we moved our seats to form a crescent moon. Off in the distance, birds were singing, and then I heard something else. Like water poured into a cup, music began to fill the air. I could hear the soft hum of an accordion accompanied by a harmony of voices telling a story and resonating with life and joy. The chorus sang about someone performing miracles for this faithful group of people—an old woman, a young girl, an older man, a mother, and a father, all from different eras and textures of life. I was wide awake, and we were all spiritual nomads.

Slowly, the group began to clap, and within moments, their hands mirrored the song and they began to sing. I tried to follow along, but the words were fleeting, like the flash of a city on a distant horizon. I felt like such an auslander. What was I doing here? What was I here for? Was I a witness or just a shadowy interloper? As I ran through these questions, the shaman dipped his head. His head fell once, twice, three times, and then—*wham*—a wave of pressure pounded against my chest, radiating from my solar plexus to my arms and legs. My heart raced, my eardrums burned, and my skin tingled with energy. I was pushed back into my seat.

The shaman slowly looked in my direction. His hands trembled. His eyes had rolled back, and only the whites were visible. His upper body shook as he declared, "I am the spirit of Niño Fidencio! Who has come to witness the miracles of our lord and savior and his blessed mother?

"Come, everyone, to witness the miracles of the Blessed Mother," the shaman slowly said, although now his voice was different. He no longer spoke in the tenor of six-foot-tall man and instead radiated a soft, sweet voice. It was soothing and comforting.

"Everyone is welcome. All are children of God. Come to be healed by the power and mystery of the Holy Spirit." And upon that command, the gathered crowd stood up and formed a line to talk to the healer, but it was not the shaman they were speaking to: it was the spirit of Niño Fidencio.

I CLOSED MY eyes and for a few seconds let go of all conscious thought. As my head nodded downwards, I was transported to another place and time. High atop a hill, perched over a desert plain, the lonely expanse was breathtaking. In the distance, on the valley floor, I could see a long and winding road broken up by pieces of scrub brush. As I shifted my sight to scan the peak, my eyes caught a glimpse of a young man dressed in white. His features were solemn, and his sincere eyes spoke of confidence and a still deeper understanding. He said, "Bring me the woman."

I looked around and could see a multitude of people standing around the man—but not near him. He was too powerful and too holy. As he gestured toward the woman, she approached, trembling. "In the name of the Father, the Son, and the Holy Ghost," spoke the healer as he placed his hand on the woman's temples. He seemed to lower her, as if to baptize her, bearing the entire weight of her body, but amazingly he was using only his right hand. Suddenly, he caught a glimpse of me, and looked straight at me, or maybe straight into me. I awoke and realized I was back in the carport. I then raised my head and broke free from the vision.

The people went to the Toltec shaman with their requests, but they weren't asking for the healer's help. They were asking for help from the spirit channeled by the shaman, and it was the spirit who was healing the sick—help to mend a broken leg, mercy to ease the pain of arthritic hands, and compassion to heal a broken heart. Each time, the spirit would listen to the faithful. The spirit would lay the vessel's trembling hands on the weary, bless the infirm, and whisper secret words to each of the people, who would humbly bow their heads and listen. Each time, the faithful would walk away with tears in their eyes and a look of hope. All the while, the shaman's hands were trembling, and his eyes were rolled to the back of his head, with only the whites visible. Then it was my mother's turn to see the healer.

"Young lady, you have a very difficult job. You are surrounded by conflict, yet you must build harmony from discord. You must unite the weary, love those that are different, and, above all, care for everyone." With those words, the channel put his right hand to my mother's forehead. As a soft green light radiated from his touch, I could see my mother's features soften. Her eyes became relaxed, her body loosened, and with a deep sigh, she seemed to release whatever thing held her in its grasp. "You are healed," spoke the learned sage. With those words, my mother returned to her seat. I was the only one left to see Niño Fidencio.

I began to approach the shaman. I felt like I was falling into a dream, and within a few steps, I was standing in front of the shaman. The spirit was with me.

"My son, you are on a journey. The road will not always be easy or clear. You will face many obstacles, and you will be challenged by forces both natural and supernatural. Yet triumph is within your reach. That thing you seek is also seeking you. And the thing you came to find is not what you are looking for. Remember: if you are confused, go within. And ask for guidance from the Holy Spirit and the Blessed Mother. I will always be with you."

The healer embraced me and put his hands on my lower back, which started to feel deeply warm. My eyes closed, and I saw a golden light in the spot where the shaman was seated. I hadn't told him, but my back muscles had been tense for weeks, and he reached right for the troublesome spot. Soon enough, the heat was gone, and the healer returned his hands to his sides.

The muscles in my lower back were loose and relaxed. I stood taller and gingerly moved side to side, ready to experience pain, but I felt nothing. The discomfort was inexplicably gone.

"All are welcome here. All are children of the Holy Spirit and the Blessed Mother. I am Niño Fidencio, and I come with peace, hope, and love," said the spirit.

Those words ended the ceremony, and the shaman dipped his head once more. After a few moments, he looked up. Sweat poured from his face as he sank his weight into the back of his chair. His breathing was rapid and shallow as he sucked in air. If I hadn't seen the occurrence with my own eyes, I would have said he'd just finished a marathon.

I heard music in the air again. "That's strange," I thought. I looked around and asked if someone had turned the music back on. The woman seated next to me replied, "The music never stopped."

The music never stopped. But how could that be? Mysteriously, the only thing I had heard after the shaman went into trance were the words of the spirit and then silence. I didn't hear anything else. Had I fallen into some sort of trance?

It would take some time to process what I had just witnessed. Those words, "The music never stopped," haunted me. Who was Niño Fidencio? Why did I only hear his words and not the music? Was that a sign? What was the spirit's message? And what was the thing I was looking for that would find me?

FOR THE NEXT several weeks, I wandered through a daze and wrestled with thoughts and dreams. I read books, spent late nights online, and talked with professors and friends about magical lore. I needed to find out exactly what I saw. Was it a dream? Was it a vision? And why did the shaman use the spirit of this healer?

In shamanism, rules fall away quickly. There may be similarities across cultures, but that is where comparisons stop. A *marakame*, or Huichol high priest, will call on different spirits and use different herbs to give a blessing than a Buddhist high lama. A Siberian shaman's songs to ensure a successful hunt are different from the songs of a Jivaro shaman. With the Toltec shaman, he heals people the only way he knows how: as a channeler shaman. This type of shaman conducts healing by channeling the spirit of a saint or holy figure. During a ceremony, a channeler shaman will release his consciousness to allow another force to enter and conduct the healing. The shaman allows his body to become a vessel for spirit. For a few moments, the essences of both entities merge, then separate. While in trance, the spirit uses the shaman's hands and body to diagnose illnesses, give advice, and communicate with the living. When the medium can no longer maintain the connection, the spirit leaves. As the shaman returns to alertness, he will sometimes cry, having been so close to divinity, then returning to everyday reality. The medium will also have great feelings of euphoria, having felt the energetic presence of a holy being.

The channeler shamans who call upon the spirit of José Fidencio are known as Fidencistas. These Toltec shamans are found only in one part of the world, the border region of the United States and Mexico. As a medium, the shaman enters an altered state of consciousness and raises his vibration while the spirit of Fidencio lowers its vibration. As the entities merge at some spiritual intersection, the shaman will lose consciousness and allow the spirit to occupy the shaman's body. Since the body is now filled with spirit, the body will then show the mannerisms, speaking style, and movements of the spirit, and the spirit is now capable of interacting with four-dimensional space. The channeler's consciousness is not trapped; it is more akin to being asleep. Most vessels describe the process as dreamlike and ethereal.

In this semi-trance state, the shaman's natural abilities become more powerful as they channel the spirit of Niño Fidencio. The spirit conducts healings with divine spiritual energy, using the bodies and energy matrices of the healers. The effects are powerful. The spirit uses the channeler's body to lay on hands. Patients experience dramatic recoveries and even more intriguing aftereffects.

*Legend*, *saint*, and *saviour* have all been used to describe José Fidencio. He was a mysterious faith healer who emerged from the foothills of the Sierra Madre in the late 1920s. The faithful call the healer Niño, or "child," because he was thought to be pure of heart and free from sin, like a child. According to accounts, when in trance, Fidencio spoke in a falsetto voice, indicating his rise in vibration and resonance with the Holy Spirit.

Born José Fidencio Sintora Constantino in 1898, from an early age he exhibited a strange and powerful understanding of medicinal herbs and healing techniques. He grew to prominence in the 1920s and '30s as a faith healer and supernatural folk hero. His healing abilities, kind disposition, and compassion became known throughout the country. Fidencio was a hero to the poor, for he would never turn anyone away for lack of money. Most healings were performed without charge, and pilgrims would leave food, clothes, and offerings for the saint and his assistants.

Fidencio saw his abilities as a gift from God that would touch and bless those afflicted by terrible disease. The healer always served the divine. And more intriguing than his healing mission is the fact that even death itself has not stopped him from healing the sick.

THE DAY AFTER the healing, my mother's headaches were gone. And the next time my mother returned to work, the problematic employee took several days off from work. The following week, the woman left. Whatever had been cast toward my mother had returned to its vicious origin.

This is an important lesson: never conjure to hurt other living beings. When a person consciously projects ill feelings toward another or goes a further step and actually crafts something, the dark energy, the dis-ease, can actually return to its source.

Evil conjurings are inherently unstable because they are dark, and one cannot truly control the forces of dis-ease. And if these negative energies return to the caster, they return many times stronger. The Wicca traditions offer a solid guiding principle: "So long as ye harm none, do as ye will." But an even better intention is to work only with light. If you live in the service of others and with a pure heart, you will always be surrounded by light, and you will have nothing to fear.

Back at school, I considered the mystery solved and returned to life as normal. But questions persisted. For instance, how did the shaman know about my mother's work? How did he know about my injury? And why did he give me that message, the one that no one else heard? I asked my mom about it, but she didn't remember. Was that a dream too? And what about the music? Why did the music stop? Or why was I the only one not to hear it?

I WENT ABOUT my days and kept to the business of my studies. New classes came along. A new girlfriend arrived and left. As I reached the end of my schoolwork, unsure of what to do, I sent out a ton of job applications, but no job ever materialized. I returned to see the shaman once more, but he was long gone. The ranch had been sold, with no forwarding address. I had read about this kind of thing happening—the mysterious healer who suddenly disappears.

I thought my shamanic adventure was over. But the spiritual world doesn't always cooperate with our plans.

# CHAPTER 2
## Not a Dream

—◄○►—

ABOUT A YEAR later, I was in Austin, Texas, on my own quest to discover the everyday meanings of life. I search for truth as much as I search for facts. Facts are the allegations of history and archaeology, while truth is the search for our immortal soul. I was welcoming a distraction from the monotony of law school and chose to visit a store that stood out orange, bright, and alive among an urban wheat field of cinder block and grass. I ventured inside, drawn in by the Spanish signs and esoteric symbols on the façade. And that's how I met Lee Cantu.

I would eventually become a frequent visitor of his store, buying incense, having my cards read, drinking coffee, and talking about ghosts, healing, and auras. Lee Cantu is the owner of the *herbería*, or magic shop. Well-known throughout Austin for his healing abilities, Lee has been a working shaman for over twenty-five years. He's been in newspapers, magazines, TV specials, and has even consulted on a couple of films. A burly man, Cantu is a certified master welder. In another life, his strong arms wielded fire and steel, and his fists, the size of pineapples, did the talking. With his strong will, he directed a young labor union in the 1960s long before he began to pray over people. It was an interesting start for a United Nations–recognized indigenous tribal elder and shaman.

His shop in South Austin is the archetypal Mexican herberia—a place to buy candles, find spiritual items, seek assistance, and gossip. It's sort of like a town hall, except the store still maintains its religious overtones. Most of its resident items are vaguely related to Catholicism. In other words, there would be no sign reading "In God We Trust, But Leave Her at the Door" in the front window of this town center.

One important aspect of shamanism is that all is often not what it appears to be. Shamans will sometimes be deceptive and not reveal what they are doing, and other shamans will downplay their abilities or heal only a select few. The idea is protection. Most shamans come from indigenous healing traditions going back hundreds of years and would rather perish than reveal their most sacred mysteries. Most shamans are also humble and live meekly—not because they don't want material comforts, but because they understand their healing mission is more important than money. If the healer drives a Rolls-Royce, then he is probably not a true shaman. Others will claim to be shamans and exaggerate their healing powers. Again, all is not as it appears to be, and although many pretenders claim shamanic ability, few indigenous healers still remain. And, of course, there is no such thing as a suburban shaman—someone who takes a few classes, installs art downtown, and then, *presto*, they're now a spiritual healer.

A person seeking out a shaman should also rely on intuition and pay attention to feelings of good and bad, light and dark, right and wrong. In my interactions with shamans, I always ask myself what my intuition tells me about this person. Is he asking for a lot of money up front? What kinds of symbols surround the shaman—crosses, holy eyes of protection, and other symbols of light? Or do they mix and match symbols of darkness and light? The Son of Man has said that a house divided against itself cannot stand, nor can a person serve two masters. If you see a shaman use symbols of light and dark or offer services of protection and hexing, I offer one word for you: *run*.

Lee Cantu is authentic. He has no reason to deceive or exaggerate, for he truly is strong and powerful. Cantu only sells items that are used for working with the light. And he always wears either a holy cross or a sacred amulet given to him by an aboriginal chief, a symbol of honor from the first worldwide meeting of indigenous people. A true follower of the spiritual path, Cantu is a shaman you can trust and confide in.

On a hot summer day, Cantu called unexpectedly and invited me in. He had been asked to conduct a healing on a woman named Ruth. From her home in Oregon, she made the long journey to Austin's grassy shore with her daughter. Beset by some of the maladies of old age, including a stroke and Alzheimer's, Ruth wanted to regain control of her life. A sprightly eighty-four-year-old, she arrived with an amazing personality and strong psychic abilities. Before the healing began, she insisted on buying us an ice cream cone to cope with the sweltering Texas heat as we waited for Cantu to arrive and open the store. The previous day, I had spent thirty minutes driving through Austin looking for just that, an ice cream cone.

Cantu arrived. We were led inside his shop, small sheep following a brawny herdsman. It was after-hours, so lights were dim. The only natural light coming into the store shimmered through two store windows and broke the darkness. In the shadows, the place was a bit disconcerting. Silhouettes almost seemed to dance upon the dark painted walls filled with herbs, signs, and flowers. I wondered if the statuary came alive late at night—one saint talking to another or checking to see if their candles were selling. Do the elementals wake at midnight, endlessly waltzing in the moonlight? With the energy of myriad people, objects, and things, the place seemed "a bit warm" psychically—not quite haunted but not quite still either. Out of the corner of my eye, I saw the shadow of one of the piñatas move on the wall. I quickly looked toward the object, but the papier-mâché menagerie was still. The doors and windows were shut to the world, so no breeze could have entered the space, but I did see something move. Shut to the wind but perhaps open to something else, the store seemed to breathe and shine. Breaking my reverie, Cantu called me to his back office.

"We're ready to start, come on," he said. I advanced toward the back of the store, past holy denizens and into his office, not quite sure what to expect. Like something out of a movie, Cantu's office was brimming with the esoteric. From a statue of Lord Shiva to a bust of Quan Yin to books by Allan Kardec, the room was like a small museum of mystic world traditions. And almost like a spiritual bakery, the scent of the ethereal filled the air. Cantu always has candles lit—holy flame purposely aligned with his healing energy.

In the back of Cantu's office stood an altar. A cross emerged from the wall, along with a picture of Christ and the Virgin Mary. The display was illuminated by two small golden lamps. The energy toward the back of the room was almost funereal, a sacred and somber place where things are removed and laid to rest. Fears and illness are cast off, old bodies discarded, spirits released. And patients walk away reborn and new.

I sat down next to Ruth. Cantu told her I was a friend and asked if I could watch. Pleasantly, Ruth agreed. I spoke to her daughter for a few moments about Ruth's condition. Ruth had suffered several strokes and had lost most of her short-term memory. I could see the strain in her daughter's eyes; her shepherdess was slowly being taken away, bit by bit, memory by memory. Events that had happened long ago were quite easy to recollect, but in the day-to-day moments, Ruth would constantly repeat herself and ask the same questions over and over again. Caught in a loop of short-term memory, Ruth was trapped. Repeating thoughts, ideas, and images, she seemed hopelessly lost. Cantu rose and gently led

Ruth to a long padded table in front of the altar. Ruth lay down, wanting to rest more than just her body; Ruth wanted to lay to rest her shackles.

The healer prepared for the ceremony. Cantu sat next to Ruth and began to pray. As he prayed, a golden light enveloped his body. Leaning forward on a small chair, the softness of his features was overcome by a radiant golden energy. Faster and faster, his hands moved, fingers kneading spark-filled air. As he continued, the round yellow glow of his face turned to a soft red. Reaching forward, he gently placed his hands on Ruth's head.

With his hands and fingers on her head, he began to penetrate her auric, or energetic, field. Fingers reached into the cosmos, into infinity. In turn, chromatic energy, the multicolored energy of the rainbow, reached into her mind. With this energy, Cantu worked frantically to revive her brain. Paths through damaged synapses were rerouted to healthy tissue. Areas of Ruth's brain affected by stroke and disease were bypassed as newer connections strengthened. Newer pathways were being created, neurons generated and buttressed. Ruth's body trembled as energy coursed through her body and soul. This was healing energy—the energy of light and miracles.

Cantu pulled his hands away from Ruth and leaned back into his chair. Still seated, Cantu began to violently jerk his hands toward his body and then away. Like being at rest, then unexpectedly receiving a tremendous jolt, his muscles contracted, let loose, and then contracted again. He suddenly dropped his head. With his chin on his chest, he grudgingly moved his jaw toward his left shoulder. As Cantu repeated this movement, he breathed in deeply and suddenly. He then raised his head and, with eyes shut, spoke in my direction:

"I am the spirit of Niño Fidencio, and I have messages for you and for the world!"

I couldn't conceal my shock. I thought I was finished speaking with Fidencio. Cantu never told me he was a trance medium. What the hell was going on?

In his high falsetto, Fidencio exclaimed, "I must heal this woman. This woman is not lost, nor is she to be thrown away. She has a good heart. And you must be patient with her. If she repeats herself, you must gently remind her of what she just said. You must then ask her new questions. The new questions allow her to open a different path in her mind. As you strengthen the new pattern of awareness, the old pattern of forgetfulness will fall away. Above all, show her kindness, compassion, and love.

"My son, the world is in a state of chaos. Great calamities and great suffering await. But rejoice, for the time of change is at hand. Humanity will undergo great suffering, but great spiritual victories will be achieved.

"Be wary of the West Coast of this country. A great earthquake will come and cause much devastation. Be wary of land next to the ocean. The next fifty years will see great storms and floods. Without change, and without the human will to change, the northern ice will melt. The earth has become sick and is begging for mercy—mercy for the birds, the fish, the plants of the land and of the sea.

"Mediums will be able to detect the changes. When the stars begin to fall, the hour will be close at hand. When the astral plane begins to shift, those of higher consciousness will survive.

"We must join together to send light and love to those in the darkness. We must join to show the way. Why is there so much hate and suffering in the world? Why is there so much anger? People are beginning to lose their minds. The world is in a state of aggression. Many tragedies will unfold. The saints and the virgin have been sending us signs.

"Instead of using ideas to kill one another, we must help each other. Don't let people pull you down. Follow the path of light, love, and God. Even family will limit you. But stay true to the path.

"My son, you are on a mission of healing, learning, and teaching. You must seek out the most powerful elders in our world. Clear the road, clear the path. Have peace in your heart. This is the path to God. And don't try to push things. What you cannot do with the strongest push, God can do effortlessly.

"You will meet a woman. She dreams of helping others. She never thinks of herself but instead lives for the benefit of all. After you meet her, my son, she will be like a piece of gum on your shoe, never leaving you. You must continue to seek her."

With that, the healer lifted his head.

I WASN'T JUST speechless, I was awestruck. I didn't expect Fidencio to re-appear and deliver a message for all of us, especially a message for me. I never told Cantu of my encounter with the spirit. Who was this woman I would be seeking? Was the first message real? Could this be happening? And what about the messages about sharing light with the world and healing our planet; could they be real too?

The message couldn't have been much clearer. The path to God is a path of peace; through peace comes healing; and through healing emerges love. And my adventure had just begun. Finally, there was no doubt in my mind. I felt as though I had my own mission: to find the elemental shamans—the powerful healers of our age and masters of the elements—and meet them, learn their secrets, and gain their wisdom for the benefit of our planet.

# PART TWO

## Earth

# CHAPTER 3
## Spiritwalker: Cherokee Shaman

———◀○▶———

**A**T THE BOTTOM of an ancient ocean lives a very special shaman. Walking the path of the Red Road, this man has an extraordinary ability to alter rules that give the world structure and order. Planetary systems exist through rules. Causality occurs because of rules. When you meet someone who can bend the rules at will and achieve great levels of change, you have found someone truly unique. Using the energy of the medicine wheel, a Cherokee Spiritwalker is this person.

I had just finished law school and didn't yet have a job, so I did what many generations had done before: I headed West to find my destiny. The desert of the American Southwest is vast and holds tremendous mystery. From the complex Anasazi ruins to the mysterious windows of Chaco Canyon that are aligned to celebrate the Summer Solstice, many enigmas reside in this locale. Hunting parties, explorers, and adventurers have all gone missing searching for untold wealth and cities of gold—Cibola and El Dorado. There were so many mysteries I wanted to explore, but there also was something else, someone I needed to see.

I had heard about a very special Native American shaman from my good friend and psychic Stacey Anne Wolf. During one of our visits, she recommended that I see Gary Gent, a Cherokee Spiritwalker and expert in soul retrieval. My soul was restless. I wanted to put aside some issues from my past, lay other things to rest, and think about my discoveries to come. Some things I just wanted to bring home. Could the Cherokee Spiritwalker and the energy of the medicine wheel help me? I was about find out. Besides, something in the desert was calling to me. It's a place so pure, so primordial. Desert sands strip away all masks and disguises, and all meaningless things fall away. To survive in the desert, you need shelter, food, and water. Everything else is unimportant—except, perhaps, the sanctity of your soul.

Energy flows freely in the desert. At nighttime, the moon casts a soft blue glow over the limitless expanse. The Joshua trees, yucca, and scrub stretch out for miles, as far as the eye can see. Wispy clouds break up the serene evening sky, and the stars are among the brightest you will ever gaze upon.

The desert reveals many things to many people. Truth, life, death, and peace are among its denizens. The desert reveals what Native Americans call the Great Mystery. To the first Americans, the path to the Great Mystery is one of knowledge, wisdom, spirituality, and compassion. They call this path Canku Luta, or the Red Road.

I had set aside three weeks for my trip. The plan was to spend a few days with Gary Gent, then drive up to Flagstaff and Sedona. I wanted to see the Spiritwalker but also find out about the enigmatic energy fields, called vortexes, in Sedona. Like other living beings, shamans require energy. To conduct supernatural feats and otherworldly tasks like bending time and appearing in two places at once, shamans require tremendous amounts of power. Vortexes can act as this energy source. So where are the vortexes?

In certain places on Earth, currents in our planet's magnetic field converge and cause heightened extrasensory perception (ESP), telekinesis, clairsentience, and out-of-body travel. Among these places are Nazca, Stonehenge, Teotihuacan, Machu Picchu, the Bermuda Triangle, and Sedona. I wanted to know if they were real. Was there an electromagnetic force, an energy crisscrossing the boundaries of our planet, that could cause rifts in space and time? Would I feel its outflow in the canyons of Sedona?

SPRINGTIME GREETED MY arrival in Phoenix with crisp desert air and lingering aromas of sage and nutmeg. Exiting the plane, I was lost in the maze of the airport and felt like a pinball thrust to and fro. As the escalator to baggage claim led me down, I glimpsed something strange on the far wall: a sand sculpture whose residents were not seashells or filaments but the bleached bones of Pleistocene piranhas and long-dead birds. Things forgotten, things left behind—like the pieces of my soul that I longed to retrieve.

Native American shamans believe in soul retrieval, the idea that our souls and identities are comprised of a dozen or more pieces. These pieces represent different stages in our development and our lives. Some soul pieces will take the shape of a five-year-old boy, for instance. This soul piece will identify and think as a five-year-old. Another soul piece may take the form of an infant. Another may look and act like our current selves. In other words, our identities are comprised of the sum of our past, present, and future experiences, both good and bad.

For the shaman, the ceremony to retrieve a soul piece is an effort to bring back something that was lost, to reintegrate that part of a person's soul and make the person whole again. But if a person isn't presently "whole," how did the soul piece shear off? What would make a part of the soul run away? The druids of the DSM-IV TR, otherwise known as psychologists, call this cognitive disassociation.

Cognitive disassociation is the idea that during periods of great stress, abuse, sadness, or loss, a person will disassociate from the trauma and pull away their consciousness as a coping mechanism to survive the traumatic event. Later on, the person will suppress the memory and may even deny it completely. This disassociation leads to a long-term feeling of emptiness, of sadness, of something not being right, because at the moment the mind pulled away, a part of the soul is left behind at the instant of trauma. And just like two lovers separated by space and time, some things belong together. The sun needs the moon, just as the house needs its master, for without the two, existence is meaningless. Souls are no different.

To bring back the missing soul piece, the shaman will use his abilities to travel through space and time and retrieve the long-lost self. Much like the Indiana Jones of the spirit world, the shaman will journey to find and recover the soul piece. And just like the misplaced animals I saw on the wall of the Phoenix airport, which probably cry at night to go back to the desert, a person's soul pieces yearn to return home and reunite with a person's soul.


AT THE RENTAL counter, I signed papers, waived fees, grabbed keys, and walked again. Moving with a sense of urgency, I felt something important was coming. Once outside, I cautiously surveyed my vehicle, a small no-frills four-door sedan. I silently hoped the five-horsepower, four-cylinder engine wouldn't strand me near the top of the first mountain range. After loading gear, I climbed in, started my weedwacker disguised as a car, and zoomed off into the great American West.

The highways in Phoenix are fantastic. In non-rush hour traffic, it's like your own private autobahn, complete with six lanes of fresh, fast blacktop on each side. The only problem is distance. Although the drives are mostly straight, it takes a blessed hour to get from point A to point B. When I finally made it to the hotel, I unpacked, showered, and organized my hiking equipment, all the while pondering why I was drawn to the Cherokee shaman and what secrets Sedona held.

I awoke the next morning with a strange feeling of peace. I didn't feel anxious about the day; everything seemed at ease. Maybe it had something to do with the location; the desert in the Valley of the Sun was once the bottom of a sea, the deep bowl of an *oceanus antiquus*, an ancient ocean brimming with life, decay, rebirth, and then more life. The residual energy of millions of years of sea life is soothing, calm, and peaceful.

On the way to Gary's, I kept thinking about caves. Mysterious cave systems are found beneath the pyramids of Teotihuacan. Celtic or Gaelic traditions tell of the fairies and nature spirits that live in caves. Maya high priests would say that caves led their souls to Xibalba, or the Road to Awe. To native cultures, caves are enigmatic and extremely important. To a shaman, caves are places to gain knowledge and commune with the spirits of nature, and they're gateways to the upper, middle, and lower worlds.

When a shaman journeys to find a missing soul piece, the shaman will travel to the upper, middle, and lower worlds. These realms are not archetypes or overlays of heaven, hell, or purgatory. Heaven and hell are human religious constructs created to describe places of energy—places of universal love and places devoid of love. Moreover, heaven and hell carry connotations of judgment, reward, and punishment. Shamanic worlds are not like this at all. When shamans journey, they use these worlds to describe areas of energy and wisdom. And yes, like others, these worlds have their own set of rules. Let me explain.

The lower world is where the shaman travels to seek guidance. If the realms could be compared to a state of being, the lower world is the place of Genesis—simply alive. Often described as lush and tropical, the lower world is abundantly green, teeming with life, animals, and vegetation. All shades of green—from emerald to jade and seafoam—await the shaman in this world. Green is associated with the heart chakra, growth, healing, and the ability to love deeply.

The infinite green hues support myriad life forms and life forces in the lower world. As the shaman begins to survey the pleasant landscape, he is on the lookout for a supernatural assistant: a power animal. The power animal is important, because it gives the shaman advice to accomplish the task at hand.

Power animals can be hawks, salamanders, fish, snails—anything. And they are not to be judged by their appearance! Many of us want to believe that the boldest-looking power animals are also the strongest. We think of eagles, condors, wolves, and bears as being masters of their realms and all-powerful. But what about lizards, caterpillars, and frogs? Are they not also mysterious?

The lizard has the ability to suffer great injury and miraculously generate another limb or tail. The caterpillar goes through great change and with faith becomes a butterfly. The frog has the ability to live on both land and water. Can an eagle live in two worlds? Can the mighty grizzly bear regenerate a limb? Of course not. Animals' meanings go beyond their appearance. A shaman will look at the power animal to give information about the healing. A jaguar will indicate strength gained by stealthiness. A raccoon shows the ability to gain success from adversity. A turtle, wisdom by moving slowly. All animals are powerful because they come from the creator and the natural world. The power animal that the shaman encounters is uniquely important because it gifts divine insight.

Once the shaman encounters a power animal, he will greet the animal, ask a question, receive an answer, and then thank the life form for its help. All life forms want to be acknowledged. They want to be appreciated. They want to know that they are completing their given tasks in the universe.

Through these encounters, and with a deep sense of kindness and awe, the shaman is reaffirming reverence for nature spirits. And by walking a road of sincerity, the shaman is paving the way for more divine insight and help from the mystic realm. As the shaman works more and more with power animals and nature spirits, she is increasing her supernatural abilities by following road signs on the highway of destiny and embracing the energy of the cosmos.

After the shaman has obtained an answer to the question in both form and word, the shaman can now begin preparations for a journey into the middle world to effectuate the change.

The middle world is fairly easy to visualize, because it can be compared to an overlay of our own reality and everyday life. The middle world has buildings, trees, people, roads, cars, money, weather, and periods of daylight and darkness. Sometimes we gain glimpses of the middle world in our dreams. If you've ever had a dream where you're in your house and a friend is visiting you, you are dreaming of the middle world. Or you're driving to a park and using your own car—you're dreaming of the middle world. The dream images of the middle world give us messages, warnings, keys, and communication from faraway friends and loved ones. There are also ways to increase our nighttime dream lucidity. Hawaiian shamans, or kahunas, will tell you to drink pineapple juice before bedtime to stay lucid as you travel to the middle world. Just don't drink too much or you will be fairly tired in the morning from living, playing, and learning all night long.

A shaman, however, doesn't travel to the middle world to play in dreams or enjoy a latte at the neighborhood coffee shop. The shaman travels to there to find his patient. If a shaman is performing a healing, the shaman must travel to the middle world to connect with the spirit of the person to be healed. If the shaman is doing soul retrieval, the shaman must find the missing soul piece and then return it to its owner. Again, the key is the overlay. The middle world is an overlay to our world. So, when the shaman goes to find a soul piece in the middle world, after receiving guidance from the power animal, the shaman must go back to that part of the overlay where the soul piece fragmented from the soul. The lost soul piece is usually found in that place of great trauma.

The soul pieces may be found in work environments, childhood places, and scenes of great loss or separation. We've all encountered some sort of emotional turmoil, but different individuals react to trauma in varying ways. Most choose to block out these painful thoughts and memories completely. And as we put these episodes aside and out of the reach of our conscious mind, psychologists say we are using our attic. In the attic, we stow away things we want to forget. The loss of a beloved pet, parents who were constantly fighting, or the death of a loved one are all times we don't want to recall. But these events become memories locked forever in our minds. Ironically, we think we are the only ones with an attic and feel ashamed for having suffered so much, but everyone puts away these painful remembrances, these secret realities, in their own attics.

So, if the trauma was the childhood loss of a favorite dog, that part of the soul fragments, and the soul piece becomes trapped at our childhood home, waiting on the porchstep for Rover to return. If the trauma was watching a best friend pass away, our soul piece is at the hospital with hands clutching our heads, wondering why Sam died.

But just as the soul piece is trapped, a person's higher soul wants integration. The higher soul wants its pieces to come back home. Again, some things are meant to be together, and time and space are just illusory walls to the wholeness of being. So the shaman will journey to find and return these missing soul pieces.

Another type of work shamans perform in the middle world are extractions. An extraction is the removal of an object from a person's auric field and energetic body. If a shaman wants to conduct an extraction, he must first locate the person in the middle world and then find the source of trouble. The shaman can quickly diagnose the patient's illness by seeing symbolic images of the dis-ease on the person's body. Problems with the throat area may appear as a magical dart hindering the person's breath. Stomach problems are seen as dark, viscous masses attacking a person's center and spreading like miniature explosions. Tumors are viewed as solid, black masses in the person's energy field.

After seeing the problem or blockage, the shaman then works to restore the vitality of the damaged area. If the shaman encounters a magical dart, then he simply pulls out the dart, removes any residual poison with his mouth, spits out the poison, and then uses his fingertips to fill the area with gold healing light. The process is almost the same for stomach disease. The shaman will find the black area, isolate it, compact it into the shape of a small ball, and then pull out the sphere. The shaman then throws the mass toward the center of Earth. The dis-ease is neutralized as the universal light in the center of Earth's core breaks down the dark components.

The shaman knows no limitations in terms of using energy healing to attack the disease. The world of shamanic healing is not limited by constructs such as downtime, recovery periods, convalescence, or phrases like "we don't have the technology yet." The healing is instant, possible, and exceptional.

The shaman then works to increase a person's aura and energetic field, which is a projection of a person's energy, thoughts, consciousness, and general well-being. The shaman pulls down universal energy from the great source or can even use energy given by the power animal. The shaman gently envelops the patient with this energetic field and then fuses this golden energy onto the body like a gentle painter with a silken brush. But instead of a brush, the shaman is using his own life force and universal energy to accomplish the task.

When the energetic healing is complete, the shaman's final step is to pass on a message. The shaman will usually whisper a secret in the patient's ear. It could be advice, a message of hope, or a directional heading—it could be anything. Once the healing is complete, or the soul piece is retrieved, the shaman returns to our waking world. The shaman emerges from the cave, slowly stirring as his consciousness rejoins normal reality.

Very rarely, the shaman will journey to the upper world for specialized information. If the shaman travels to the lower world for guidance, then the shaman travels to the upper world for revelation. The upper world is the land of archangels, master guides, Akashic records, and deity. In this world, the shaman can encounter the spirits of legends, gods, and transdimensional beings. Examples of the spirits in the upper world include Quan Yin, Buddha, the Virgin Mary, Jesus, and Zoroaster. These cosmic masters give messages and provide a touch of themselves, the godlike and sublime *logos*, or divine essence, to the shaman.

The upper world is so magnificent that shamans will sometimes have difficulty describing it. No words exist for the sheer sense of joy, bliss, peace, harmony, and love that is found there. Although information gained in the upper world is extraordinary, the danger is that the shaman's soul will not want to return to the world of waking reality. This occurs because the upper realm's beauty is so profound that the shaman's consciousness doesn't want to leave. For this reason, some shamans are not allowed upper-world access until many years into their training. If the upper world is closed to the shaman, he instead will be taken to a gateway room to allow spirits of the upper realm to communicate with him.

When they come back to ordinary reality after journeying to the upper world, some shamans cry profusely or even go through periods of depression. This happens because the shaman has left a place of cosmic consciousness, a zone of such pure love, that returning to the problems and malaise of the waking world is inescapably tragic. And this is why the shaman weeps . . .

AFTER LOSING MYSELF in thoughts of shamanic caves, I was back in the car and on the way to visit Gary the Cherokee Spiritwalker. As I pulled up to his home, I noticed that the lawn was well kept but not overly artificial. Walking closer to the house, I could tell it had been remodeled. The darker slab of a new concrete foundation was pressed next to the older and lighter-colored slab of the previous foundation. A shaman that does home improvement; I could live with that.

I expected to meet an older man. I knew Gent was a Vietnam veteran in his late fifties, and most veterans of the era had not aged well. The trauma of fighting an unwanted and losing war took their toll on sons and daughters of the '60s. Instead, I was greeted by a young man, seemingly in his early forties. With a full head of brown hair, a powerful person held out his hand to me. "Hello, you must be Omar. My name is Gary," said the shaman.

Gary invited me into his house and led me to the sacred space. The home was clean, without excess décor or clutter busying the area like unwanted thoughts through an overactive mind. This was another place where chi flowed freely. As I walked to the back, I saw some Native American objects, a painting, and a rug on the wall. I wondered if they were power objects, guardians to Gary's inner chamber. The warrior in the painting—was he ready to jump out and frighten unwanted ghosts? Was the rug ready to come off the wall and envelop a trespasser with heat to dispatch them?

Gary's office contained a small desk and a converted massage table, which was more akin to a horse with colorful blankets. There was no discernable décor in the room except for a large drum on the floor, next to the table. And what a drum! I had seen the design before—a medicine wheel with arrows and colors and people. The beautiful designs represent the Four Corners, Grandmother Earth, and Grandfather Sky. But this medicine wheel was different, for each quadrant was radiating with energy feathers in blue, red, white, and black. If you were to spin the design and stare intently, it would create a vortex effect—almost the same vortex you would see as you were entering a shamanic cave. The design, when still, looked as if it been delivered from the clouds, a final token from the thunderbird.

The leather of the drum was unique. The natural pattern of the animal skin formed dark spots around a clear center like truth emerging from the chaos of a darkened sky. The drum was a device to open a doorway, an energetic symbol shining through darkness.

Not all is what it appears to be. The world of the shaman is the world of the unseen. Only through childlike eyes and an open soul can one fully grasp the world not as it exists but as it resonates—because not all things are as they appear. A long, thin, clear quartz crystal is actually a wand that glows different colors when it is used. An eagle feather, when waved in the air, is a magical brush used to construct the frame of a spirit house. A drum, when awakened, actually grows to ten times its size and then becomes a portal to the middle world. Everything, anything, all power objects, all symbols, every gesture resonates with life-force energy and has a secret purpose.

Gary invited me to sit on the table while he asked questions about my goal. What did I want to accomplish? What was I looking for? I told him I was on a journey, unsure of the destination and looking for the path. He stared at me intently. I could feel his eyes peering into my heart. Could he see my hidden soul, the part of me I don't share with others? Would he help me? Was I in the right place?

I had been asking myself these questions for the last few days, but this time, something was different. A wave of energy suddenly washed and flowed through my body. Still a young learner but no longer the first card of the Major Arcana, I felt a bit more confident. Gary then nodded and began the ceremony.

Before we embarked on the soul retrieval, Gary began by clearing the sacred space. Native American shamans traditionally burn sage to raise the vibration and rid an area of negativity. Sage leaves have a light green color, a velvety texture, and a sharp, fragrant scent. After lighting a sage wand, Gary began the ceremony.

"Grandmother Earth, Grandfather Sky, the spirits of the North, the South, the East, and the West: we ask that you protect us on this journey. Guide us to the answers that we need. Help us safely into the tunnel of our ancestors. We honor you and the spirits of those that have passed." For a split second, I could hear a drumbeat and someone chanting or singing. The sound was something distant but also very familiar. But of course, Gary's drum was still on the ground, and we were the only ones in the house. Gary asked me to close my eyes as he began to journey.

His instructions were simple: close your eyes, don't meditate, don't fall asleep, just relax. As Gary picked up the drum, my mind drifted off . . .

TO ENTER ALTERED states of consciousness, shamans use different means to open gateways into the spirit world. Traditionally, shamans use herbs such as ayahuasca and peyote to open the door, but these aren't always the best tools, as plants can vary in quality and potency from season to season. Too much of the herbs and the shaman can suffer brain damage or even die. A shaman must also appease the spirit of the plant. If the plant is taken for the wrong reasons or without the proper ceremony, the shaman risks angering the spirit, or the essence, of the plant. This results in an unwanted and nightmarish trip. A better and safer method to journey shamanically is to use a sonic driver, such as a drumbeat.

The way a sonic driver works is that the constant sound, at a specific frequency and the right harmonic tone, produces a synchronization in brain activity between the left and right hemispheres. With both hemispheres working together, the human brain is better able to access higher thought processes, letting go of the life-saving yet spiritually debilitating and primitive thoughts of our reptilian brain stem. Drumbeats, heartbeats, and hemi-sync music are all examples of sounds that magnify this connection to higher thought. With both hemispheres firing, the brain experiences an altered state of consciousness, because normally the human brain doesn't work this way. And so a simple drum beat allows journeys into the shamanic world without the danger and inconsistencies of plants.

With my eyes closed, I tried not to focus on anything in particular; I merely followed the drumbeats. Whereas most shamans would take thirty minutes to enter an altered state of consciousness, Gary can do it in five. And that's what makes him so unique: he has the ability to understand the rules, rewrite them, and use them in a way that doesn't upset the natural order of the cosmos. In other words, Gary is so powerful that he can create his own operating system for shamanic healing. Gary uses a system that transcends traditions that are thousands of years old. He's developed a system that works but does not upset the balance. Only someone with true mastery can accomplish this herculean task, and only much later did I fully understand this distinction and comprehend Gary's power. But even during my first visit with Gary, I knew I had found the right shaman.

I began to drift off, gently slipping away, and then someone grabbed my left hand. I was in front of a large fire, set beside a teepee. The night air was cool against my skin. I saw brown grass beneath my feet. As the fire crackled, I could see the alternating red, yellow, and gold tones of the firelight sweep across the earth's down. I looked to my left and saw a young woman dancing around the fire. She was wearing a beautiful red robe embroidered with gold leaf trim. As the soft features of her gentle shape swayed to the drumbeat, her long, dark hair swayed on her shoulders—left, then right, then a turn.

Rhythm became form, then form became movement. And the form was lovely! She smiled at me. It was her eyes that caught my attention. Were they brown or green? Or orange? I couldn't quite make it out. With a soft pull, she grabbed my hand as we began to dance around the fire. Suddenly, someone tugged at my right hand. I looked, and there was a little girl with jet black hair.

Who were these people? We were smiling, laughing, and dancing around the fire. Suddenly, the little one was gone, and the beautiful woman stopped. She looked directly at me with eyes of orange-green, hues of breathtaking iridescence. She was about to tell me something when I awoke to Gary expending his breath over my heart.

"Omar, we're done. You can get up now," he said.

What? Did that just happen? But I just laid down on the blanketed horse that was pretending to be a massage table. Who was that woman? Where did she go? How could I see her again? And how, in the great expanse of time and space, do I find her? And what was she about to tell me?

The answers, or puzzle pieces it seemed, started to come together. I was never looking for a path. The whole time I was *on* the path. And not only did I need to find the healers of our age, I was also looking for a woman—a young woman with dark hair, soft eyes, a kind heart, and a beautiful soul. A woman who would be my destiny.

# CHAPTER 4
## Bring Them Home

———◆◇◆———

**W**HEN GARY FINISHED, I looked at my watch: what had seemed like two minutes of drumming was actually around ten. Another characteristic of shamanic work is the altered sense of time. Both shaman and patient can experience time shifts. The time shifts are sometimes a matter of perception—the sense that time has gone faster or more slowly. Or it can be an actual time shift, where a localized anomaly is created, and clocks and watches in the sacred space will actually be minutes ahead or behind other timepieces in the room.

In the upper, middle, and lower worlds, the rules of time are different as well. Shamans will sometimes talk about journeying for three years in the middle world, when in normal waking time they have been in an altered state of consciousness for one hour. And this is possible because in nonordinary worlds, time as we know it does not exist. Time is merely another tool used by the spiritual traveler. I sat up and listened to Gary, who said he had brought back five soul pieces.

## First Soul Piece

"At five, you were on a street, sitting down, looking at the dusty earth. No one else was around you. I arrived with my spirit guides and van. (Gary later told me he travels the middle world with his spirit guides in a cool VW van from 1960, painted yellow with flowers.) We spoke to you and then told you it was time to come home. What was going on in your life at that time?" he asked.

When I was five, I spent a lot of time alone. I didn't have other kids to play with, so I ended up creating adventures in my mind. I was the pirate king of a fleet of captured Spanish galleons or I was the knight of the enchanted forest, living among my grandmother's peach and ash trees. I would often look out at western orange sunsets beyond green spires, wondering and asking what the next day would bring. Imagination got me through that period of isolation. I wanted to be someone else. I wanted to be somewhere else. I wasn't sad, but I wasn't happy either. It was a world I constructed in my mind, and to this day a part of me is always wandering the horizon of endless dreamscapes, looking for a new adventure.

The vital lesson of the five-year-old soul piece is this: imagination alone does not a life make. There is a world out there that must be explored, lived in, walked through, and healed. Wisdom comes from living in the waking world. Books may give us inspiration or material, but it's the decisions we make in the day-to-day world that are the exam, for it's the waking world that needs the most healing.

"Make sure you welcome your soul piece every day for the next thirty days. Do something that you enjoyed as a kid. Make your soul piece feel at home," were Gary's instructions. A shaman tells you to welcome a soul piece back for a specific period of time. This assures that the reintegration is successful, since it takes time for the missing soul piece to rejoin fully.

## Second Soul Piece

"Then I found you in an empty room, in a uniform, staring at blank walls, not quite sure of what you were doing and not quite happy with where you were. You were without form or purpose, like water looking for a glass," noted Gary. "Where were you at this time?"

At the age of twenty-three, I was a second lieutenant in the Marine Corps, stationed in Okinawa, Japan. I joined the Marines to save the world, foster democracy, and bring freedom and hope to others. Instead, stationed in deep Southern Japan, we were seen more as trespassers. The Okinawans disliked us, and they made sure we knew it. We were the imperialists, the last vestige of mainland Japan's abuse of its southern-most citizens.

And so I spent most days disappointed. I lived in a small room on-base in the BOQ (Bachelor's Officer Quarters). The space was bare; I didn't decorate it. Not a single painting, picture, poster, or wall hanging covered the walls—nothing. All was bare and empty, just like me.

When Gary brought back this second soul piece, I learned that everyone has a role to play in the great drama of life. All jobs, gestures, thoughts, and actions are significant. From the butterfly that flutters its wings to the greatest thunderstorm bringing rain to parched fields, all things have purpose. What about that butterfly? How can its life be purposeful? Imagine you're coming home from a long day at work. Frustrations are mounting, a project is behind schedule, a deadline is coming up. On your drive, you see a small monarch butterfly travel past you in a gentle waltz, and your mind drifts. Where did that butterfly come from? Was it born in a grove of trees? How many flowers has it seen? Has it ever danced upon a curtain of orange blossoms and honeysuckle? And for a few seconds, your mind is elsewhere. Your troubles are gone, and everything is beautiful once more. You're reminded about the innerconnectedness of life, the elegance of nature, the simplicity of the cosmos. All because of one little butterfly.

"Make sure you tell this soul piece that everyone has a role to play in life. No job is insignificant. We make the best with what we have. Work to help others. In this way, you spread the healing energy, the energy of light, health, and goodness," said Gary.

## Third Soul Piece

"I next found you as an eighteen-year-old, again in an empty room, not understanding why the room was so empty. What were you doing at this time?" asked the shaman.

Ahhh . . . I was a freshman in college. The world was strange, unknown, and foreign. That first year, I felt out of place—a hawk thrust out of the thermal. I debated going back to Texas, back to my family and friends, back to a world I knew.

I didn't find anthropology until my second semester. What I did find the first semester was loneliness. I wasn't sure how to function in the world of tribes where people wouldn't talk to you if you didn't wear the right letters on your chest. I thought college was supposed to be fun, a place to meet new people, to grow, and to share ideas. I made it through by wearing a mask of strength and toughness. My outer, projected persona was a contrast to my inner feelings of fear and not belonging.

The lesson of the third soul piece is this: we all have the ability to change and to direct the force of change in our lives. If you don't like where you live, move. If you don't like what you are studying, find something else. In other words, accept change as a part of your life, and utilize it! If you want to learn more about ancient Egypt, buy books. If you want to travel to the Alps, then start putting some money aside, even just thirty dollars a month. Start taking action! The longest journey begins with a single step; the largest course correction with a simple nudge.

The key is direction. Once you set about accomplishing something important, if your intent is proper, the forces of the unseen world will assist you. You will begin to consciously, and more importantly subconsciously, work toward your goal. Chance encounters will take you by surprise, and opportunities will fall out of nowhere. Doors once under the heavy bolt of mammoth timbers will effortlessly open.

"Do something fun for this soul piece. Make sure you take it for a drive, take it on a trip, do something fun. This piece was very ready to come home," said Gary.

Gary then told me how he retrieved my fourth soul piece.

## Fourth Soul Piece

"I found you when you were ten years old. You were standing in front of your mom and dad. They were fighting. You had your arms held out. Your father placed a heavy load in your hands while your mother looked on."

Once again, I was awestruck by Gary's ability to zero in on my experiences. Growing up, I remember my parents' divorce. I can, but I prefer not to, remember the long nights of them fighting, yelling, and shouting at each another. For years, this memory remained locked away in an old trunk, hidden in a place where we stow things we are ashamed of. It seemed Gary found my attic very quickly.

Like most children of divorce, I blamed myself. I didn't know any better, and I thought it was my fault. When a child's world is falling apart and the two people you love most become filled with hate, you blame yourself. And I'm not sure if I've ever really come to terms with what happened.

"We brought him home," Gary said. "He was happy to get back. He was a very relieved ten-year-old. Now you will see a shift in your family dynamics. You will also see a shift in the relationship with your parents."

Gary was right. In my interactions with my parents after the soul retrieval, I was much stronger. I refused to shoulder their burdens. If they started a disagreement, I didn't take sides. It was neither my place nor my dispute to resolve. And I wasn't about to be trapped by a Chinese finger puzzle, where the more you struggled, the worse the situation became.

Reconnecting with this soul piece also had the effect of making me more directive about choosing my path. I realized that I was never cut out to be a "suit" and that my real passion lies with travel and exploration.

The lesson of this soul piece is that there are no victims, just volunteers. Only you can take back your power—no one will give it to you. And at times, others will want to pull you into their conflicts. Resist! Don't give in. Keep your power! Live your dream and follow your path. Listen to your spirit guides, and align yourself with the higher power of the cosmos. It is your destiny.

Then Gary retrieved yet another piece of my soul.

## Fifth Soul Piece

"I last found you at fifteen to sixteen years old. You were trapped in a corner by other kids. There was a problem with your peer group dynamic. Two emotions, fear and anger, froze you. You pulled away, and away you stayed."

Gary was describing how I typically deal with situations I'm not accustomed to. When I'm thrust somewhere I don't want to be, I put up a good façade and then pull away. High school was where it began. I only had a few close friends. I limited my interactions, and instead of engaging others, I sometimes pulled inward. If I was thrown into an unknown situation, I put up a brave front, and then I pulled away. It later became a mantra to deal with stress.

The lesson of this soul piece is that we cannot just do spiritual work in the spiritual world. We cannot talk about concepts of soul retrieval, shamanic healing, healing the planet, healing our karma, and so on if we never apply these lessons to our waking reality. The key to saving the planet and achieving our shared destiny will be using strength of purpose, shared focus, and beliefs to change the world. We cannot just live in the spiritual realm, chant "om mani padme hung," and never apply what we learn. We must get out and use this knowledge as we interact with plants, air, trees, amoebas, spirit guides, shamans, and even the stars!

NONE OF THESE spiritual lessons require life-altering events. The lessons of my soul pieces showed me that any time or day of the week we can practice healing. Any hour, any minute, every minute, we can walk the Canku Luta, the Red Road. You want to know how? It's easy. Pick up a piece of garbage as you are walking down the street. Recycle a plastic bottle. Give a friend a phone call. Hold open the door for someone. Show an animal kindness. Put your hand on the trunk of a tree. Greet a stranger. Let peace and serenity fill your heart! This is the true path to liberation and healing the earth. Simple actions, done everywhere, will ultimately lead to planetary restoration.

I thanked Gary for these illuminating truths. Before I left, Gary showed me a bowl of water. "I also performed some extractions on you. I found a magical dart in your throat and a lump of blackness in your stomach. I took these out and put them into the water. Now I want you to take the water to the bathroom and drink it."

*What?* In all of my studies of shamanism, I had never heard of anyone saying that you had to ingest the things that the shaman had just taken out of you. And these things were not appealing. A magical dart is an indicator of someone not wanting to hear what you had to say. A stomach mass represents feelings of remorse you may have internalized. And now I was supposed to drink them?

BRING THEM HOME

47

"Just kidding. I just wanted to see the look on your face," he laughed.

I laughed too. Shamans can be funny and laugh just like the rest of us. My mind immediately shifted to thoughts of the Buddha, who taught with laughter. Shamanically, laughter is also a good way to ward off evil. By laughing, we raise our vibration and we release good energy into the world. Conversely, if you respond to evil with force, sometimes that force will only be redirected toward you. Laughter, on the other hand, dissipates the dis-ease and the evil. It is another useful tool in a shaman's pouch of wisdom.

I emptied the water into the toilet, thanked the universe, and then flushed it. Down, down, down—back to the planet. Down, down, down—to the earth's core, to be broken into component pieces and cleansed by our Mother. I thanked Gary, picked up my belongings, and left.

ON THE HIGHWAY to Sedona, I carried heavy thoughts. Things done, things undone, ideas I wanted to change, and differences I wanted to create. I also remembered what Gary had told me about some of the aftereffects of soul retrieval. Patients can feel lethargic or dizzy, emotions may be heightened, colors may appear brighter, smells may be more distinct, people from the past may attempt to reconnect, and many times, vestiges of the traumatic experience will once again reemerge. The aftereffects vary from person to person and are not meant to cause suffering. Instead, the phenomena is a way for the soul to acknowledge that it is becoming whole. It is a way for the person to understand that the period of conflict is over. As the soul piece comes back, the patient understands that the trauma which caused the separation is gone forever. And most importantly, the person can finally put to rest the period of pain or suffering that caused the soul piece to fragment in the first place.

Sure enough, as I was driving, an ex-girlfriend called me. I remembered Gary talking about things from the past coming back to the surface. I spoke to her for a bit, thanked her for the call, and sent the thought on its way. Some things are best left in the past, best looked at through the distance and tinge of yellowish photographs, because at a distance is the only way they appear pleasant. The long, desolate highway stretched before me into the horizon. The road to Sedona lay beyond mountains and valleys, farther beyond boulders of rust and earth.

# CHAPTER 5
## Mysteries in the Earth

———◄O►———

THERE EXIST IN Sedona four main vortexes and a smaller, secret vortex. The four are Bell Rock, Cathedral Rock, Airport Mesa, and Boynton Canyon. Proximity to a powerful vortex is characterized by a marked increase in telekinesis, psychokinesis, ESP, clairsentience, audiosentience, and otherworldy phenomena. As of yet, there are no scientific instruments that can measure the energy released by these particle storms. But that doesn't mean vortex energy isn't real; it just means that we don't necessarily have the proper advanced technology to detect these magnetic anomalies.

The best way to understand a vortex is to think of a whirlpool. The top of the whirlpool appears wild and powerful, with a large swirl; yet the bottom of the whirlpool is equally as powerful but compact and spins very rapidly. And through the spinning

———◄◇►———

tunnel that is created, the intense energy from the bottom explodes rapidly upwards. In terms of magnetics, vortex energy radiates and is projected up from the bowels of the earth. It's simply a matter of fluid dynamics. If we remember that the earth's core is made up of molten liquid, and the earth spins on its axis at a speed of 5,000 mph, then we see that the earth's spinning motion creates instability and subsequent anomalies in the liquid core. And since most of the earth's core is metal, the spinning also creates hyperenergetic magnetic fields. And the vortex is nothing more than these magnetic fields coming deep from inside the earth, being funneled to the surface by a whirlpool spin.

Vortexes are split into three types: negative, positive, and balanced. Each type describes the effect that the vortex causes. The energy of the negative vortex is said to be grounding. This type draws out a person's conflicts to alleviate pain. A negative vortex will focus, concentrate, contain, and then release a person's issues, spiritual angst, maladies, and past hurt. But to heal, it must first cut. Like a Japanese swordsman, the negative vortex will pull out the diseased limb and then effortlessly hack it away with a blade of energy. The vortex cuts through the cloud of defenses straight to the cancerous heart of one's issues and then swiftly dispatches the burden. Sedona's Cathedral Rock and Bell Rock are negative vortexes.

Positive vortexes, on the other hand, are uplifting, awe-inspiring, and powerful energy forces that can course through a person's soul and being. Like an electrical storm, the positive vortex bestows power. After visiting the positive vortex, a person will have boundless energy and a renewed sense of hope and optimism. A positive vortex bestows the energy of the warrior, the spirit of the sun, and the aura of strength, thereby empowering the will. The positive vortex in Sedona is Airport Mesa.

The balanced vortex brings calm and serenity. After spending time at a balanced vortex, a person will usually feel sleepy and at ease. The sense is sort of like being wrapped up in a warm blanket on a cool evening. The soft, radiant heat envelops you, warms you, and holds you. Balanced vortexes remind us what it feels like to be free from mental clutter and chatter. They provide us a relaxed state of being, allowing us to accept and understand the forces of the universe. These vortexes give us a reference point for a world in slumber, balance, and harmony. In Sedona, the balanced vortex is Boynton Canyon.

My goal in Sedona was to visit these vortexes. I had traveled from the Spiritwalker's toward the Great Mystery for about four hours. It's a desolate drive from Phoenix but a good time to think. Arriving in the late evening, I was ready for bed and the next day's hike.

In the early morning, I drove to Bell Rock first. The engine of my Rent-a-Runt protested in agony as it traversed the small mountain range. Sedona looks like a miniature Grand Canyon, complete with similar colors of rock, shapes of the formations, and blowing winds with cloud cover. I reached the nature park area, stopping in the visitor's lot, and unloaded my gear.

Putting on a light jacket to block the crisp mountain air, I shouldered my pack. With a brief stretch of my legs and arms, my hike began. Taking a deep breath of desert air, I inhaled the dryness and lingering aromas of cinnamon and nutmeg. Before me stretched an expanse of boulders, cactus trees, and rock awash in a sea of red. Deep ochres and siennas filled my view—reds so vibrant, you almost wanted to pick them up and rub them into your skin. The contrasting colors of red earth and blue sky colored the world, mixing and mingling the vital ingredients of life's sacred dance.

Native Americans talk about walking the Red Road. The road is a metaphor for living in harmony with nature. Certain things put us on the Red Road: reverence for Grandmother Earth and Grandfather Sky; respect for the waters; awe for our sacred brothers the otter, the wolf, the bison, the birds; and reverence for the living spirit in all things. This living spirit common to all is called the Great Mystery. And there are things that take us off the Red Road: commercialization, exploitation of natural resources, war against our fellow brothers and sisters, and apathy for the planet. So was I still on the path?

The hiking trail was smooth, gradual, and kind—like the first sip from a glass of merlot, lingering, slightly vanilla, and ever so sweet. Part of the trail appeared to snake through someone's backyard. A subdivision had recently sprung up—true civilization rising above the sand—and the path led so close to someone's home that I could easily count the individual barrel tiles upon the clay tile roof. I continued up the trail.

After crossing several dry stream beds, testament to the swift fury of desert rain, I approached the mountain. There seemed to be no trail leading to the summit, so I located the next best thing.

On the left face of Bell Rock was a dry stream bed leading to the top that created a small and accessible opening into the formation. I carefully hiked up the stream bed, dodging the low, grasping arms of tree branches and roots. Like miscreant hands reaching for my left boot, the growths were tricky to navigate. I went up about fifty feet at a thirty-five-degree slope, navigated left, then turned right to enter the body of the mountain. I felt like a small bacterium going through flesh and bone on the way to a hidden inner chamber.

My eyes scanned this amazing rock formation. It looked like three stacked donuts, each increasingly smaller in size, leading to the summit. I looked for a handhold and spider-crawled my way inside. I removed my pack and walked around for a bit. Since the formation was behind the main face of Bell Rock, I carefully found my way along the outcropping, moving outwards and right, until I was at the front of the formation.

The view was tremendous. I was forty feet tall and strong. I WAS the mountain! I could look out into the distant expanse and see other hikers along the path. With my earth-toned clothing, no one would see me if I stood still and didn't break the outline of the terrain with movement. Is this what it feels like to be a mountain? Standing tall, weathering away, yet looking out at humanity for millions of years?

Carefully navigating back to the chamber behind the rock face, I stopped and rested for a moment. Suddenly, something caught my eye. On the second ledge, at the bottom edge of the dusty donut, there was something that looked like white scratch marks upon an ochre wall. Moving closer, I discovered the design to be a series of white letters, which formed a sentence. At the level of my knees, in script two inches tall, was written "The only prisons are the ones we make." Interesting.

In the entire rock formation, in the whole grid square, I managed to find a small bit of writing, a few inches of philosophy trapped in time. If the only prisons are the ones we make, then there are no prisons. Our only limitations are the ones we create. There are no limits in terms of our humanity, our capacity for caring, or our love for fellow beings. We are only limited by, and are prisoners to, our minds and the blind dislike for those things we fear or those things we don't understand.

Those things that are foreign, those things that are strange, and those things that are different are all things we fear. And more often than not, our initial reaction to this fear is aggression. So, in effect, we've created our own prisons. We are the prisoner, the warden, and the guard. Interesting. The only prisons are the ones we make.

I began my descent after a few minutes of journaling. I loaded my pack, adjusted straps, and found the way down. After about thirty minutes, I was back at the trailhead, in front of the car. Amongst the entire mountain range, did that message from the earth just mysteriously appear? That was amazing. But the day wasn't over yet. Next I drove to Cathedral Rock.

Earlier in the morning, I overheard an employee at the ranger station describe the hike to Cathedral Rock. "That's a very hard climb. Steep ascent. Not for the weak of heart." I thought, "Yeah, right. What does this guy know? Gimme a break, I'm a former Marine. I can do this climb easily. Bring it on!" And you know what? The ranger was right. Cathedral Rock was a hard climb, every single inch of it. But not for the reasons he said.

Every muscle, every sinew, every fiber of my being was screaming in agony as I crawled up the mountain. I had hiked and climbed before. In the Marines, we routinely completed twenty-mile hikes called "humps" with full combat loads—up to ninety pounds of gear. We perspired so much that when we finished, our uniforms and boots were stained with salt. Yet none of those hikes was ever as difficult as that twenty-minute climb up Cathedral Rock.

Shaped like a mammoth staircase, Cathedral Rock is a formation with mini ledges that become taller and taller. The climb up the 400-foot megalith isn't hard. You go up about forty feet at a slight slope, climb ten feet vertically, then repeat. Along the way, you must find handholds and footholds. But it's not the terrain that makes it hard. It's the negative vortex.

Near the summit, I was mentally and spiritually exhausted. Other climbers were at the top. I saw a sixty-year-old man, a young family, and some teenagers. I quickly turned my head away so they wouldn't see the single tear stream down the right side of my face.

What did Cathedral Rock show me? What was so difficult about bounding over this small piece of boulder? Climbing Cathedral Rock, I was faced with my deepest fears and my most painful failures. Everything came back to me all at once, like reliving all my painful experiences in hyperdrive. All the mistakes, all the heartache, and all the lost dreams coursed through the core of my being like a river of fire. I wanted to give up so desperately, but I had to continue. I had to scale that mountain.

When I made it to the top, I rested a few moments, gathered my composure, and put my mask of strength back on. I made small talk with the other hikers to lessen the pain and control my unease. This mountain had conquered me. "I" was no more; there was nothing left to lose. All had been shown to me, and all had been taken away.

As the hikers turned to start down the mountain, I stood up and raised my hands in a Y-shape over the summit. I then lowered my hands slowly and dropped to one knee, touching my hands to stone, bringing my heart to the earth. I asked Cathedral Rock to take away my burdens and lift my pain. As I pushed my hands down on the rock, I felt a bit of warmth at my feet, and then a lifting in my chest, and then slowly, ever so slowly, a release downward. Down, down, down my energy went. Down, down, down toward the earth. And down, down, away from me. Like sheets of rain from a passing storm, the pain slowly receded. I sighed deeply and began my descent.

At the bottom of Cathedral Rock, I turned around and cast one last glance toward my liberator. I noticed the shape. What increased the vortex's power was the size and shape of the mountain. The Cathedral Rock formation is much taller and larger than Bell Rock. This causes a greater release of energy at the summit of Cathedral Rock, since the rock formation rises high above the desert floor. Comparing energy levels, Bell Rock is a nine-volt battery; Cathedral Rock is a lightning bolt. And if that's what Cathedral Rock feels like, I never want to go back again.

That was enough for one day. I shared my dinner that evening with a curtain of nighttime sky, and a million years of starlight shined down upon my thoughts.


I AWOKE THE next day ready to conquer the vortexes. But something had changed. I wasn't sad or gloomy anymore. I felt more enthusiastic about life. I felt optimistic. I had changed. I was transformed by the energy of Cathedral Rock.

Airport Mesa was next on the list. It's called Airport Mesa because the top of the mountain is large and flat, and has, you've guessed it, an airport. The Sedona Municipal Airport is nestled here and has a very short runway—not for the amateur pilot or the faint of heart. If you ever think of flying to Sedona, just take the silver skybird to Phoenix and drive up. I promise you will thank me.

I parked my car, paid the metallic attendant, and began walking the steep trail. A short distance from the start of the trail, the path split into two smaller trails. The first trail led to the left and upwards about thirty feet to an outcrop of rock topped by a table-like, flat surface. The second trail led clockwise around the small mountain and stopped at the summit, near the airport landing strip.

I started with the second trail, which held the longer path and gave a good view of the valley. The vegetation on both formations was sparse. Small piñon trees and juniper intermittently broke the rocky outline. After climbing up the trail and gaining some altitude, I surveyed the valley. I didn't realize it till then, but all the vortexes within view of Airport Mesa have very little vegetation. Bell Rock, Cathedral Rock, and Airport Mesa are mostly barren. The other rock formations in the valley were almost fully green. It's almost as if the vortex energy stunts or alters normal plant growth.

As I hiked across the mountain, I wondered when the trail might end. After reaching each far and away precipice in the distance, I would turn the corner to find another precipice further into the horizon. And after hiking to that ledge, I would only turn and find another, and then another. The trail seemed to stretch endlessly to the right. After about thirty minutes, I spotted an overhead ledge jutting out of the mountain slope and decided it was time for a break. Climbing fifteen feet up the mountain, I stopped and removed my pack. From the outcrop, at about 300 feet above the valley floor, I could see the whole city: Northern Sedona, Old Sedona, the rock vortexes, trees, everything. I sat down.

What happened to the first Native Americans, the Sinagua, that occupied the valley? When the city of Sedona was settled in the 1800s, the first tribes were long gone, and all that remained were a few scattered ruins built into the mountains. But the valley was beautiful, safe, green, and abundant—the valley provided life. So why did the first tribes leave? Like so many ancient capitals—such as Tikal, Palenque, Teotihuacan, and Machu Picchu—the place of sanctuary had been suddenly abandoned.

In my mind's eye, I looked down into the valley and saw a red snake run across the land, and then sickness followed by a great loss. The snake seemed to follow the outline of the river. Was it disease that wiped out the Sinagua? Was it warfare with a neighboring tribe? Did the inhabitants offend the sacred spirits or spirits of the ancestors? Will we ever know or understand? Something happened to make the ancient ones leave. Another riddle lost to time . . .

A gust from the valley quickly broke my thoughts. I gathered my gear and carefully walked down the slope. Slipping and falling on my arse a few times, I had a good laugh. Once more conquered by nature, I was reminded that even though we reside on the planet and ostensibly take care of it, we will never own or control it. We belong to the earth, not the other way around. We can only work with nature to sustain ourselves and our future. And with a short few steps, I was back on the endless trail that kept turning to the right.

After about another twenty minutes, I arrived at the end of the trailhead. A small sign read, "You have reached the end of the trail. This is the airport. Please control your jackelopes and sea nymphs, and kindly return the way from which you came."

No, there wasn't a line about the jackelope, next-door neighbor to the *homo sasquatchis*, but that would have been funny. I followed the fence line for a bit, though, and noticed it was pretty solid chainlink. I thought about performing a special Marine party skill entitled "how to climb over a chainlink fence in two seconds" or perhaps even altering the sign with electrical tape to make it say something REALLY FUNNY. Common sense prevailed; however, those few seconds seemed an eternity.

I decided to unshoulder my pack and rest for a few moments. Backpacking the Airport Mesa trail took about fifty minutes, not including time for stops. It was a decent hike. Easy and kind, just long. I scribbled a few notes in my journal, took some pictures, and then loaded my gear. Shouldering my pack, I began the descent.

As I was walking, I felt great. I bounded down the trail in large strides, the wind in my face, feeling confident. Everything looked brighter, felt better, and was simply vibrant. I was superlatively aware of the sounds, the colors of the mountain, the crispness in the air. Something was off, but I felt great, and at this point, I just didn't care. On the way down, I encountered several hikers and eagerly went off-trail, climbing around them. *Man, oh man,* I felt awesome. So absolutely alive! And within a few minutes more, I was back at the start of the trailhead.

What? How could I be back at the beginning already? I had just started walking down the trail. And then I looked at my watch. It read 12:40. *12:40? That's not right.* I began my descent from the top of the mountain at 12:25. Had I just finished the return trip in fifteen minutes? But that's not possible, because it took me fifty minutes to walk up the mountain in the first place. How could I complete one leg of a hike in fifty minutes, and then turn around and come back the same way in fifteen?

To this day, I can't explain time differential. I've been hiking about fourteen years, and I think I know what I'm doing (or at least what not to do). But it's physically impossible to have such a difference in completion times when a person is hiking somewhere and then hiking back. An uphill climb generally takes longer than the descent, but not to this extreme. It just doesn't happen.

The only thing I can possibly think of is that around certain vortexes, unusual electromagnetic phenomena occurs. These phenomena include shifts in plants, people, and time. Everything that has an electric field, bioelectric field, or magnetic field can be affected. For me, time actually slowed down or I sped faster through time. What seemed like an hour was only fifteen minutes. Moreover, I completed the 2½- mile return hike while walking at a rate of 8 mph. At full sprint, I can only run that fast for about two minutes. In other words, it's just not possible.

I remembered something else. The telltale sign of a Sedona vortex is this: an axial twist in juniper tree branches. Instead of a normal straight growth pattern, the branches of the juniper trees near and around vortexes twist spirally along the branch. The closer you are to vortex energy, the more spirally a twist you will see. And the closer you are to the vortex, the more likely you will experience a shift in energy.

I must have walked through a rift in time, a window outside of the normal ebb and flow of space and thought. It is something few people have done, and if you believe Bermuda Triangle legend, something that few people come back from. I was a bit dazed by the experience, but I took a deep breath and continued on. I would later spend hours wondering about that day, trying to figure out exactly what happened.

Once again at the start of the trail, I decided to take the leftward path. Bounding my way up the thirty-foot boulder, I quickly scaled the rock and stood on its table. Approaching the foremost section, I gazed across the valley. My face was buffeted by a strong wind, gusting about 40 knots, as a deep roar filled my eardrums. I raised my hands upwards in a Y and thanked the mountain for its energy.

I WAS ALIVE! Anything was possible. Everything was possible. All my dreams were within reach. They were simply orders to be placed at the counter of the Destiny Diner. I felt the energy. I WAS the energy. I felt a great connectedness, a sense of peace and strength. It was a knowingness—a simple idea that everything would be okay, and that we are all one. Plants, animals, amoebas, humans; plankton, redwood trees, dolphins, seagulls; howler monkeys, rhinos, manatees, snails. All different yet all the same. All part of the energy of the cosmos. I simply realized that all our shared hopes and dreams are within our grasp. And for this feeling, I thank the mountain and the vortex for their energy.

# CHAPTER 6
## Dream Date

———•⟨O⟩•———

WHEN A SHAMAN learns to astral travel, the first step is to secure release from the confines of the body. During sleep, our spirit is loosely connected to our physical form. Once in a while, we become conscious, experiencing awareness through this spirit-double, which ancient Egyptians called the *ba*. We feel paralyzed—able to wake but not stir. The shaman will control this state to smoothly free themselves from the sheath of the physical form. By concentrating, a shaman can direct his astral form to any country, any continent, any time on Earth. The ultimate journey is travel amongst the cosmos. Once the shaman has broken the bonds of the planet, limitless space travel is possible—planetary space, interstellar space, and intergalactic space are all pathways on the road to touch the face of God.

———•⟨O⟩•———

Back at the hotel after my journey to Airport Mesa, I sat on the balcony beneath the stars, pondering the day's hike and the magnificence of starlight. In the night sky, I could make out the blue stars and the gold stars, the red ones and the yellows, and the infinite starfield that lay beyond. After about a half-hour, the air once again became crisp. Zipping my fleece for warmth, I headed back inside. With my gear packed and ready for tomorrow's hike, I climbed into bed. The gentleness of deep sleep soon overtook me.

I AWOKE IN my hotel room, but I was not quite in my body. I was floating, more like fluttering, a few feet off the floor. I could feel my body riding currents of ether, going up and down, bobbing on some type of energy wave, and then I was quickly pulled outside my window. I found myself in a city block with red brick all around me.

I had experienced astral dreams before, but not quite like this one. And the brick was not just red, it was bathed in a red glow, as if saturated with deep red light. A woman emerged from the shadows. She was Asian, in her mid-forties, with fine shoulder-length black hair. She was not surprised to see me.

"May I go see her?" I instinctively asked.

The woman replied, "Yes, my son, you may."

I was then in a living room. A young woman had fallen asleep on the sofa, with a movie playing on the television. Long, dark hair framed her face. She was the most gentle, the most beautiful, and the kindest woman that I had ever seen. The entire room was filled with a soft red glow. I tenderly put my hand on her shoulder and gently woke her.

"My name is Omar, and I wanted to see you."

She gazed at me with a soft look, her features Asian but not Asian. Could she be like me? I'm Hispanic on my father's side, and Scottish and Irish on my mother's. Could she be like me, with feet in different worlds? In her eyes I saw kindness and a deep sense of peace and knowingness that touched my soul. She seemed to radiate serenity.

The lovely woman took my hand as we began to walk outside. With each step, we talked about ourselves and the world. As we walked, I noticed that she kept looking down, which meant to me that she was introspective. I could tell that she was the kind of person who truly cared about the world and thought through her actions so as not to harm another. She stopped walking and looked straight at me.

I looked at her, and for a moment, I knew. Then, painfully, I awoke. I remembered she had said her favorite color was blue, because light blue was the color of the sky—and something about blue flowers, the kind with the small petals.

COULD IT BE? Could I have just met the woman of my dreams *in* my dreams? The raven-haired lady with eyes of orange, blue, and green? Was this the same woman I had met during my soul retrieval? My mind raced. A sense of warmth radiated throughout my body. But who was she, and where would I find her?

Hoping for more clues, I went back to sleep.

After a few moments, it seemed I was once again at Vanderbilt University. I was walking along the common lawn area, from the dining hall to the student theater. I looked down, and a stream cut my forward progress.

As I followed the stream to the right with my eyes, I noticed a small, swirling vortex reaching up to the heavens. A mixture of leaves and water droplets was spinning, twirling infinitely higher and higher. The vortex was lilliputian, with a diameter of about four inches. Yet it rhythmically danced and undulated, and I could easily follow the leaves as they slowly wound their way up, up, and up in a circular motion, farther and farther into the sky.

I then saw movement out of the corner of my eye. In the distance, I scanned the horizon and saw four gigantic vortexes spiraling toward the heavens. Like dancing tornadoes, the dark masses swirled upwards. Their girth was indescribable; they were bigger than cities, churning and turning like four mega-tornadoes. It was just amazing.

And in the center of the four leviathans was this one small vortex next to a stream, reaching to God.

THE NEXT TIME I awoke was eight AM. The whole night, I had been given very specific answers to questions that haunted me. The energy of Airport Mesa allowed me to lay to rest my past, chart my future, and walk the path. When I first started opening up to messages in dreams, I would get maybe one or two dreams a month. Nothing startling, but things that were important—check your tires, study for this exam, be careful with this person, and so on. But that evening in Sedona, the vortex energy fed me precognitive dream after dream.

Receiving dream messages is like diving into a pool. You get the strongest and most accurate messages right as you fall asleep. The next best messages come right before you wake up, as you emerge from the dream waters. The time spent at Airport Mesa magnified this effect. I didn't have the normal ebb and flow of dream sleep; instead, I was held in place at the water's surface. Gently bobbing up and down, I gathered many dream messages, learning immensely. But if there were four gigantic vortexes in Sedona, as my dreams told me, where was the smaller hidden one?

After taking a couple days to rest after the ether of vortex sleep, I decided to finish my tour of Sedona and visit Boynton Canyon.

ACCORDING TO SEDONA mystics, the energy of Boynton Canyon is neutral. If I had experienced the negative and difficult energies of Cathedral and Bell Rock and the positive and uplifting energies of Airport Mesa, what would the neutral energy of Boynton Canyon hold for me?

Starting my hike toward Boynton Canyon in the early morning, I walked down a small, lonely asphalt road bordered by intermittent houses. At the end of the road, literally and figuratively, I saw an open field bordered by a high fence with a solitary gate about 100 feet away. I crossed the field of green grass—out of place in the land of reds and yellows—and approached the barrier. This was the final moment. I had the feeling that if I crossed the gate, everything I knew would change. I would be forever changed.

The symbolic consequence was daunting. Everything I thought I knew—everything that I believed to know about life, the world, the cosmos, about the experience of living—*everything* would change. And if I crossed the gate, this part of the journey would quickly come to an end. Where would I find the next adventure, the next horizon, the next mystery? Would I be called somewhere? Would I dream again? And the woman—would I ever find her?

So, with a mixture of sadness and nostalgia, uncertainty, but most importantly hope, I approached the gate, unlocked the barrier, and crossed over to the other side.

I hiked for several miles along the small trail. The farther along I went, the smaller and rockier the path became, until finally very little trail remained. Curiously, I found myself walking through an emerald green forest at the bottom of a desert canyon. *Underground stream. There must be an underground stream.* This must be the same water that feeds the trees and is the source of the mysterious rock spring in the canyon. Legend says there is a sacred rock spring hidden at the back of the canyon. With its stone lips, the spring provides the sacred kiss of healing. The water is something magical, the spring something special. To this day, Apache tribal members still visit the canyon, carrying plastic bottles, to collect the mountain's tears. As the trail ended, I scoured the area for signs of the spring.

Two hours later, after numerous scrapes and scratches, I gave up. The mysterious spring, at least for me, would remain hidden. I began my hike out of the canyon. After about fifteen minutes, I spotted something along the cliff wall. Out of the corner of my right eye, I saw something shimmering and sparkling in the sun rays. I quickly gained my bearings and moved toward the rocky ledge.

Climbing about fifty feet up and navigating through a waist-tall labyrinth of small trees, roots, and aloe-like plants with razor-sharp needles, I found myself near the ledge and saw a small cave, or at least a diminutive hollow into the mountain. It measured about two feet high and four feet deep. Moss was growing around the mouth like a small unkempt beard, and fresh water glistened around the opening. I touched a little bit of the moisture and put it on my forehead, my heart, and my hands for good measure.

As I glanced around and looked toward the opposite side of the immense chasm, I saw the layers of earth that made up Boynton Canyon. Like magnificent swirls, the sheets of white, tan, brown, and sienna were a testament to the power of time. The captured color wheel of this incredible place held the secrets to our past and the keys to our future. I remembered Gary's drum and its colorful design.

On the drum, feathers of blue, red, white, and black sprout from the center skin. From the center also emerge four arrows that partition but also link the colored feathers. And at the very center of the mandala was a human being with its head radiating knowledge. The design was a true medicine wheel—a tool of strength, healing, unity, and teaching.

A medicine wheel is filled with symbols. To Native Americans, the medicine wheel is a sacred map of the cosmos, showing the four directions of existence. It is also a record of creation, a symbol of protogenesis capturing the formation of the universe, when a single thought radiated from the mind of the Great Spirit. With its symbol of a radiant mind conquering the unknown, the medicine wheel is also a metaphor for strength, showing how knowledge can help humankind overcome ignorance. And finally, the medicine wheel shows unity, that the four races on the planet can live together by overcoming fear.

In its true and elemental form, the Native American medicine wheel existed long before humanity took its first steps on the planet. It's a blueprint of our past and a key to our present. Most importantly, it is a map to our future, for the knowledge and destiny of the sacred wheel will continue to guide us along our collective path long after we leave the planet, as long as we listen to and heed the words of the Great Spirit.

With our limited time on this earth, we must care for it and each other. The earth does not know us as tribes, races, or colors; it knows us as its children. And as its children, we must protect it. We must care for it. We must love the earth. Our journey as a species will not end here. We will surely float into the heavens on ships bearing masts of victory and discovery. From logs of math and physics, we are destined to ride swiftly on currents of hope and exploration. But will we bring enlightenment or devastation? Will we come as friends from a distant galaxy or refugees from a destroyed home?

OUR DESTINY, AND the earth's destiny, is one and the same. There is no separation. The earth is who we are, it's where we're from, and it reflects our greater humanity. The earth is the sum of our collective thoughts. The planet is a mirror unto our dreams. The earth is us, and we are the earth. And earth will always be home.

With that understanding, I left Boynton Canyon, and Sedona, forever.

# CHAPTER 7
## Song of the Elders

———————◄O►———————

**S**HAMANS HAVE BEEN healing humanity for over twenty thousand years. From as far as Oceana to the near jungles of the Yucatan, indigenous shamans can be found throughout the planet. They perform rituals to soothe, ceremonies to mend, and magic to fix the complex physical and mental illnesses that plague humankind. To alleviate suffering is the shaman's ultimate goal. To promote spiritual resilience and transcend suffering is their soul's calling. For ages, shamans have provided us healing, communicated with the gods, and given us the keys to understand the elusive concept of consciousness. But are we listening to their messages?

My journey wasn't yet complete. I needed to visit Gary Gent one last time. I wanted to find out more about the Spiritwalker and his messages for humanity. I told him that my goals were simple: just to learn. So I began with his beginning.

"Gary, how did you start shamanic healing? How were you trained?" I asked.

"I started when I was a young boy. My father trained me with concentration exercises. He would have me focus on things in the natural world, like leaves or trees or water. Clouds were special. We were taught to concentrate on clouds and change their shape. Eventually, we could change their shapes and directions of movement.

"I wasn't always on the path. I stopped at about my mid-teens. After the war, I felt like I needed to return to my roots—to return to my family and heritage. That's how I got started."

"How is it that you can travel to the other realms so quickly?"

"It's like falling off a log. I've done it so many times in my mind, it becomes second nature. I visualize balancing on a log, resting in a body of water. As I spin the log with my feet, my kundalini energy rises. As the log spins faster and faster, I wait for the right time to just let go. This is when I purposely fall off the log and into the waters of the non-ordinary realms."

"Why do you travel with so many spirit guides in the middle world?" I asked.

"I travel with a big group because it offers me protection. I can easily ask multiple guides for help, and it also helps to arrive in a group when I negotiate to reclaim or return a soul piece. Imagine if you are lost somewhere and a single person shows up to greet you and lead you home. You might first feel suspicious. 'Who is this person?' you might ask, or 'What do they want?' So instead, I arrive with a big group. The soul piece sees a family and cheering section. Instead of just one person welcoming you, it's a whole medley of sounds and whistles and claps that are all filled with joy. It's like a big birthday party welcoming you back."

"So when you encounter the soul pieces, what do they look like?" I asked.

"It depends on the situation and the person. Many times when I encounter a person's soul piece, it looks like a younger version of themselves. It's more a function of what time in their lives that person was in when that soul piece was lost.

"I also see soul pieces in the context of their situation. If someone had a traumatic event when they were working as a police officer, I will see them in a police uniform. If they witnessed something as a nurse, I will see them in their nursing gear. It just depends on the person and situation. The appearance of the soul piece is similar to a marker identifying that particular period during a person's life."

"Do you see other entities in the middle world as well?" I asked.

"Yes, sometimes I can see spirit guides traveling in the middle world. Other times, I see negative entities. The spirit guides appear as glowing or pearlescent. The negative entities appear as dark shades or shadows. Sometimes, if they are advanced, they will appear as normal beings. Other times, they will cover their eyes. The eyes will always give negative creatures away. Negative beings have eyes that are glowing red, glowing blue, or snake-like. Saints, or highly realized beings, have glowing white eyes. That's how you know they are saints."

"So you're saying you actually see beings in context of a religious belief system?" I asked.

"Of course. I've seen buddhas, I've seen angels, I've seen saints. It's not a matter of giving preference to one single religion but in recognizing the commonality to all religions."

"In Native American beliefs, are there overriding concepts such as good and evil?" I continued.

"Yes, but it's more complicated. Everything has its purpose in the universe. That's how the universe was created by the Great Mystery, through God. For example, you may see a rattlesnake while walking along a trail. You then assume the rattlesnake is bad because it can bite you. Yet, in reality, the rattlesnake has its purpose. It may be part of a larger design that we cannot comprehend. Just because we don't understand something doesn't mean that it's without purpose. And, of course, I'm not saying to pick up the rattlesnake. But instead, understand that it is there for a reason. Understand what it can do. And then just avoid it. Even negative entities serve a purpose. They confront us with our worst fears and teach us that our souls are pure light, and that we cannot live in fear or be victims of fear."

"If a person isn't able to visit a shaman, what can they do to cleanse negativity?" I asked.

"Well, you can always go to a sweat lodge. The heat serves to release toxins, to purify a person's system by making the auric and energetic field too hot for the negative attachments. The negativity is then sweated out and released. You can also eat hot chiles like jalapeños or chile piquin. This does the same thing. By increasing the core temperature of the body, we are raising the corresponding vibration of the auric and energetic field. Doing this, we are burning away the toxins, ridding us of the negative attachments to our energy field. Smudging yourself with sage also works."

"How do you tweak rules without upsetting the balance of universal laws?" I asked.

"Well, it's not that I break the rules, but I know what questions to ask so that I can get around them. I always consult with my spirit guides on the best course of action, the best way to conduct a healing, and the best way to get someone's soul piece back. Some of the lessons I've learned include that an entity cannot lie to you three times in a row. That is, if you ask it to tell you its name, it cannot tell you another name three times over.

"Some things in the middle world are there to trick you; they are there to take you off your path. That's why you rely on your spirit guides to help you. The spirit guides will tell you which roads to take and what things you can do without violating the treaties. What you think of as rules can also be thought of as treaties. There are treaties between worlds, between realms, and between entities that live in these realms. It's a matter of maintaining order—these rules maintain balance. If these treaties were to be broken, there would be widespread catastrophe in our waking world. The fabric of space and time would break down. The impossible would become commonplace. And the stress on humanity would be too great. Some call this the end time. Others call this the Apocalypse."

"Is it guaranteed that the end will occur?" I asked.

"Of course not. If we work on spiritual evolution—if we work on living in harmony with the forces of nature and being human instead of humans simply being—we will ascend to the next level of evolution, the next level of manifestation."

"You mean beings of light?" I asked.

"Yes, but capable of transcending space and time. Capable of traveling to distant worlds to assist other beings. Capable of walking with the Great Mystery."

"Gary, what do you most want people to remember?" I asked.

"I want people to remember that life is about action. Buddhists say life is like falling forward. But instead of falling on your face, you put your foot out. And then because of your forward motion, you must put your other foot out. And so on and so on. In other words, life is about movement. We must understand this motion and gain momentum as we move forward.

"It's also important not to hide behind dogma or use dogma as an excuse to foster inactivity or lack of action. In other words, you cannot encounter problems in the waking world and then use dogma as an excuse to ignore these challenges. For example, you cannot say, 'I pray to the Great Mystery every day. I go to the sweat lodge. I honor the earth. So, therefore, I respect nature.' And then do nothing when a new chemical factory goes up or skip a town hall meeting about water pollution.

"Why aren't you there protesting? Why isn't your voice being heard? Just because you fulfilled the basic actions required by dogma doesn't let you off the hook. You must act on your beliefs every single day. You honor nature by thoughts and actions. You walk upon the earth based on your deeds. Same thing with going to church, temple, or even the forest. There is no difference. Participating in religious activities doesn't get us off the hook. We must act every day, so don't get trapped by dogma," said the Spiritwalker.

"Have fun with the world. Enjoy your journey. Don't be so hard on yourself, and don't take life too seriously. Buddha laughed and scared away the negative spirits. Do the same. Laugh, learn, enjoy life, smile! Learn and smile."

With that, Gary completed the teaching, and I felt good about receiving the answers I'd searched for. We are from the earth, and to the earth we shall return. It is the firmament that holds the roots of the shamanic tree. It is the ground that connects us to our past and our subconscious. By dealing with past events, we can grow and gain the gifts of the earth—strength and sustenance. It was a rewarding journey to the deserts of Arizona, escaping prisons of my mind to emerge in forests of possibility.

# PART THREE

*Water*

# CHAPTER 8
## Madre Luna

———◄O►———

THE ANCIENT MAYA are per-
haps one of the most mysterious
civilizations. With a culture that spanned the jungles, or *selva*, of Central America to the west coast
of Mexico, the Maya occupied an area of more than
150,000 square miles. The names of its rulers were
intriguing—*Ajaw B'akab*, or Lord of the Fire, and *Yax
Pasaj*, or First Dawn, who collected tribute from
distant shores and raised stones to the sky. Their
acts were forever immortalized on megaliths called
stelae, which have withstood the selva's appetite for
more than 1500 years.

The first archaeologists to rediscover the ancient
Maya were stunned by the beautiful paintings,
glyphs, and monumental architecture that emerged
from beneath the jungle canopy. First thought to be
hills, entire pyramids were uncovered, revealing inner burial chambers filled with exquisite jade, gold,

and other ornaments. The murals were breathtaking, depicting rulers, creation, and magic.

It was an advanced culture that developed higher mathematics, astronomy, and architecture. A place where priests abstracted the concept of zero, predicted eclipses, and surmised a calendar more accurate than our own. Yet, equally shocking was the discovery that the Maya elite were not peaceful astronomer-priests, as initially imagined, but royal dynasties obsessed with rulership and power. It was blood that fed the earth and caused the sun to rise. It was the kings who provided the sacred fluid and lifeforce for the gods' sustenance—and royal blood was favored above all, to the point where rulers invoked their gods with ritual bloodletting, pulling thorns and stingray spines through tongues and other fleshy parts of their bodies.

For the ancient Maya, religion was such an integral part of daily life that there was no separate word or glyph for the concept of religion. The mystics of these orders, the ancient psychonauts seeking to bridge the realms of divinity and flesh, were the shamans. It was the shamans who communicated with gods, the shamans who guided the kings as the rulers burned their offerings of blood and paper on sacred scrolls to the gods, the shamans who foretold of great triumphs and catastrophes.

Most intriguing of all was the Maya astronomy and calendrical system developed by the shaman-priests. The Maya ("Mayan" is used when referring to the language, "Maya" is the proper term for the people and civilization) were able to predict solar eclipses, the rise of Venus, and cycles of the moon. The culture had no less than three calendars—a ceremonial calendar called the *Tzolk'in*, a solar calendar called the *Ha'ab*, and a great calendar that combined the two. And to chart the great distances of time and space from the act of creation, the Maya used epochs of time called *baktuns*. The shamans foretold that after thirteen baktuns, the world would end violently, only to be repopulated by the next race of supernatural beings.

To the great Maya, the end of the Age of Humans would come on December 23, 2012. It would seem the day of our Apocalypse, the end of the current thirteenth baktun, was predicted more than 1,000 years ago.

A FEW MONTHS after my travels in the Southwest, dreams again pervaded my nightscapes. Like velvety wine, they enchanted my mind and soul, beckoning me to begin a new search. These dreams showed me a lake—a body of tears, but not tears of sadness. I saw water that could be a turbulent blue, then suddenly change to a peaceful, soft green hue. I saw glimpses of something on the lake's southern shore—it appeared to be a highway in the midst of a jungle. Then there would be a school bus coming to pick me up and me nearly missing it. All I could remember of the dreams were bits and pieces of color and shape, nothing more. But something was wrong. I also kept seeing the shapes of caimans lurking beneath dark waters, ready to strike, and the visions wouldn't stop. Where would my next expedition take me?

I also dreamt of a shaman who was exquisitely gentle. I kept seeing an ancient woman with black hair and a blue face—a daughter of the moon, with arms and hands of bronze and cacao. She would appear next to a volcano, holding a staff and calling to me. I could never make out what she was saying, yet the words were soothing, calming, comforting. But where was this place? The lake was perhaps the best clue.

I began looking at maps, reading books, and searching the Internet. After a few weeks, I found my answer. In the jungles of Central America, near the center of the world, lies a mysterious lake. Worshipped by the Maya, the lake is thought to be the place of genesis. The name of the lake: Atitlan. And on its elemental and misty shores stood a city of shamans, a place known as Santiago Atitlan.

Other than archaeology, I knew very little about Guatemala. I had never traveled there. I didn't have any family there. My knowledge came from book study of an ancient race. Virtually wiped out by AD 780, all that remained of the Maya were burial sites, artifacts, and iconography. But why was I being called? What were the secrets of the Maya? How did a culture capable of predicting eclipses and the astronomical path of Venus disappear? And what about the calendar and the secret of 2012— would the world truly end?

I tried to put the thoughts out of my mind, but the dreams wouldn't stop. I had to find this ancient woman, this shaman. I was compelled to locate this oracle and keeper of a guarded religious tradition, one almost lost to the black shroud of time. What secrets about our world did she know, and where would I find her? Would she believe my story? The journey sounded far-fetched, but the dreams didn't stop. I had an appointment to meet Madre Luna in Guatemala, and I couldn't be late.

I arrived in Guatemala City in early November, about three months after last speaking with Gary. The plan was to meet with a local Maya guide from Panajachel and travel on to Santiago in search of the woman. I was going to look for her on the south end of Lake Atitlan and then hike into the mountains if needed. Without topographic maps or GPS, I had a plan if I became lost or disoriented: hike toward a valley and then follow the eventual draw back to the lake. I knew that the journey to find the Maya woman would be easy, but the voyage back would be hard. In dreams, I would become lost on the return trip home, or I would be running from someone chasing me in a market.

When I arrived in Guatemala City, the airport was like something out of a movie set. As we landed, we drifted past rusting hulks of long-dead birds. This airfield was an oubliette—a place where things are left to be forgotten, its prisoners bits and pieces of discarded wings and dreams. After the plane finally stopped, the aircrew opened the door, and we were greeted by humid jungle air. We slowly filed out of the silver tube of artificial surfaces, polyester, and remanufactured air and made our way into the airport, past blank walls, picture frames with no pictures, and florescent lights older than Eve. At customs, a pleasant-looking woman in her mid-thirties was my inspector. The conversation I had been expecting—"*Buenos días*, what is the reason for your visit?" "Oh, just to find an ancient woman with black hair and a blue face who lives on a lake, who speaks to me in my dreams"—never happened. Instead, she greeted me politely and stamped my passport with the darkest, blackest ink and boldest stamp I had ever seen. Welcome to Guatemala.

Picking up my bags in the arrival salon, I was greeted by my guide—a small man with graying temples and thin stature. Wearing the blue jeans and blue shirt disguise of a city dweller, he shook my hand when I approached and heaved my bag over his shoulder. A small Toyota was our slow, no-frills bullet out of the city. Off into destiny we went. Driving about thirty minutes through a maze of brightly colored one- and two-story block buildings and past lurching, growling, and grunting trucks, we hit the open road and began to climb. The memory of the city faded as we approached the clouds. Within a few moments, the temperature dropped, traffic dispersed, and we continued our ascent of the first mountain range. Gazing at majestic thirty-foot cedar trees, small copses of maize fields, and mists, my mind began to drift back to the beginning of Maya cosmology.

The Maya believe that the gods created humans a total of four times. The first time, the Maya gods created human beings in the form of animals—animals that could move, run, burrow, and fly. Animals that could laugh, bark, swim, and eat populated the earth. Caves became daytime dens for bats. Lakes were filled with fish, frogs, and amoebas, happily chirping their swim songs. The air was filled with birds of all kinds— robins, eagles, ducks, and cranes. And the animals were happy. But the only thing the animals could not do was communicate with the gods. So instead of offering prayers, the animals could only grunt, growl, and caw. The gods soon became dissatisfied and bored with the indistinguishable animal-speak and decided to try again.

The second time, the gods created human beings in the form of clay. The clay was rich in color, matching the vivid tones of the earth. The clay was easily sculpted, creating beautiful forms of faces, muscles, legs, and arms. Yet the clay was soft, and softer still were the minds within the clay bodies—incapable of thought, speech, or love. And when the clay met water, the humans dissolved, forming pools of streaking mud, gently trickling down the hillside. And so the gods brought forth the rains and destroyed the entire crop of humans so that they could try again.

The third time, the gods created human beings from wood. The wood was strong, held its form, and was wise. The wood carried the knowledge of countless trees—the mighty oak, the flexible willow, the grand scented cedar. And the wood could speak intelligently to the gods. The wood could convey knowledge and prayers, as its roots came from the earth. But the wood had no heart. Without hearts to experience life's joys, sadness, and beauty, the prayers of the wood people were hollow and meaningless. The gods soon became bored with the insincere prayers and destroyed the wood people. In a rain of judgment, the gods brought down the stars, which crashed to the earth and caused fire and explosions that quickly consumed the wood people. Then something curious happened.

As the stars fell, bits and pieces of starlight matter scattered across lush fields of vegetation. Most of the crops were destroyed in the fires, yet one crop began to thrive. When night would fall upon the earth, the gods noticed the new strange glow emanating from the fields of maize. Instead of black stalks and black leaves brought on by nighttime's paintbrush, the field of maize began to glow soft white, then light blue, then yellow. The gods, puzzled by this new maize with its soft colors, came down from the heavens and held the maize in their hands.

"Look how beautiful you are," said the gods to the maize. "See this maize! It's so precious," said the gods to one another.

And as the gods held the maize, they began to whisper secret prayers to the ears of corn. As the prayers went into the fields and up to the heavens, something else happened: the maize began to tremble with the first signs of life. At that moment, at that single moment, the gods knew maize was perfect to house the hearts and souls of their children.

So for the fourth creation, the Maya gods made the humans out of maize. And like the maize itself, the people of the maize can be cut, grow, leave seeds, feed, die, laugh, sing, and be reborn. Most importantly, they can cry, because as the gods knew, if the maize people can cry, it means that they have a heart. Tears come from only one place, and that's deep inside a person's heart. And only from a beating heart can prayers to the gods be made.

The gods were pleased with these new people of maize. They also knew that since the maize people were made from part starlight, the people were destined to return to the stars someday and walk amongst the gods.

TWO AND A half hours later, we arrived in Antigua. A beautiful city, more out of time than in, Antigua was once the colonial capital of Guatemala. However, rocked by severe earthquakes, or *terremotos*, the capital was moved in the late 1700s. The only true reminder of the city's battle with the earth is the unrestored Catholic church, whose ruins are the resting place for the great cleric-adventurer-chronicler Bernal Diaz. By edict now, all buildings in Antigua are one-story, except for significant government offices or special structures. And as all roads are cobblestone, I was thankful to be riding in a car and not a hard-planked horse wagon.

We reached the transfer station, one building amongst an age of buildings, all brick with barrel-tile roofs. In front of the structure, a road crew was repairing ancient basalt pavestones, not with asphalt or concrete or gravel but with other pavestones. All of the surrounding paving stones had to be dug up and out, the earth recompacted and stones reseated. In four hundred years, little had changed in Antigua. The same stones trodden on by countless Maya and Spanish, missionaries and traders, libertines and traitors, would be trodden upon by me.

I waited in the courtyard of the transfer station amongst travel posters and certificates, booklets, and brochures, for about thirty minutes before the next transport arrived. The various backpackers, natives, evangelicals, and I, all en route to Solola, then Panajachel, were picked up by a small bus. On the road, each traveler chatted about their lives and their likes. After about two hours, several mountain ranges, and a couple of greasy spoons, we reached the outskirts of Solola. Dusk had already fallen from nighttime's breath, and beyond the mix of artificial moons and small cityscapes, stars emerged from the woven fabric of the evening sky. Bigger in name than in breadth, Solola was more of a crossroads than a city. Maybe that's how gates into other worlds are—large in reputation yet ironically small and almost unnoticeable in actuality, perhaps to disguise the shift from the waking world of books and silicon to the realm of gods and creation. In the blink of an eye, we arrived in Solola, were greeted, and then were on our way again.

Like an overloaded pack mule, heaving to and fro with innumerous tack and supply, we reached the edge of a deep ravine, driving deeper and deeper into the bowl of the lake. Further and further we traveled, starlost wanderers whose only comfort was the seemingly graphite depths and even quicker deaths from a sudden plunge into the ravine. Although we were descending, the enveloping darkness of the lake was broken only by minute flashes of light from the city below, which gave us the feeling we were ascending into nighttime sky.

We arrived in Panajachel. More tourist stop and departure point than Maya village, the streets were bustling with late-night markets, vendors, cooked meats, illicit meets, and the pack o' dogs from any small and popular destination. This is how peripheral cities appear after thresholds into other worlds are crossed: seemingly benign yet totally dangerous.

That evening was 13 Cornstalk, 6 Ceh in the Maya calendar. Cogs within cogs, circles hurling arcs, the Maya calendar is a collection of wheels spinning endlessly into eternity. The calendar is comprised of three separate cycles of time: the Tzolk'in, the Ha'ab, and the intersection of the two, known as the Calendar Round. Day dates were made by the spinning of wheels that churn and rotate forever. And just as songs tell us which offerings the gods prefer, the sacred calendar tells us which days to feed the gods. Some days were special. Other days were extraordinary. The most mysterious days marked the end of the epic cycle, the completion of the great baktun. And the next end date is December 23, 2012.

I was let off at the front entrance to the Posada de los Volcanes, my home away from home. Once inside, I prepped my gear and hit the bed. I slept soundly that evening. No significant dreams. No insignificant dreams. No dreams whatsoever. Was I near a cave? I had no idea. Was I already in the cave? I didn't know. And so, like a character from a great adventure book, I slept like a fossil.

# CHAPTER 9
## Into the Jungle

O NE OF THE MOST important shamanic skills is the ability to communicate through dreams. By focusing their consciousness, a shaman can appear to another shaman, a family member, a village elder, or a distant relative via dreams. The shaman faces two challenges when communicating to others through dreams: recollection and fear on the part of the receiver. First, the recipient must remember the dream. The shaman must communicate the message to the recipient over and over so the receiver will remember the dream message. Secondly, the shaman must appear benign so as not to startle the receiver.

The next morning, I awoke with a mission to find a hearty breakfast and a steaming cup of freshly ground coffee. There was time before I was set to meet the Maya guide, so I walked down the arcade, past the hustle and bustle of a small market town. Vendors were already assembling their displays of garments, necklaces, and fruits. I passed several open booths of masks and stoneware, flanked by sellers of oranges and woven broadcloth. I hurried past the stalls. Choosing a restaurant, I navigated past a labyrinthine outlay of tables, It seemed I was in a box with orange-painted stucco walls. I sat down and eagerly awaited the staff.

"*Buenos días, señor. Algo para almuerzo?* Good morning, sir. Something for breakfast?" chirped the waiter. He was tall for a Maya, about five foot three with long jet-black hair and copper skin. He was dressed formally in a tuxedo vest but no jacket. I quickly ordered *huevos rancheros con frijoles*—eggs with tomato sauce, chile, bacon, and black beans. The waiter brought out a cup of hot dark coffee with steamed milk, and I let my thoughts drift.

The woman with black hair and a blue face had to live along the lakeshore, somewhere near a highway, perhaps near one of the volcanoes. Was she known by the local community? It couldn't be just a dream; it was too real—the recurring theme of leaving home, of being summoned by the ancient Maya woman. The daughter of the moon was beckoning me, calling me. She had to exist. Now I just needed to find her.

The arrival of food broke my contemplation. Guatemalan breakfasts are actually very hearty. The meal had been artfully arranged on the plate, but being too hungry to admire it for long, I broke down the formation as soon as the waiter left. The beans were creamy, the eggs firm, the bacon crisp, and the chile hot. In other words, the food was good.

I finished breakfast, paid in the colorful blue and red hues of quetzales, and walked away. I had quite a bit of time before I was to meet David, my local guide. We were to meet in the one place all adventurers go to meet their guides—a place with paneled wood, lots of glass, stainless steel, and residents from Scotland, Puerto Rico, and Russia; in other words, a bar.

I figured that if I had several hours to spend, I could at least get a good walking tour of the city. Leaving the arcade, I headed up Calle

Santander. At the northernmost end of the street, I hit a *T*, channeling any further travel only left or right. At the intersection, there was a bank, a motorcycle vendor, and a small grocery. I made a mental note of the two armed guards at the bank, holding stainless-steel shotguns at the ready. You don't see that at the Bank of America in Burbank, next to Sardo's. Turning right, I made my way up the street. A block farther, I turned left and walked northward again. Another three blocks, and I was at the center of town. To the north was the police station, and to the east, surrounded by a small stone wall about three feet high, stood a very old church. The layout of most Spanish towns in the New World is strikingly similar. Most houses and shops are arranged around a town square. The town square forms the heart of the city and almost always contains a church.

The church is usually built atop the ruins of a pre-Columbian temple. And the church, most of the time, is built with pieces of the conquered ceremonial center. The idea is to keep the flock going to the same well, just change the façade. Wood gives way to clay, clay becomes stone, stone changes to steel, and steel is transformed to silicon. Old gods give way to new. Has it ever been any different? Will it ever be?

The Catholic Church's decision to build over the old places of worship was brilliant. In doing so, the Spanish utilized the most important secret that's at the core of any religion: it's the faith from believers that gives the institutions power, not the other way around. Because the new churches were simply built atop the old sacred sites and much older sacrosanct caves—hallowed ground that had been worshipped for untold generations—the people already believed in the power of the place. The church simply harnessed the energy connected to the sacred spaces. It was the power of faith, the belief in faith, just shifted in a new direction. Incorporating the most important sources of mystic energy, faith and knowingness, the church kept the religious sites the same; all they did was change the outer shell.

Looking at the church in the town square, I noticed that the stone was different. The church wasn't built out of concrete or brick; it was constructed out of basaltic stone, the same stone from the mountain, a weathered steel-gray relic of the earth that was everlasting. If anything, the church said, "I am of the earth. Look at me. Look at my skin and bones. I *am* the mountain." And behind the church was nothing except sheer cliff—just a stone curtain stretching 300 feet into the heavens.

The church was also at the highest elevation in the village. Only by accepting this new religion could the villagers scale the mountain. Only by accepting God would their souls ascend the heavens. This was the symbolic message of the church, designed by foreigners to control native beliefs. But control was merely an illusion, for the true control and destiny of the church stood with the indigenous people, as it always had. And culture would find a way to survive.

I walked up the steps before the church and entered through its old wooden doors. Blackened by time, the timbers bore witness to hundreds of years of baptisms and marriages, deaths and sermons, salvation and sainthood. The unholy and the devout, the questioning and the faithful had all passed under them.

Nowhere to be seen was the ostentatious decoration of Mexican churches. Gone was the thrice-melted Aztec gold that had passed through ancient hands as tribute, been melted to form idols, and finally been melted one last time by the Spanish to venerate saints. From ceilings to floor, crosses to chalices, garments to icons, all the gold in Mexican churches came from the Mexica. But in this Guatemalan church, there was not a single drop of gold adorning even a nail head. The church was spectacularly ordinary. As I walked into the stone cave, searching for destiny, my eyes darted to the ceiling.

At the front of the church there was something strange. Though the space was mostly empty, I encountered an overwhelming sense of fullness, like sound with no source, waves with no ocean. And although the church was vacant, I didn't feel alone. So what saint or ghost was with me that day in the Church of San Francisco de Assisi in Panajachel? To this hour, I am unsure.

I knelt down before the main altar. I bowed my head and clasped my hands. Silently, I prayed. I asked for a safe journey, for signs to light the path, for happiness and fullness. I prayed for truth, that I would stay on my road. I prayed for life, that all living beings would feel joy. And I prayed that the dark-haired woman—the one I saw from my first soul retrieval with the Spiritwalker, the one that comforts me—that wherever she was, that she be kept safe. As I rose, a sense of knowingness pervaded my center. Whatever happened, this journey would work out well. And whatever may come was destined.

After rising and leaving the church, I wandered the streets. I visited chocolate shops and tortilla makers, coffee roasters and street vendors. The sights and sounds of the village reminded me that I was far from home. Eventually the time came to meet my Maya guide, David.

I was meeting my guide at the PanaRock, or the Panajachel Hard Rock Café. It was a knockoff, complete with nightly music, T-shirts for sale, and a school bus—yes, a school bus—inside of it. As I walked into the bar, up the steps, and past the first line of tables, to the right was the sawed-off half of an entire school bus, either welded, Super Glued, or bubble-gummed to the wall. That was interesting, because before I left, I kept dreaming of being picked up by a school bus. In Guatemala, the most widely found transport is a converted school bus, more commonly known as the chicken bus. Its notorious because (1) it's usually colorfully painted and tricked out to match the secret identities, whims, and desires of its drivers, (2) it usually carries many more people than it was designed to, and (3) since it's exceeded its driving lifetime and monies are put into paint rather than shocks or tires, the ride is about as comfortable as sitting on a cast-iron plate with worn springs.

And yes, they do carry chickens—and pigs, goats, monkeys, roosters, iguanas, and everything else. The buses were born in the United States, took countless children millions of miles, and then were sold and transported to Latin American countries to begin a new life, or at least to finish an old one. Once, I even saw a yellow bus with an old insignia of "Rock Falls Illinois ISD" on its side. But most chicken busses are painted bright hues of pink, red, green, or orange. They actually look cool, with custom chrome rims, special lights, custom paint. It's like a bus that artsy beatniks or rebellious youth would ride. But the ride is punishing, since the modifications are only superficial and little money is actually put into improving or even maintaining the ride of the bus. So most busses have worn-out shocks, bad brakes, paper-thin seats, and frenetic drivers. In other words, a chicken bus.

I looked around the bar for a while, getting my bearings and thinking about my next move. I didn't quite know what my guide looked like, but I knew his name. So I ordered a Coke and asked for David. The sodas in Latin American countries are crisp and refreshing, made with old-fashioned sugar cane, not high-fructose corn sweeteners. A moment later, David walked in.

He was unmistakable. With arms the size of saguaro cactus and the chest of a tree stump, he was perhaps one of the largest Guatemalans I had ever seen. Ordering rum, we spoke for hours. I first asked David about the civil war. Lasting over thirty years, the episode was a dark stain on Guatemalan conscience and consciousness. When I asked what eventually happened to the *guerilleros* (the guerillas) and the nationalist groups, David just shrugged his shoulders and didn't answer.

David said I needed to visit the Chichicastenango market, a gathering place for trade goods, fresh vegetables, people, and woodwork. David also talked about shamans in Guatemala. Most use candles with their magic. The colors of the candle represent intent—red for love, green for prosperity, blue for health. Fire was important too. Most ceremonies were performed with fire and copal, just as the ancient Maya had worshipped their ancestors almost fifteen hundred years ago. Prayers were chanted and sung—the gods craved attention, song, liquor, and music, just as human beings did.

David also said there was a mysterious elder we needed to see. Some called him the Lord of the Lake. The effigy was worshipped in homes around the shore, but its main altar was in Santiago Atitlan, on the opposite side of the water. I asked David about 2012 in the Maya calendar and if he was ready for the great apocalypse. He just smiled and ordered another round. David and I talked for hours—about legends, shamans, and mystical powers. About journeys, magic, and objects devoured. We even talked about the school bus welded to the wall.

David knew of several powerful healers around Lake Atitlan. We would first visit villages on the shore, then search the hills for the lady of the moon, the Madre Luna, if need be.

Our exploration would begin in a few days, as David was scheduled to work the two following mornings. I could use the time to journal, review travel books, and study the language. Or I could just go on ahead to Chichicastenango and then Santiago Atitlan.

Well, I'm in the jungle, a travel guidebook isn't going to answer my questions, and I've got a day or two. Let's go!

Besides, I had arranged for another local guide, just in case.

# CHAPTER 10
## Pagan Market

———◆◯◆———

$S$YNCRETISM IS WHAT anthropologists call the blending or infusing of diametrically opposing religious or belief systems. When two different cultures meet, one does not always completely subjugate the other. Many times, the weaker belief system will go underground and remain hidden. Using and appropriating the symbology of the new religion or new culture, the old religion will find a way to survive. Stone gargoyles and snakes found in Catholic churches built during the Dark Ages remind us of the nature religions of Europe. In Santería and Palo, the old gods, or orishas, were given the new names of Catholic saints to appease the church. Even time-honored symbols of the Christian faith, such as the Christmas tree and All Saints' Day, were once Pagan traditions.

My itinerary in Guatemala now included visiting the largest indigenous market in Central America, in Chichicastenango. I waited for the shuttle in the hotel's outdoor courtyard, conversing with my new-found friend, a yellow-headed Amazon parrot named Paco. After pecking me a few times, the wily bird dipped its head, down and to the left, and allowed me to scratch the downy feathers behind its ear. I talked to Paco until he finally whistled the all-too-familiar "Wheee-whooo" that men make when an attractive female walks by. Paco was a male parrot, of course, and I quickly turned around just to see if by some twist of fate a beauty was behind us. No such luck. I returned to the business of waiting.

As the cool mountain air drifted into the valley of Lake Atitlan, the hustle and bustle of the city soon overtook dawn's silence. The sun grew brighter, mountain mists began to evaporate, colors were clearer, and the grittiness of the town sharpened. In the early dawn hours, the city became the blade of a hoe whose freshly shorn shavings were blown off into the nothingness of empty memory. After a few more minutes, the bus arrived and picked up its passengers, including a couple from New York, some tourists from Canada, a small group from France, and a young man from Spain.

The van headed northwest to the outskirts of town and then up the mountain highway leading to Solola. The small white transport slowly lurched up the steep trail. With no guardrails, all our eyes could focus on were mountain, road, foliage, and a sheer drop into brown-gray stone. We were all travelers searching for something, eagerly awaiting the market's color and shape.

Every so often, I would look back over my left shoulder and see the expanse of the lake. Like a small ocean held firm in a cereal bowl, the deep blue waters were ringed by aggressive and towering volcanoes. Lake Atitlan, visible from space, was created 80,000 years ago when a mega-volcano exploded, sending ejecta as far away as Florida. The lake was formed when water filled the magma depression created during the explosion. With depths of 350 meters, it's difficult to fathom how so much water could leach, fall, and seep its way into the pit.

Coming off the mountain, we reached the flat lands and rolling hills of the countryside. Gazing out the window, I observed the sights of a typical day in Guatemala—small fields of giant corn with stalks reaching ten feet high, woodcutters hunched over from the weight of packs on their backs, and plenty of stray dogs, goats, and chickens. After about an hour of driving, we approached the outskirts of Chichicastenago, or Chichi. The most striking feature of the city was the lack of ever-present cinderblock buildings. Instead, dotting the landscape were older buildings of stone and stucco. As we entered the city, asphalt-paved streets gave way to cobblestone and basalt.

Finally, the van came to a halt. We eagerly departed and went our separate ways. Looking across the landscape, something immediately caught my eye: a small wisp of smoke on the side of a faraway hill, a cottony vapor slowly rising and undulating against the azure sky.

Walking toward the smoke, I could make out a person amongst the great expanse. The small figure was burning an offering. I could tell by the arm movements—the person would kneel and gesture toward the earth, then stand and make sweeping motions toward the sky. I wondered what prayers were made among ancient forests as grayish smoke rose to the sky in stair-step formation. Offerings are best made on certain days of the week. Wednesdays are good, and so are Mondays. But not on Sundays, as this would offend the saints. Hundreds of years ago, the Maya taught us the best days to present offerings to ancient gods . . .

THE PRIMARY MAYAN calendar is the Tzolk'in, or ceremonial calendar. It was used to forecast auspicious days for gifts of copal and flowers to the deities, enthronement of kings, days to begin military campaigns, and occasions for festival. The Tzolk'in consists of 260 days, which

Mayanists also say correlates to the period of time that a human fetus stays within the womb. There are twenty months of thirteen days each in the Tzolk'in. But the Maya also used two other calendars.

A young boy approached me and broke the thought. "*Buenos días, señor. Necesita usted un guía por su viaje? Mi nombre es Martín.* Good morning, sir, do you need a guide for your journey? My name is Martin," chirped the young sparrow while holding out his right wingtip for a handshake. It was actually a very good sign. Hindu gurus would say it was auspicious, for I had just finished reading a travel book by an author with the same name. And so, after discussing a schedule and making arrangements, Martin and I headed out into the vastness of Chichi, a young bird leading a lost tiger into the vast mystery. Martin was about seventeen years old, although he looked about twelve. Small in stature and thin, his short black hair framed an elegant coffee-colored face. He was well-spoken, polite, and wore pressed clothes. Attired more like a golf pro than Maya boy, he quickly pointed out his government-issue photo badge, identifying him as a professional tour guide. We planned to see churches and the market, and I especially wanted to see the enigmatic *Pascal Abaj*, or Stone Mountain God, that had been worshiped for over a thousand years on a small hill near the city.

The young man led the way through the first octopus-like row of people and market stalls. Guatemalans from all provinces descended on the Thursday fair. The booths were simple—just wooden tables with plywood walls, no longer the bright yellow color of new pine but instead a faded grayish-brown from rain and passing seasons. And the variety was impressive. We passed booths of wooden masks, jewelry, and *huipiles,* or woven dresses; vendors of carvings, rice, grain, breads, and coffee.

After several turns through the market, we reached the outer edge of a white two-story building. We walked inside, climbed two rows of stairs, and turned right. Through the doorway, the noise and faint scent of the vegetable market began to seep into our spheres. A few steps later and we were on a balcony overlooking the entire symphony. And the aromas! I smelled the most fragrant vegetables ever. It was like smelling life. I could make out the soft aroma of corn and tomatoes, the deep smell of squash, the sharp smell of celery, and the brightness of oranges and grapes. I could make out the crispness of the onions, the green scent of nopal, or cactus, and even the soft perfume of roses.

This was the smell of the earth itself. Everything was natural and alive! Beauty replaced the heavy, dull odors of metal, the chemical wafts secreted by plastics and polyester carpet, and the sickly and thick flatulence of diesel engines and unnatural fire. Instead, all I smelled was the beautiful smell of the earth. I wish I could have somehow placed the scent in a bottle, just to open it up every morning and breathe it in.

From this vantage point, I scanned the market and spotted more types of fruits and vegetables. Roma tomatoes, jalapeño chiles, red grapes, butternut squash, shallots, avocado, and pineapple. Onions, bananas, strawberries. Yellow corn, mangoes, and watermelons! It was just a heaven of colors and flavors. And each pile was carefully arranged as women and men eagerly sifted through earth's offerings, gathering food to feed their families and loved ones.

I took my camera out and started to take pictures, but something curious happened. I began to have problems with one area of the room and one person in particular—a man dressed in the traditional attire of the Tzutujil Maya. The Tzutujil are the mysterious Maya ethnic group that live among the shores of Lake Atitlan. The man wore the unique embroidered shirt, black cowboy hat, red sash, and knee-length white pants of the order. And every time I tried to take his picture, my photos blurred. After about three attempts, the man turned round, looked straight at me, smiled, and then turned back around to continue his vegetable quest.

"The photos aren't coming out, are they?" asked Martin.

"No, they're not." I replied.

"That's because he's a shaman," the bird chirped, smiling.

This had happened before. I had the same problem with Lee Cantu in Austin, when he was healing a patient. When I took his picture without asking, the photo didn't turn out and about twelve other pictures in my digital camera were wiped out. The pictures were saved on a memory card, but it didn't matter—they were still erased! I had to ask Cantu's permission before I took his photo. After I asked, the new pictures came out fine, and I was a believer once more.

Here in Guatemala, I didn't want to lose any pictures, or—worse—my camera. I quickly erased the shaman's blurry pictures and then mentally asked him to pardon my transgression. I regained my composure and took a few more pictures of the vegetable market, being careful not to include the shaman in any of the shots. After a few minutes, I told Martin I was ready to see the church.

Once outside, the dustiness of the town quickly replaced the pleasant smells of the market. Walking slowly, we eventually reached the main church. At the top of a platform, past twelve steps, stood the entrance to the Iglesia de Santo Tomás, or the Church of Saint Thomas. Yet what stood out was not the church itself but the stone altar halfway up the stairs to the entrance. The altar burned the sweet sweat of native trees. And as bits of copal and balsam were touched by fire and turned to smoke, countless untold prayers reached the heavens.

I eagerly ascended the stairs, and an unusual but known sense of dizziness and vertigo overtook my body. The feeling is unusual in that I don't normally get this feeling. The feeling is known, however, because I feel this way only when I'm near powerful magic. It's sort of like vertigo or being dangled off the side of a tall building on a bungee cord. Just as you're starting to feel steady, *whoom*, the cord pulls you up and dizzies you again.

As I reached the top of the stairs, I peeked through doors to gain a glimpse of the church's innards. I strained my neck, and like a tan brontosaurus, my head ventured in while my eyes eagerly searched for food. As my vision adjusted, I decided to cross the threshold of the church and was amazed.

If the church at Panajachel was left of normal, the Iglesia de Santo Tomás in Chichicastenango was out of the heavens. If I could only use one word to describe the scene, it would be *pagan*. For inside the enormous cavern was not a Catholic church but a ritual cave. And in the mouth were magics, collections of arcane knowledge, secret incantations, and faith that had remained unchanged for over a thousand years. Even though the ceremonies were performed in a public setting, few understood what was really going on.

In the middle of the church, spanning from the entry doors to the pulpit, were eight wooden squares on the floor, arranged by twos about three feet by three feet in size, holding various sticks of colored candles and being prayed over by no less than four shamans. And as the light of the candles saturated the room, I could also make out the faint smell of copal while the layered sounds of prayers and chanting were sung over and over again.

As my eyes continued to adjust, I walked closer to one of the shaman's squares and sat in a pew to observe her work. The movements were slow and deliberate, cautious and reverent. Dressed in a traditional *huipil*, she carefully took ten candles out of a canvas bag. While on her knees, she placed each one of the candles atop the wooden square. The mini-stage of faux stone was ebony after years of offerings, smoke, wax, and use. As she placed the last candle on the wood by drip-melting it, then seating it, I leaned in for a better look and turned my head to hear magical blue speech: "*Tuc ac, mac lic. Tuc ac teen-o. Siempre dos rujin. Tuc ac hamee.*"

I could only make out one word in Spanish out of every ten; the rest were Mayan. In Guatemala, there are over twenty subdialects of the Mayan language; the majority of the country doesn't even speak Spanish. The shaman continued: "*Tuc ac, tin lo volver. Tuc ac lin ac neeh.*"

I looked to Martin for an explanation. He just shook his head and shrugged his shoulders in the universal *I don't know* expression.

Once in a while, I can tune in to the sounds and hear in my mind what the shaman is saying. It's similar to drifting off into wakeful sleep, resting, and then tuning in. I slowed my breathing and listened for a few minutes. Nothing.

Sometimes I can also see when shamans are transferring energy. This is how I see what the shamans do. This is how I saw Lee Cantu perform psychic surgery on Ruth. This is how I observed Gary Gent use his drum to open the portal to the lower world. I lowered my eyelids and started to relax. Nothing.

Today, in this church, with this shaman, I didn't hear or see anything. No sounds, no feelings, no impressions. No smells, textures, nothing in my mind. Just sheer nothingness. It could actually be some sort of a cloaking spell. The shamans envelop their mind with a type of fog so you can't just stop in and say, "Hey, how are you? So, that's a love spell, right?"

The same thing happened in the market with the shaman and photo. It's as if the shamans in Guatemala try to protect their images, their minds, their thoughts. And some of the protective shield must come from the land itself. How else can a culture and magical tradition survive hidden for so long? A bit mystified, I sat back in the pew and instead began to look at the arrangement of the candles.

As the shaman lit and placed the candles on the square, a shape began to emerge. Two columns of white candles were placed perpendicularly to a pair of yellow candles. The colors were angled slightly outwards as the outline of a pyramid formed. Both the white and yellow candles were small, each about five inches high. The shaman would take a candle from her pouch, light it using the center candles, allow the wax to drip, and then place the new candle in one of the columns. "This is a marriage ceremony. The shaman is asking for life, happiness, and joy," Martin noted.

That made sense. Two become one, and from one emerge many. Each side represented male and female.

"The white candles are the children, aren't they?" I asked Martin. And just as Martin began to nod his head, the shaman looked up at me and smiled—and for about a split second, faster than a flea's breath, I could have sworn the shaman winked at me. I quickly looked at Martin and then toward the shaman once more. Her head was back down, intently focused on the work.

After a few more minutes, I moved to another pew and looked as another shaman began spellcasting. Once more, learned hands of leathery mocha began to slowly pull out candles and arrange them in a form. And as the candles took the form of an arc, with hues of purple, blue, green, yellow, orange, and red spaced around a white candle, the shaman slowly began speaking to her creation.

"*Been-ah. Mos tee, tuc ac. Mos tee been ah,*" the gentle voice whispered to the candles. And as the last candle was placed on the wooden square, the soft flames began to sway—at first one, then a couple, then a few more, until all the candlelight was dancing in unison.

"That's for healing, isn't it?" I asked Martin.

"Yes, how did you know?" he replied.

"The colors. You can always tell by the colors," I said. The white candle was the patient. The colored candles represented the chakras. The shaman was using the candles to realign and reenergize the person's energetic body to bring about healing.

I spent a good thirty to forty minutes in the cathedral, watching as people came and left, prayers were formed and released, and thoughts and speech were directed toward the gods. Occasionally tourists would enter the church and watch as a shaman was praying. The tourist would quietly utter a few words to their traveling companion, the companion would snicker and laugh, and then the pair would leave.

It irritated me that some tourists looked at the indigenous people as if the Maya were prisoners to the past, locked in a meaningless ceremony and unwilling to accept the powerful gods of Technology and Convenience, Silicon and Chaos. They didn't see that this place was a mesmerizing periscope into a culture thousands of years old. Words ancient and beautiful. Hands powerful and soft. Lifeforce, essence, and energy. Transcendence was at hand, but enlightenment was trivial in the eyes of the blind. Melancholy and sad, I walked out of the church. So beautiful and so tragic. Would we ever transcend our world to walk amongst the holy? Would we break free of our bonds? Perhaps I was most upset at myself, for I am just as guilty, if not more so, as anyone else of fighting to keep the shackles on. Of mindfully forgetting the true nature of life. Of not remembering the mystery and beauty.

I deeply exhaled and looked at a puzzled Martin. It would take me some time to digest a bitter meal of thoughts, epiphany, and regret.

As we walked out of the church and down the steps, Martin asked where I wanted to go next. Something significant had happened in the church, I just felt it. And I needed to continue along this path. I asked Martin to take me to the other church in town, the Iglesia de Calvario, or Church of the Calvary. I was led by Martin back through the rich sights and smells of the market. We eventually made it to the second church after dodging woodcutters, small babes, and other marketgoers. Once again, I was greeted by steps leading up to a platform.

After a thousand years, had anything really changed? A temple holding ancient mysteries stood at the top of a hill as a solitary man walked up stone stairs, searching for God. I was reminded that for the Maya, the form and shape of a temple isn't important, isn't necessary to commune with the gods. The importance lies in the sacred prayers, the spiritual essence that's given from one's heart. It's the divine breath that is spoken—the words and thoughts that originated with the gods—that is given back to the gods in the form of prayer.

And why is breath so important? Because it was through breath that the Maya gods first gave the sacred lifeforce to the people of maize. The gods talked the Maya people into existence. The gods sang life into their souls. The breath of the gods infused the maize with consciousness, and the maize became alive. And just as the gods talked to the maize, so do the people of maize talk to their gods.

The Maya communicate to their gods through breath—with sounds of sacred prayers, songs of majesty, and words of faith. For Maya shamans, it is the most powerful way to communicate to the gods. It's the breath that makes it special, because the breath carries the words from a person's soul. It's faith that makes prayers holy, not the temples, statues, or even candles. It's the words and breath that convey life, but the words have to be energized with faith. It's the energized words that feed the gods, speech both holy and sacred.

Inside the Iglesia de Calvario, I found the scene extremely ordinary. This church had no sacred prayers emanating from different voices, no candles in secret formations flickering amongst soft, bronzed hands, caressing color and fire. My lungs were no longer filled with the sweet smell of copal, thick as peanut butter mixed with molasses. Instead, at the head of the church, near the pulpit, a small line of people were waiting their turn to approach what looked like . . . seemed like . . . was it . . . a glass coffin?

Quickly, my mind turned to scenes from nineteenth-century England, when the dead were displayed in glass coffins, dressed in black, surrounded by small black drapes, on a black coach led by a black horse with a black-dressed steward riding onwards to the cemetery. I approached the horizontal dais at the front of the church with a bit of caution. As I walked up the platform and closer to the sepulcher, my sense of dread was replaced by a sense of awe and peace, for the person inside the coffin was very familiar.

I noticed the features on the statue lying down in eternal waiting. A beard. Wounds on the wrists and feet. Brownish hair. Flowing robes. Sad eyes filled with human suffering. Wearing a crown of thorns. The statue, the body, the deity was Jesus Christ.

No longer was God an abstract concept, something placed high above you upon a wall, looking down. This god rested at eye-level with the faithful. This god shared their anguish, felt their tears, sensed their pain. All of the Guatemalans that approached Jesus that day prayed in the same mesmerizing way. They dropped down to their knees, made the sign of the cross, clasped their hands, prayed deep prayers, and when finished, every one of them placed their right hand on the glass coffin and touched God.

After two thousand years, through turmoil, upheaval, and the crashing of the heavens, very little had changed. The Maya still needed to touch their gods. It was touch that connected the people to God and gave them comfort. It made people feel they were not alone; instead, divinity was all around them, touching their souls. For just as the gods touched the maize, the people of the maize needed to touch the gods. We all need that connection to the sacred.

But where are the gods? Are the gods in temples? No. Are the gods only in statues? No. Are the gods in sacred relics maintained only by chosen priests? Of course not. The spirit of God is in the chirp of birds in trees, the cool mists enveloping the mountains, the strong gusts of the air, and the endless folds of whitecapped ocean waves. These are all natural things that were created by divinity and reflect divinity; thus, God is in nature. And touching God is as easy as touching nature. If all of nature is a creation of divinity, then all of nature is a connection to the divine. By connecting to living things and respecting nature, we touch the holy.

This is another aspect of Maya shamanism. Although it may appear that the Maya need to physically touch their gods, in reality the Maya don't require statues, or idols, or physical forms to worship. The Maya don't require stone temples, or churches, or even altars. All the Maya require is nature. For the Maya, the gods are nature, and nature is God.

The Maya gods are found in the air, the soil, the plants, and the lake waters. The Maya pantheon gives us Chaac, the god of rain. It also tells us of Cay, the god of water. And then there is Ixchel, the goddess of the moon. These are all nature spirits. Why? Because God is in nature.

If a Maya wants to worship the rain god Chaac, they don't go to Chaac's temple, they go outside and pray for rain. If the Maya want to pray to Ixchel, they wait until the moon is high above, lighting the valleys with a soft blue hue. That way, the Maya can worship their gods anywhere and everywhere. By touching the spirit of nature, the spirit *in* nature, the Maya connect to the divine.

As I WATCHED the last pilgrim rise from her prayers, I noticed her hand-woven dress of blue violet, embroidered with flowers, corn, and birds. It spoke of a deep faith in nature. I then heard a soft voice behind me. Turning around, I saw a small doorway near the front of the church. Leaning in for a closer look, I saw a small figure in the corner with fire and shadows, sitting at a table.

I stood up and walked toward the small room on the right side of the church. Seated at a small pine table, gray with years, was a man dressed in traditional Tzutujil attire of embroidered shirt, short white pants, and a sash. He was speaking down, toward the table, while his right hand made careful up-and-down movements across the wooden surface. And as a flickering flame of candlelight danced, I began to make out his features. The ensuing collage of his many faces filled my mind. This man was a farmer, his dark skin stretched tightly over his face. He was also a father who had watched his sons and daughters grow old and pass. And he was a sage, his voice steady, his movements fluid, a keeper of ancient wisdom who didn't need to wear trinkets or amulets of shiny gold.

With calloused and leathery hands more akin to claws than fingers, he kept reaching for things on the table. The Maya seated at the table was a fortune teller. Shamans routinely use tools such as bones, shells, and runes to portend the future. The Maya seer repeated the cycle, the spinning of objects over and over. My mind again returned to the Maya calendar.

The second Maya calendar is the Ha'ab. The Ha'ab is the solar calendar used to time harvests, identify the solstices, and track astronomical phenomena such as eclipses. The Ha'ab consists of 365 days. Together, the Tzolk'in and the Ha'ab make up the Calendar Round. Like interlocking fingers, or bi-directional cogs, the Tzolk'in and Ha'ab spin together to create over 18,980 combinations of day names. Some of the day names include Batz (Monkey), Ajpu (Sun), and Ak'bal (Night). For example, a Ha'ab date for August 1, 2007, would be 19 Xul (Dog); the Tzolk'in date would be 11 Chuen (Frog). But when both the Tzolk'in and the Ha'ab come together in the Calendar Round, another date is formed. The proper Maya name for August 1, 2007, is 4 Ahaw 8 Kumk'u, a name that honors both the will of the gods and the dreams of humans.

At the church, the seer's digits kept the shape of a T. rex's head as they reached for something, picked it up, and then placed it back down. The pattern was repeated as he spoke a mysterious language of rhyming words and coarser words. I walked toward the table and saw that he was reaching down and moving small beans.

The beans were colors of deep red and crimson, some with black eyes, some with white, that formed pools atop a pine table. And the larger pattern that emerged was a square with five columns and five rows. The beans were moved from pile to pile. Color and shape began to fill my eyes, just as another message emerged from the vastness of eternity.

The man stopped, let out a deep sigh, and then looked straight at me. He said something in Mayan and then waited for my reply. I quickly looked around for Martin, but the sparrow had momentarily flown away. This was something important, and my translator was gone.

I sat down at the empty chair. With a wave of his right arm, fabric swooshing on wood, the seer cleared the table. And when all the beans were once again in a big crimson pile, the man began to mix the eyes by moving the pool in a clockwise swirling motion. Clockwise is how water drains in the Northern Hemisphere. Clockwise is how rooms are saged by Cherokee Spiritwalkers. And clockwise is the direction vortexes spin in Sedona, reaching upwards toward infinity.

With determined motions, the seer began to pour smaller pools. First, five pools were poured into a column on the far left. And then another column, and another, until twenty-five small crimson pools dotted the table. When a pool was fully formed, the man would reach to that pile, pull out a bean, and then place it back into the larger pile. And from the larger pile, the man would pick out another bean and place it back into the smaller pile. The scene was repeated, over and over, until I was dizzy and lost track of which bean went where. I became mesmerized by the movements and the slow, subtle prayers emerging from the man's mouth.

Every once in a while, the man would stop, open his eyes in amazement, and then say something that wasn't a part of the prayer. Or he would see something in the beans, pull his body back, raise his chest, widen his eyes again, and mutter something. Then he stopped dead as a lump of coal and said, "*Tuc lín, mish nosh. Tuc ac lín ac. Leen meeh aj hun.*"

Out of the stillness of my confusion, I heard another voice:

"He says your destiny is close at hand, but destiny can cut two ways." It was Martin. "He says your destiny is close."

The message stunned me. I sat back in my chair to let it sink in as the echoes of candlelight began to show the other denizens of the room.

Stacked to my left like bundles of wood were four large objects. At once shiny, then matte, I began to notice more and more of them. As I turned fully toward them, I saw the truth of what my eyes had struggled to see. The objects were not blocks of wood. They were lacquered coffins.

Quickly, I reached for my wallet to pay the seer. I felt my entire soul shudder. I needed to leave quickly! Without even thanking the sage, I sped out of the room and into the larger church. Regaining my composure, I slowed down a bit at the midway point of the temple. I needed some air, and my chest was pounding. Outside the church, my eyes readjusted to the light and the reassuring presence of people. Beautiful people. Market people. Maya people. Living people.

Martin was behind me. "*Todo está bien?* Is everything okay?"

I nodded my head. "*Sí, no más necesito aire.* Everything's fine, just needed to get some air."

Yeah, right. That was total bullshit. I was trembling. Note to self: before you have your fortune read, make sure the room is not a holding area for coffins, cadavers, or other things categorized under the heading "formerly living, now dead and very likely to haunt you."

And the message—what did it mean? "Your destiny is close at hand, but destiny can cut two ways." Two ways? What two ways? Martin quickly broke me from the spell.

"*Estás listo a ver Pascal Abaj?* Are you ready to see Pascal Abaj, the stone of the mountain?" chirped the bird.

"*Seguro que sí!* Let's go," I hastily replied.

I'm brave and mostly fearless. But that time, I was faking it. I was shaken by the coffins and the prophecy. Destiny can cut two ways—both good and bad. I knew about the good outcome, which was finding the woman in the middle of the jungle. Completing the impossible quest, I would find her and ask her about healing, the Maya calendar, her prophecies, and the messages for humanity. And then there was her connection to the moon.

When I dreamt of her, the Maya shaman, I would see her with a light blue face, but that didn't quite make sense. The only thing I could think of was the moon. The light the moon casts upon the earth is pale blue. On nights of the full moon, the effect is magnified, with the entire earth—from deserts to forests, from snowbanks to rivers, all of creation—bathed in a ghostly blue light. So, if the color of moonlight is pale blue, and the woman's face was blue, there had to be some sort of strong connection to the moon. The energy of the moon is soothing—yin, gentle, and nurturing. In contrast to the strong yang of the sun and heat that obliterates, the moon soothes and nourishes. It is the moon that gives us tides, and the cycle of the moon marks the passage of a month. A woman's time corresponds to the moon. And it is the moon that gives us gossamer dreams upon shamanic wings.

But what exactly would explain the woman's blue face and her connection to the moon? More importantly, if this was the good outcome —finding the woman of the moon, the Madre Luna—what was the bad augury as foretold by the Maya soothsayer?

# CHAPTER 11
## God of the Mountain

ONE OF THE most misunderstood shamanic abilities is shapeshifting. With a focused and concentrated will, a shaman can change the appearance and the abilities of their consciousness. To develop hunting skills, a shaman will assume the shape of a jaguar and then track down prey for nourishment. To increase their abilities as a seer, the shaman will transform into a bird and fly to enemies' camps to learn of adversaries' plans and desires. Reports say that when in trance, the shapeshifting shaman will begin to move and undulate like the desired animal. Even more mysterious are legends saying that while shamans are shapeshifting, the healer will disappear completely, only to have the target animal appear in the shaman's home.

LEAVING THE CHURCH, we navigated through town to the city's edge, where streets opened up to a wider expanse with stray dogs, dust, and faded yellow buildings. A small culvert ran along the street. Chichicastenango was a place of rain, and when the tears of the god Chaac came, water needed to be diverted quickly or there would be mudslides and more tears.

On the final curve of the road, we came upon a small sign pointing the way to the mountain deity. Follow the arrow—the *anuncio* seemed almost comical. Are signposts to God so clear? Or is the journey to divinity supposed to be difficult? Leaving the road, we reached a small trail that led down, then up, toward the mountain. The path reflected one's own struggle to achieve closeness to God. First the inner conflicts, a journey into the murky depths of a person's psyche, then a challenging climb to enlightenment, to the eventual connection with the all.

A forest of switchbacks greeted our ascent. Upward and upward we hiked, and as we climbed, I began to feel lightheaded. My pulse increased, and my breathing was labored. My lungs struggled for oxygen. Having grown up a flatlander on sea-level topography, my body wasn't used to the altitude. And we weren't even than high up—just 8,000 feet.

At the top of the mountain was a path leading toward something mysterious. Rows of towering trees—more sentinels than welcoming committee—lined bare ground toward a clearing. As we approached a large circle of open earth, I began to see more and more people. Maya and non-Maya filled the vast space.

The people's gaze was intently focused on what appeared to be a small group of stones, and we approached for a closer look. The basalt enigma revealed itself to be a large stone mesa, or table, about a foot above the ground, with a headlike outcrop at the center. Smaller gray stones on both sides framed the face. On the altar were offerings of copal, flowers, alcohol, and tobacco. This was Pascal Abaj, literally "the stone of the mountain." A Maya deity, Pascal Abaj has been revered for over a thou-

sand years. I could see in my mind's eye the artifacts that an archaeological dig at this site would yield: pot shards, gold, and beads would be the
offerings found underneath myriad layers of earth.

From the crowd emerged a lone shaman who stepped toward the
altar. Dressed in blue jeans and a blue cotton shirt, he had longish black
hair, a moustache, and coffee-colored skin. By his build, he looked more
like a boxer than a holy man. When he reached the circle of offerings
on the ground, he stopped. He removed his shoulder bag and took out
a red scarf. In one fluid motion, he dropped to both knees, stretched
upwards, and began to tie the scarf on his head. With purposeful movements, he formed the trademark knotted headscarf of the Tzutujil Maya,
the people of Lake Atitlan.

The man stood and in his right hand held an immense bottle of *aguardiente*, alcohol made from sugar cane. The joyful glass, holding a turbulent
ocean, easily dwarfed the man's paw. Within seconds, the jaguar emptied out the crystal liquid on the rainbow of color adorning the earth.
In my mind's eye, I knew the shaman to be a shapeshifter, quickly taking
the persona of the powerful jungle cat as he cast spells. The aguardiente
went first toward the cardinal directions, then clockwise. Clockwise, as
always. Raising the bottle first toward the heavens, then down to the
earth, the jaguar uttered a prayer. Resting the bottle on the ground, the
cat reached into his spots and pulled out a box of flame. Holding the box
with his left foreleg against his chest, the shaman reached in and contracted his body. As a white teardrop rubbed against rattlesnake wafer,
a spark emerged and was cast toward the sky. The flame danced into
eternity as it arced upwards, then down to the mandala.

At the jaguar's feet was the most unique *quema*, or offering, I had ever
seen. Laid out in a thunderburst of light and color, candles were arranged
atop a sea of copal. The dried sap was generously laid out in corn-husk
bundles and pebbles. Colors of red, blue, yellow, light blue, green, purple,

orange, light purple, pink, and peach broke up the white ocean. There were no black candles, and that was a good sign.

This was an earth mandala, a quema for life. And around the circle were placed thirteen eggs, just past the copal. Thirteen is a lucky number in the realm of the Maya. Every month in the Maya Tzolk'in, or Sacred Round Calendar, has thirteen days. The Tzolk'in was used for divination and ceremonies. Thirteen is also the number of primary moon phases that are observed during a modern 365.25-day solar year.

The eggs represent life and are given as a sacrifice of lifeforce. They symbolize something that has the essence of life but will not suffer when offered to the gods. The same goes for corn and flowers, for they too are considered to be living things that can be given without harming one's karma. And the offerings, as sacred gifts, are still cosmically important.

As the fire grew, the shaman began to chant. Some prayers were in Spanish, some were Mayan. Other prayers seemed to come from some other language entirely. The prayers were offered quietly at first, gently addressing, waking, and rousing the gods. Next, his voice was raised. The louder sounds brought forth acknowledgement and compliments, telling the gods how powerful they were. And his voice was raised again as the shaman shouted and called forth the spirits of the ancestors. Each loud crescendo rallied the gods and denizens of the ancient world.

After the louder cycle of prayer, the shaman dramatically rose and reached toward the heavens. Clouds in his fists, sunlight bouncing off his scarf, the jaguar let out a long string of color disguised as syllables. And in more of a roar than a voice, the cat let out further incantations at the top of his lungs. His pulse was pounding as he stood to the heavens. Suddenly, the flames that had been burning at about knee level lept up a full eight feet. His prayers so strong, his will so pure, I saw the flames rise and explode. With no additional aguardiente, gasoline, or other fuel, the flames jumped and danced of their own accord.

And out of the distance, from the eastern sky, approached a speck of color amidst a sea of blue. Closer and closer the thread came, until I could make out wings. Then a body. Then a head and a tail. And as the eagle approached the clearing, it rose, then circled once, twice, three times about a hundred feet over the fire. Suddenly swooping downward, the eagle crossed the mandala's smoke trail, then soared off into the southern sky.

I was awestruck. World cultures from the Haida of the Northwest Coast to the Inca of the Andes revere eagles as messengers that bring spiritual manna and wisdom from the gods. Maya beliefs are the same. To the Maya, eagles are sacred messengers and intermediaries between the lands of human beings and the gods. Master of both realms of spirit and flesh, the eagle can soar to vast heights, then hover and land amongst trees and streams. Into the clearing, and directly over the altar to Pascal Abaj, a lone eagle mysteriously flew in and carried the shaman's prayers, just as the jaguar completed his ceremony. Watching the eagle's grasp, I felt a profound connectedness to the universe, a knowledge that all things are sacred—and that the spirits of the ancestors do hear our prayers.

The voice of the shaman changed as his songs faded and lullabied the gods back to their eternal slumber. The ceremony was complete. Turning away from the clearing and descending the mountain, my thoughts reflected on the role of the eggs in the mandala. Sacrifices and offerings to the gods do not require suffering or pain on the part of any being; it's the spirit of the offering that's important. The spirit of the corn sings when it is offered to the gods. The spirit of the flower dances when it is given with kindness and joy. Offerings are much more powerful when they come from love and devotion rather than fear and pain. The buzzing of the hummingbird, the laughter of the monkeys, and the singing of macaws—the gods are nature and want to hear the beauty of prayers, not the agony of screams.

So the ancient Maya, who became trapped in a nightmare of blood, were wrong. The ancient Maya thought that blood was required to feed the gods, that blood kept the sun in the sky, and that the gods favored royal blood above all other. But it was just an elaborate lie that kept warring rulers in place. Eventually the illusion tore a civilization apart, for as adept as the Maya were with astronomy, science, and calendrics, they couldn't overcome an unquenchable thirst for power and the resulting quest for blood. And over a thousand years later, have we really changed?

Emerging from the base of the mountain after the descent, we were once again walking toward town. After a few moments, the familiar cinderblock buildings came into view. I asked Martin to stop so we could visit the mask shops along the way.

Martin led me into a yellow block building. The owner quickly emerged. With his large eyes, hair in a ponytail, and vertical mouth, he looked like a toad. Speaking to Martin in Mayan, the two began to haggle over prices.

I began my search. Some of the masks were very ornate, with white horns and green tongues. Others were simple, with features that mimicked the normal curve and shape of a man's face. I looked for something special.

Toward the back, one mask stood out. It was a creation of cobalt and serpentine mother-of-pearl inlay, with a gemstone slightly above the center of the eyes. After purchasing it, I asked Martin which deity, god, or nature spirit I had picked up. Martin asked the store owner in Mayan, then translated:

"*Es el Maya díos de sueños.* It's the Maya god of dreams," he said.

To the ancient Greeks, this deity would be Morpheus, providing prophetic dreams to the Oracle at Delphi and other soothsayers. It seemed that Morpheus had successfully led me this far. But did any unexpected and unpleasant surprises lurk around the corner?

## CHAPTER 12
### Lake of Destiny

———◀〇▶———

I WAS NOT AT all surprised that I chose the mask for the Maya god of dreams. In fact, it reminded me that I still needed to find the hauntingly real object of my sacred quest —the woman of the moon, the Madre Luna of Lake Atitlan, who spoke to me in dreams. And there was something mysterious about Lake Atitlan. Its deep blue depths bothered me as we descended the mountain highway back from the market. After arriving at home base from my day of visiting the market and churches, the lake was calling to me with its soft scent and gentle *olas*, or waves. What was it about the lake? What did its waters symbolize? And why had it been important to the Maya for over a thousand years? I decided to find out.

I walked south toward the lakeshore, passing narrowing streets and dark stone walls. The slope

———◀〇▶———

gradually dropped as I approached the water. When I reached the edge of the lake, I stood upon a stone lip that jutted outwards and overlooked the massive expanse of a landlocked sea. Farther—within my view but beyond my grasp—I looked beyond the sapphire waters that held up towering volcanoes. Up, past the dense green beard of the mountain, up, up, my gaze turned toward the sun and moon.

The clouds were magnificent. They had taken on a form most bold. Amongst the rays of sun and hovering above the three volcanoes, the silvery cotton took the appearance of a grand explosion. It looked as if the moment of first eruption had been forever saved in time. The clouds were no longer hazy pools of water but pyroclastic smoke and ash bellowing from giants. And in the chaos, in the ensuing *Sturm und Drang* of fire and liquefied stone that obliterated the landscape, more life would emerge from the mountain's blood. As a huge earthen bowl appeared, then filled with water, blue-green fins would now wave hello in the waters. When the forests grew new leaves, monkeys would sing in the trees and butterflies would throw yellow and orange spots against a blue sky. From an ending emerged a new beginning. And that's how the Maya gods were created . . .

IN THE FIRST creation, two sparks emerged out of the nothingness of empty thought. Before, the universe was unconscious, not even asleep. The nothingness wasn't black; black would indicate the absence of something. The nothingness was simply nothing, a void.

As the two sparks started to glow, one red and one gold, they began to gently drift in the newly formed expanse. Spinning and floating, the sparks were happy. But not knowing what to do and not understanding how to act in the mindfulness of existence, the sparks eventually faded away. And like two chirps of a small bird, the sparks were gone. But they did exist: two forces, Passion and Holiness. Yet, not knowing what to do, they both blinked out of existence.

From out of the now-formed mindfulness, what we know of as the mind of God, two sparks were formed once again, a red one for Passion and a blue one for Force. There was no concept of time passing, because time did not yet exist. It might have been nanoseconds between the first and second creations or it might have been epochs of eternity. Without a measure of time, there was no passing of time.

After a while, not knowing what to do, the two sparks simply began to fight one another. The struggle might have been for control, supremacy, or even favor before God, but the two forces fought and fought desperately. Their energies eventually faded. The struggle wore out the sparks, and they once again winked out of existence.

For the third creation, two sparks were formed and danced into existence. This time they were gold and green. Gold was Holiness and green was Lifeforce. This time, the sparks created a world to occupy and filled it with lesser sparks in hues of yellow and plant shades of green. These lesser beings became lower gods and nature spirits. And the lesser gods danced and chirped and worshipped the higher gods. But once again, the gods didn't know what else to do, so they fought. The higher gods created armies out of the lower gods. The lesser gods were organized and managed into rows, columns, and battalions. With weapons of golden arrows, green vines, and tidal waves, each army fought the other into oblivion, until all the lesser gods were gone. The higher gods, in their fury, joined the war at the last moment and fought one another until they, too, faded out of existence.

In the fourth creation, something special happened. Whether it was by magic or divine plan, providence or luck, two sparks once again formed in the void. This time, the sparks were gold for Holiness and violet for Spirituality. These sparks joined together to honor the God-light, the mind that imagined them into existence. The mind of God was pleased, and the sparks were tasked to fight yet again—but this time, to join forces and fight the darkness amongst the void and lead others to the light. This was God's intent the whole time. And from the mind of the One, two lights emerged to lead the way.

These new sparks created our Earth and the planets, the moon and the stars, the animals and the humans. And as the Godlight force breathed life into the humans, the dual energies of Holiness and Spirituality were tasked to lead humanity, and all living beings, back to the light. The humans would need help, because when the second creation failed, and the sparks of Passion and Force faded, there was something left over; there is always something left after the fire. What emerged was Fear and Hate, which would forever plague all living beings and lie in shadows lurking and ready to strike.

BACK ON THE lake, I looked toward the opposite shore. The moment of the lake's creation appeared captured by the clouds; I could almost see the huge eruption of magma, earth, and fire roaring out of the three peaks. With the lush trees blown to bits and water in the roots of jungle flora evaporating instantly, this creation had been sudden, difficult, and violent. Yet this place was special, because its destruction brought more life, more lifeforce, and more Godlight.

And as the last ray of sunlight sank effortlessly against a rose-tangerine sky, the world turned into a dreamscape of grayish blue. The waters now matched the colors of the mountains, which were the same color as smoke and sky. The world was at peace; the world was one.

After the sunset dream, I left for the tavern and a meeting with David. It was a long night of tall tales, rum, and singing epic poems to fill storybooks. I said goodbye to David, and on the walk back to base, I even managed to liberate a piece of blackberry pie from a street vendor. David was working the following day, so I would once again be on my own. I awoke the next morning feeling reckless and daring, ready to cross the Lake of Dreams, Lake Atitlan.

I DECIDED TO charter my own *lancha*, or boat, across the lake and arrive in the city of Santiago Atitlan alone. Looking back, this would be a significant mistake. The Kwakiutl of the Northwest Coast say that when one is in the house of raven, it is better to scurry about as a small field mouse than come crashing through on wings of eagles. In other words, move silently, be still. But today I didn't listen. This day, painted in khaki, I boldly sat at the bow of my chartered boat, ready to storm the opposing shore. But was I in time or out of it? I noticed the waves gently lapping upon the shores. Wave after wave signaled a completion of cycle after cycle. My thoughts returned to the enigma of the Maya calendar. I still needed to find the answer.

The Calendar Round is created as the days of the Ha'ab and Tzolk'in intersect, providing a unique day-date with two Maya names. With 18,890 combinations of Ha'ab and Tzolk'in dates in the Calendar Round, the cycle repeats every fifty-two years. Once the calendar completed a cycle, the cycle continues, but there is no way to differentiate between alternating fifty-two-year periods, so the Maya used the Long Count. The Long Count calendar counts the number of days that have passed since creation. According to noted Mayanist Allen Christenson, the Maya calculated the beginning of the universe at over 41,000,000,000, 000,000,000,000,000,000 years ago. But the Long Count calendar also measures time in epicycles of 144,000 days, known as baktuns.

The baktuns were important. The Maya believe that cycles of creation last thirteen baktuns, or a period of 5,125 years. After thirteen baktuns, the world would be destroyed, then re-emerge in another cycle of creation. We are now in the thirteenth baktun, with an end date of December 23, 2012. Yes, an end date to the present age. So, will the world end? Will we see an omega to the age of humans? Will meteors rain from the sky, dropping the heavens? And will great cataclysms reclaim the earth for other life forms? I was soon to find out . . .

As I APPROACHED the other side of the lake, towering volcanoes came into view. Our eyes were dominated by the large and slumbering sentinels that were green as peat moss. The small boat rounded a cove, and to the left emerged the unwieldy city of Santiago Atitlan. I was taken aback by the unnerving sight. From the opposite shore, Santiago is hidden by lush green mountaintops, and I expected to find a Garden of Eden. But the layout of the city was a sharp contrast to the beautiful eclipse of the earthen lords and enchanting siren song of the boatmasters on its opposite shore, releasing a melodious "San-teee-ahhhh-go." From the distance, the array of houses looked more like matchboxes, incoherently stacked one atop the other by drunken hands. Smoke wafted toward the heavens from several brush fires. All of the colors within view were gray, grayish-white, and grayish-yellow. Describing the city with one word, I would choose *gritty*.

Before I left for Guatemala, I had made arrangements for a backup guide. Some of my dreams were troubling—getting lost in the jungle, being chased in the market, and kayaking around caimans. Wanting to find another source who lived in Santiago—and who knew a thing or two about shamans—I searched the Internet and found some information about a town leader named Nicolas Chavez. After calling the professor who wrote the article, I was given Chavez's contact information. If anyone in Santiago knew about a woman who worked with the moon, a Maya *aj' r'ij*, or healer, it would be Nicolas Chavez.

After the boatmaster docked and tied the lancha to the pier, I was greeted by a troupe of young boys. They seemed more actors than children from a hardscrabble existence, each eagerly vying for my attention and wanting to play guide for a day. The ensemble spoke and asked me which sights I wanted to visit. I selected one of the boys to be my guide and asked him a few questions: which site was closest, where was the church (by the city center, of course), and if he knew Nicolas Chavez. The boy said that we could find Chavez in the late afternoon, so I set off with my young guide to visit out first destination, the mysterious Maximón. One of the most interesting and misunderstood deities in Central America, Maximón is the patron saint of Lake Atitlan and the Solola region of Guatemala. I had read about Maximón before I left for Guatemala, but it's a god that's not in any anthropology or archeaology text.

My guide led me through back alleys and streets that rose up at a 45-degree angle. We encountered stray dogs amidst passed-out drunks and trod-on stones made slippery by unknown liquids. Santiago appeared in sharp contrast to Panajachel or the other Guatemalan towns I had seen. The extreme poverty was grinding and rendered a sense of malaise throughout the city. So much suffering was overwhelming. Instantly, I felt guilty for my good fortune. I get frustrated when an Internet connection goes down, when my coffee is burned, or when I can't find Harp Lager at the grocery store. Yet here, in this blessed city, mere survival is a challenge.

Soon we approached the sacred citadel of the ancient lord, the *rílaj mam*, or Maximón. Entering a nondescript cinderblock house, we found three stone steps that led to a secret inner chamber. Hidden from the world by a woven cloth curtain, closer and closer into the heart we advanced.

As I walked up the stairs, I recognized the heavy scent of copal enveloping the air like a sweet ribbon. A group from within began to chant. I could hear old, trumpety voices bringing forth their prayers. Pushing the curtain away, my eyes adjusted to the light as I saw a waist-high figure alone in the center of the room. Dressed in two black cowboy hats, beautiful scarves, and a fine woolen suit, the patron deity of the Tzutujil Maya stood watch. The Maximón (pronounced mosh-ee-mon) was attended to by ministers, servants, and courtesans, with vestiges of his power spread about in a small throne room. Quickly, I took off my hat in respect and walked toward the figure with deep reverence and awe.

AMONG THE MOST enigmatic figures in Mesoamerican religion, Maximón is the Quetzalcoatl of the modern age, a symbol and presence representing many things to many people. More than a bundle of sticks and stone, the deity stands for one thing: survival over tyranny.

A good place to meet Maximón would be at the beginning, in the year 1592. The Spanish had been in the jungle highlands for seventy years. The hardships of tribute, slavery, and conquest religion were thrust upon the Maya. It was foretold that during a time of great upheaval and suffering, a figure would emerge to protect the people—a ruler who could embody the spirit of the ancient Nahuales, the shamans and progenitors of the Maya race. Someone the people could turn to in moments of weakness and suffering. And someone who would live forever . . .

With empires in ruins, belief systems in disarray, and new rulers that were obsessed with riches and gold, the people of Lake Atitlan turned to one another for help. It was in the hands of two brothers, in gentle and small copper hands working long into the night, that faith became realized. These two brothers, Salvador and Juan, were chosen by the Maya gods to craft a deity.

Nature spirits called to the brothers in dreams. The two brothers dreamt of smoke and embers, trees filled with jaguars, and ancient Maya kings. They were beckoned to the forest by something that needed a vessel, something that wanted to live. The spirits of the Nahuales wanted to be seen, wanted to be worshipped, and wanted to survive. And so they found a way.

The brothers followed the call into the forest in search of something that could hold the spirits of the Nahuales. Could it be a jaguar pelt, or a bird to sing the songs of the ancients? Would bones hold the essence of gods? No, the brothers needed something sturdy that could withstand the onslaught of time. They needed to find something that could be formed—a thing that could at once be empty but also full. The brothers began searching for . . . a tree.

But what tree was strong enough, could be ancient enough and wise enough, to be a vessel for deity? The brothers roamed the jungle from the highest peak to the lowest stream, searching for weeks. Then one day, as the brothers entered a clearing, they noticed a tree that was different. There was nothing outwardly spectacular about this tree, one of the many residents of the forest. It was just an ordinary *palo de pito*, or coral tree. But as the brothers walked closer, they began to feel a sense of peace. And as the brothers walked closer, secrets began to emerge from the tree's grayish skin.

"Look, there—the third branch has an arm with an open hand."

"And look, there, near the trunk, is a turtle."

"Up there, at the crown, do you see the clouds?"

As the brothers marveled upon the tree, more secrets were revealed. In its bark the tree held the shapes of snakes, quetzal birds, and jaguars. On its skin it held rain clouds, the moon, and the sun. And near the roots was a stalk of maize and a two-headed eagle. The tree carried the symbols of the Nahuales, the ancients who brought astronomy and farming, architecture and art to the highlands. This was the right tree to hold the spirits of the Nahuales. This *was* the tree of the Nahuales.

After felling the tree, the brothers began the creation. Into the night, they worked with their knives and hands, carving and shaping a figure. As they toiled, sweat from their foreheads dripped upon the wood, leaving their hopes and dreams, their DNA—their life. And as their essences dripped onto the wood, so did life rise by shamans' hands.

Within two months of nighttime work, the brothers were finally done. They positioned the deity for the first time with his feet on the earth and his head toward the sky. At that moment, a miracle happened.

Gusts of air from all four directions came together around the wooden figure, and a whirlwind began to whipsaw the brothers to and fro. The whirlwind grew larger and larger until it stretched to the heavens and filled the entire clearing. As the winds grew, a giant hurling, spinning mass of raw energy undulated around the figure. Energy bolts from the forest emerged, lightning filled the skies, and the earth began to tremble. The lifeforce from the forest rose in vibration until it could no longer be contained. All at once, the entire clearing was filled with a huge explosion enveloping every living being in a blinding illumination. Then, faster than a flea can blink, the energy collapsed inward. The lifeforce came to a single point, hovering right above the wooden figure's heart. Then, in a split second, the flash of energy was gone; all was silent. The brothers knew their work was done. The mam was alive, seething with lifeforce and energy.

Exhausted from the creation, the brothers' next step was to transport the deity to the village. The Lord of the Lake, the Maximón, could only be shouldered, for that was the way in which all great Maya rulers were moved. The new Maya lord would require ceremonies with sweet copal and incense, tobacco and sacred water. Moreover, he would need someone to attend to him, wash his clothes, and care for him. The older of the two brothers, Salvador, was chosen as the deity's *telinel*, or shoulderer. And so it would be for centuries: wherever Maximón stood, the telinel was nearby. The telinel would be the guardian, attendant, sage, and chief shaman who had the closest connection to the effigy.

Back in the village, the people were happy. The brothers had brought forth a new ruler, protector, confidante, and helper from the forest. The telinel began a weekly ceremony for the mam. Maximón became a symbol for the Maya—that in the midst of turmoil, unquenchable suffering, and untold anguish, the gods listened. Thus, the will of the gods—that the Maya would survive—was made real in Maximón.

But something was amiss in the village. Rumors began to swirl of a mysterious stranger who appeared only during the night. He lurked in the shadows and would call out to the women of the village when husbands were away on hunting parties.

"Beautiful lady, where is your husband? Why would anyone leave such a fine woman alone in the nighttime?"

The stranger would entice the women with perfumed words and nighttime embraces, kissing and touching private spaces. And in the morning, when the women awoke, the mysterious stranger would be gone from their beds, leaving nothing but a sweet, lingering scent.

When the men of the village heard the stories, they became angry. Who was this man of the night, coming to take the women and gamble with his life? Who was this bold thief, anxious to meet his fate? And so, the men, as men often do, decided to lay a trap. Instead of leaving for the usual hunt, the men stayed and sent the women away to a neighboring village.

That evening, the men waited for the stranger in their beds, with obsidian axes and stone knives. As they drifted off to sleep, someone did climb into their beds, but it wasn't a man. The men instead felt the soft, fleshy feel of a woman's breasts. On their thighs, the men felt the smoothness of a woman's legs. As the men began their slumber, they wrapped their hands around the curvy features of a woman's form. And as the men relaxed their shoulders, they felt long, silken hair upon their chests.

The men thought "This is good" and dropped their axes and knives. The attitude about the stranger quickly changed. Instead of complaining when the women left overnight for the neighboring village's market, the men now looked forward to the day. But the women of the village were wise and knew something was wrong. They decided to hatch their own plan.

And on a day when the women were supposed to travel to the neighboring village, one woman disguised herself in men's clothes and cut her long hair. As evening fell, she stayed behind in an abandoned hut and waited. No sooner had she drifted off to sleep than a warmth entered the bed. To her back, the woman felt the soft, fleshy feel of a woman's breast. On the back of her legs, the woman felt the curvy features of a woman's thighs. And as the visitor in the night lay next to the disguised woman in the bed, the woman in the bed felt long strands of silken hair caress her back.

"So this is how the men are spending their time. How dare this woman enter my home, my bed, to sleep with my man!" thought the village woman.

In a fit of rage, the village woman turned around and attacked the nighttime visitor. And quicker than two starving jaguars fighting over a monkey's leg, the women were locked in mortal battle. Kicking and thrashing, scratching and biting, howling and screaming, the women fought until the stranger made one key mistake.

In an attempt to silence the village woman's shrieks, the stranger put a hand over the villager's mouth. In response, the village woman raised her head and quickly—suddenly, ferociously—bit down. Her teeth chomped down on the stranger's smallest finger. As teeth cut through flesh, flesh gave way to bone, and bone was cut in twain.

Howling in pain, the stranger fled into the jungle. The screams had been so loud, so strange, so fierce, that all of the men of the village awoke and emerged from their huts. When the village woman explained the encounter with the stranger, the men of the village were angry. They thought the stranger to be a shapeshifting jaguar, or shaman from another village, playing tricks on them.

The search began! The men sought the stranger in fields, paths, streams, and caves. The villagers looked for the visitor in valleys, trees, brush, and near the lake. Three days of searching passed, and the men returned exhausted and empty-handed. In the jungle, they hadn't found any trace of the stranger—not a drop of blood or piece of hair or any footprints. It was almost as if the stranger had vanished. But back at the village there was one clue: splinters where the woman had bit off the stranger's finger.

Resuming their weekly worship of Maximón, the men brought fresh copal, tobacco, forest fruit, and nectars. But the telinel eventually noticed something strange: the mam was missing a finger from his right hand, a pinky finger! And as the villagers looked closer, they saw what appeared to be teeth marks on the remaining stump. And as they looked closer, closer into their hearts, the Maya understood what had happened.

Since Maximón was formed from nature and nature spirits, the mam was a child of nature. And just as a child is a reflection of the parents, so must the child have the parents' good qualities and bad qualities. So, if Maximón reflects the good forces of nature, such as growth, life, and rebirth, he must also reflect humor in nature and the other nature spirit: the trickster. It is the humor in nature that gives the anteater its long tongue, the porcupine its quills, and the pig its curly tail.

When the brothers bound the forest spirits into the wooden figure, they forgot one key thing about the magic. Maximón had been infused with strength, a sense of renewal, and abundance. But he also had a sense of humor, a desire to play, and a need to laugh. And since the brothers were also creations of nature, being people of the maize, they too had a part of the trickster spirit in them! So the brothers gave Maximón an extra dose of the trickster spirit by the sweat from their brows.

Thus it was Maximón who tricked the men and women at night. But what may seem funny to the trickster is not always funny to the recipients of the trick. So the brothers decided to act.

With quick thoughts and faster hands, the creators knew what they had to do. They brought out some vines and their carving tools. They brought out knives and fire. And late into the night, after numerous offerings of copal and liquor in which to get Maximón drunk, they tied up the mam's hands and cut off his feet but otherwise left him intact, sans one pinky finger. Thereafter, the Lord of the Lake would forever have difficulty walking around the village and would be bound to fulfill the will of the shamans. And although the mam, the holy boy, would still travel by flight, communicate through dreams, harness supernatural powers, and summon spirits of the lake, he would never again be mistaken for a man or a woman. This is the legend of Maximón and the explanation for his rope-bound hands, lack of feet, and missing finger.

I SPENT THE rest of the afternoon at the *Cofradía de Santa Cruz,* or Brotherhood of the Holy Cross, studying, learning, and observing Maximón. The cofradías are the religious orders, or brotherhoods, in Santiago Atitlan who are tasked with the upkeep and shelter of the mam. Descendants of the original village families, the cofradías are a tight-knit group of men and women with a recognized shaman for each family. In the daytime, they are laborers, traders, and farmers, but their spiritual profession and nightly activities include the secretive worship and veneration of the lake spirit.

There are twelve cofradías in Santiago Atitlan, and in May the groups throw an enormous festival and move Maximón to another cofradía. That is, Maximón stays with each group for only one year before he is moved to another group. This maintains a tenuous balance of power between rival families. The exact order or rotation amongst the cofradías is unknown. Usually, Maximón will speak to the telinel in dreams and tell the head shaman where he wants to stay for the next year. If the saint isn't moved according to its wishes, members of the cofradía will become ill. This has only happened once or twice in a hundred years, when the Maya villagers defied the will of the mam.

To hold Maximón is a great honor. He brings the cofradía guests, visitors, prestige, accolades, and money. When pilgrims come to see Maximón, they usually leave gifts of tobacco, aguardiente (which the mam actually drinks), and hard currency. The money is used to buy beer, copal, and more aguardiente for the mam and members of the cofradía. The funds are also used to throw elaborate fiestas, complete with musicians, food, and dance, to celebrate the mam. It's not dissimilar to the potlatch ceremony held by Northwest Coast Indians. As the cofradía takes in money, the brotherhood shares its bounty with allies of the cofradía. The cofradía that takes care of the mam receives great auguries in the material and physical world. It brings the cofradía status and power because the cofradía decides how and where the money and offerings left for the mam are spent.

In practical terms, holding and caring for the mam brings the telinel great control over the shamans in the village. The telinel of the cofradía is now the gatekeeper to the local shamans, who must now ask the telinel's permission to perform spellcraft or healings using Maximón. As to the statue itself, today's Maximón is a collection of bundled branches, stones, and wood. The mask, or what you see as the face, is removable. And the mask is not the original. The first mask was used continuously since the sixteenth century but was stolen by Catholic priests in the 1960s and then donated to an Austrian museum. Returned to Santiago Atitlan in 1982, the original mask is hidden amongst the cofradía's lock-boxes, while the second mask is placed over the effigy we know of as the current Maximón.

In the sacred shrines of the cofradías, Maximón will always be placed on the right side of Jesus. The Christ is usually displayed in a glass coffin, just like in the Iglesia de Calvario, and is adorned with flowers, blinking Christmas lights, and colorful banners. If you ask the telinel, he will tell you that Christ is Maximón's father. This isn't quite true. It's just a way to appease the local Catholic Church. The use of the Christ is a way to frame the worship of Maximón as permitted under the watchful gaze of Christ's eyes. But again, the Maximón is not Christian; the deity is more akin to an amalgamation of pre-Columbian nature spirits.

Villagers also refer to Maximón as San Simon, or Saint Simon. This is another way to pacify the Catholic Church. In New World Catholicism, if you honor or venerate a saint, the spiritual practice is acceptable. But if you honor a pagan deity, you are committing a great transgression of faith. Alas, there is no Saint Simon and there has never been.

Others would describe Maximón as a version of Ponce de León. Some would say the mam is a representation of Judas Iscariot. Still others would say Maximón is the supreme god of the Tzutujil. These are all oversimplifications and are quite wrong. We cannot place a Western religious framework over a pre-Columbian deity and expect the construct to make sense. Moreover, Maximón is better described as an intermediary, passing prayers and giving offerings to higher gods. In other words, Maximón is an ancient saint, a native saint, crafted by indigenous hands to endure the cosmologic onslaught of the Catholic Church.

The statue exhibits some strange physical capabilities. The statue smokes cigarettes (by itself) and drinks liquor. When a lit cigarette is placed in the mam's mouth as an offering, the cigarette remains lit, and the telinel has to flick off the cigarette ash as the cig burns down. The statue also drinks aguardiente. Entire shot glasses will be poured into the statue with no fluid collecting on the ground. Maximón doesn't have containers to hold the liquor—the mam just drinks the alcohol.

I can remember all the details of the room as if my visit had only been yesterday. But what I remember most about the shrine was the faith in people's hearts. As I stayed in the room for several hours, watching ceremony after ceremony, the one thing that didn't change was the faith and devotion to the mam. Believer after believer came hoping for a miracle and praying to the effigy with complete reverence. And the prayers! Some prayed for rain and help with the harvest. Others prayed for assistance with a difficult childbirth. Still others prayed so their loved ones would be safe in distant lands. The prayers were all sincere.

Witnessing this ceremony provided me with a sense of hope that culture was able to maintain its sacred traditions in spite of colonialism, materialism, and religious holocaust. The spirits of the Maya gods never disappeared from Lake Atitlan, they just changed form. And after two thousand years, they were still there, while so many other great traditions were lost to time.

SOON IT WAS time to move to our next destination, the church. Walking out of the shrine, I was glad to be free of the heavy scent of copal. Climbing further up an alley, we found a main road and arrived at the church within a few minutes. Once again, the temple was next to the mountains and underneath the shadow of the highest peak. The curtain wall and entire church complex was raised twelve feet into the air. At the center of the square, the church itself was built atop a platform five feet higher and made of basaltic stone. I walked toward the outdoor dais, up to the platform, and was once again reminded of God's separation from humanity. This is the god of judgment, the god of wrath, contrasted to the Christ in the glass coffin, a deity which could be touched and felt. It's another subtle duality in post-Conquest religion. You have to complete the journey to the imposing temple of God to feel the love and warmth of his son, Jesus Christ.

I opened the doors of the great home and stepped inside the white cave. I didn't notice anything spectacular at first. It took me a few moments to perceive the statues of saints along the walls, adorned with beautiful robes of turquoise and teal, magenta and red, blue and green. The saints were the patron saints of the cofradías. San Jose was dressed in blue, San Miguel in red, San Francisco in teal. On Catholic feast days, such as the feast day of San Jose, the cofradías sponsor elaborate celebrations for the local community. This is how the cofradías are allowed to exist: by maintaining connection to the church and by venerating Catholic saints, the cofradías are able to keep practicing their pre-Columbian faith.

Unfortunately, I didn't have much time left in Santiago. The last lancha was set to leave in forty minutes, and I still needed to find Nicolas Chavez. So I quickly scribbled some notes, took some photos, and left the church. A gambler, woodcarver, troubadour, and shopkeeper, Nicolas Chavez is a local superstar and good person to know. I spent the remaining moments looking for him on side streets, visiting his cofradía, leaving messages for him, and finally meeting his family at the outdoor market near the pier. I spoke to his wife, Magdalena, who was a very sweet lady. I told her I would return the following day and if she could please relay the message to Chavez. I also wanted to find the secret of 2012 in the Maya calendar. Would Santiago and Lake Atitlan disappear in an instant? Would a new creation emerge to populate the earth? And with that, I said my farewells and boarded the last lancha leaving Santiago, one step closer to my destiny.

# CHAPTER 13
## Morpheus Unleashed

SHAMANIC JOURNEYS AND quests for sacred knowledge are perilous and best done clandestinely. Not everyone will want to share secrets with you. Not everyone will show you the power of the ancestors and spirits. Not everyone will bestow upon you the contents of their sacred bundles and heart's desire. Too often, foreigners arrive with smiling faces masking greedy hands. Whole societies have been decimated by people who arrive with a cross in one hand and an atom bomb in the other. So now, legacy and secrets are more tightly guarded. How far would someone go to protect knowledge both holy and profound? What is a person capable of? Would they go so far as to harm another to preserve ancient wisdom? What about kill? What is the value of a single human life in a place so mysterious, so dangerous?

I AWOKE EARLY the next day, ready to return to Santiago Atitlan and meet Nicolas Chavez. I hoped Chavez would help me locate the Madre Luna—the woman of the moon with black hair and blue face that I dreamt of. The air was chilly as I crossed the Lake of Dreams. The other passengers on the lancha wore either traditional Tzutujil Maya attire or Western wear. We were accompanied by sacks of flour, grain, and bundles of rope from Panajachel. Today, I noticed the difference in the lake's ripples and curls. For the most part, the lake waters appeared calm, with small rolling waves. But past the center of the lake and closer to Santiago, there was a section where the water became black glass. There were no waves and no movement, just a flat nothingness, indicating the deepest part of the lake. The water, more obsidian than fluid, was level and still. For the Tzutujil, Lake Atitlan is the center of the universe, the center of creation. The tribe relies on the lake for sustenance and cleansing. It washes their bodies and purifies their souls. Even Maximon's clothes are washed weekly in lake water.

We arrived early Saturday morning in Santiago, and the city was quiet. Walking to the wooden market stalls, I was greeted by a tall and thin Maya with salt-and-pepper hair, wearing a black hat, custom embroidered *pantalones,* or pants, and a crisp white shirt. This was Nicolas Chavez.

After exchanging greetings, I told Chavez about my quest, about starting off with a Toltec curandero, spending time in the desert with a Cherokee Spiritwalker, and being led to Lake Atitlan. I told Chavez about the dreams I had been having all summer—of the lake, volcanoes, and visions of the woman with black hair and a blue face. She was a healer with a connection to the moon and gentle hands. She lived among nature—her home was near a highway, possibly next to a volcano, and she used a magical staff.

I also told Chavez about my trip and traveling two thousand miles to Central America based solely on dreams and intuition. With each explanation, his eyes grew wider and wider. By his expression, he either thought I was actually guided by the spirits of the ancient Nahuales or that I was dancing on moonbeams. In other words, I was afraid he thought me a lunatic. Finally, when I finished explaining the last detail of my journey, I took a deep breath, let out a deeper sigh, and waited for a response.

It felt like I'd been at confessional for an entire day. In a way, I felt relieved. Fortunately, Chavez's faith in the spirit world was greater than mine. In a nonchalant way, he spoke. "Oh, I think I know the woman you're looking for. She lives in Cerro de Oro."

*Whew!* Finally, thankfully, here was the first major signpost that I was on the right track. After talking to Chavez for a few more minutes, he made some phone calls and travel arrangements, and we were ready to go. But first, we needed to see visit Maximón one more time. To ask the grandfather for good fortune and success on our journey.

For the first time on this trip, I felt that I was on track—being led by the spirit world and destined to meet Madre Luna. Back inside the cofradía, I purchased cigarettes, beer, and aguardiente for the mam. Maximón, like most men, drinks beer. His favorite is Gallo, which comes in a large brown bottle with a picture of a big black rooster on a red background. I distributed the booty, poured beer in the plastic cups of the telinel and members of the cofradía, gave some beer to Maximon, and took to both knees. I prayed for protection, safety, and help on my journey. And I thanked my hosts, the spirits of the Nahuales, for guiding me. As I finished, I remember the telinel uttering a few words of an ancient Maya prayer, complete with the distinctive "sh," "k," and "oo" sounds of the language. Afterwards, more beer was given to the mam, a cigarette was placed in his mouth, and we were off.

At the center of town, we boarded a *camioneta* headed to Cerro de Oro. A camioneta is an exceptional way to travel. It's a pickup truck with a framework of wood and steel on top of the bed. The framework rises above you, so when you are standing on the bed, you grab onto the over-head rails and hold on for your life. And it's a great ride! Standing up with the truck in motion, you feel the air rushing by, smell the trees and earth, and see vibrant green hues from the forest. You're taller than you've ever been, the wind is in your face, and you cannot help but feel alive and part of nature—like a hawk or sparrow gliding through energy and time.

The road twisted as we climbed higher into the sky, past coffee plantations, and after dropping off passengers, we turned onto a dirt road. We then passed a newly discovered archaeological dig site. The field was marked off with small flags and the beginnings of grid squares for mapping and excavation. After the preliminary construction of new homes, local builders had found a collection of Maya ruins underneath. Guatemala is filled with Maya ceremonial structures. From the Peten jungle to the western highlands, there are literally thousands of temples dotting the landscape. Further ahead, the dirt road changed to a street paved with stone and asphalt. Winding its way past a small town square, the camioneta dropped us off.

Walking back a bit, we approached the town center, and I made mental notes of our surroundings. Taking a side street, we passed the requisite Catholic church perched atop a small hill. Next to the church was an enigma: twenty feet above us stood a large solitary tree stretching toward the heavens. And underneath the tree was a cave that opened into the mountain below the church. There was no mention of this tree or cave in any travel guide, book, webpage, or other source I had researched before the trip. Still, there was something important about the tree and its mysterious portal. What was it? We continued our hike.

About half a mile after the town, past fences, cattle gates, and more coffee trees, we came to a small collection of gray cinderblock buildings. On a small slope overlooking the lake, there stood a single cinderblock home with an aluminum awning and no less than twenty people seated on benches outside. And there was something remarkable in their faces.

I looked closer, in their eyes I saw the same look I had seen so many times before. These were the believers, the pilgrims, looking for one last bit of magic in a hopeless world, believing beyond faith that they could still petition the earth and its elementals for assistance, asking for something that couldn't be provided by doctors, computers, or modern medicine. They were looking for nothing short of a miracle.

We found empty seats underneath the awning. Chavez began talking to the others waiting to enter the stone heart. His friendly, easygoing nature gave him access to just about anyone in the community. Chavez told me the others had journeyed from as far away as Honduras, Chiapas, and distant coastal regions to visit the woman. He was able to tell by their speech as well as their attire. Most people in Guatemala wear embroidered clothing unique to their region or province.

After a couple of minutes, a steel door swung open from the cinderblock, and a voice sweet but powerful ushered forth a command.

"Gring, gring!" said the woman. In beautiful Cachiquel mixed with a perfume vapor of Spanish, I was being summoned by the elderly Maya woman. Every non-Maya in Guatemala is a gringo, especially me. And even though I had lived and breathed myth, and spent years studying the Maya and Mesoamerica, I was easily given away by my reddish-brown hair. I chuckled as I silently thanked my mom for my Scottish roots. Taking a deep breath, I walked toward the door. I had been expected.

Once inside the room, I came face to face with the woman I'd been dreaming of for months. Could I actually be here? Was this really happening? Gently, she ushered me to a cot covered with woolen blankets. Standing five feet tall, the woman had a quiet dignity about her and a presence of softness and strength.

Long black hair framed a copper face with eyes brimming with starlight: this was Doña Pancha, the Madre Luna of Cerro de Oro. And as soon as I sat down, the elegant woman dressed in hand-embroidered garments of cobalt-painted birds and sungold flowers dropped to her knees and removed a small bundle from an altar. Placing the bundle before us, she unfolded a cloth that tenderly hid a sphere.

"*Mir, es la luna.* Look, it is the moon," said the mother in broken Spanish as she pointed to the sphere.

As I looked toward the sphere, I saw a glass crystal ball with small vines inside. The globe was about the size of my palm, and the plants within were smaller still. I saw green stalks crowned by blue petals—like miniature flowering irises upon corn plants, if there were such a thing. This was the moon, the lifeforce of the woman who had summoned me from thousands of miles away.

"*Mir, tu venir ayudar.* Look, you have come to help," said the woman, with her arms outstretched. "*Ya dijo luna.* As the moon has foretold."

I was awestruck by this revelation and almost cried. Everything had been happening according to plan. I was supposed to come and meet Madre Luna. I was supposed to come to Guatemala, to Lake Atitlan, in search of my destiny. That's why I kept encountering obstacle after obstacle until I decided to journey. Before, I couldn't find a steady job, I had problems with my car, and I even couldn't sleep because of the recurring dreams. Now it all made sense. *This* was the journey that was important. *This* was the mission to accomplish.

More important still, if the Madre Luna existed, if the dreams had been real all along, then the other woman existed, too—the woman I had been dreaming of for almost a year, perhaps even all of my life. The woman with orange eyes and long, dark hair, who visited me in dreams. I had been looking for her for what felt like an eternity. Had she been looking for me, too?

Chavez explained to Madre Luna my quests, my mission, and why I had come to Guatemala. Chavez told her of my dreams about the magical staff and her connection to the moon. Without a look of surprise, Madre Luna looked toward Chavez and nodded her head as he explained my adventure. Intermittently, she looked downward, seemingly lost in thought, and then quickly looked up. She replied with a few words here and there. Her speech was poetry, responding to Chavez's frantic scattershot. When the exchange was finished, Chavez looked at me with eyes wider than flying saucers.

"She says she already knew you were coming," gasped Chavez.

"Sí," replied Madre Luna effortlessly, as she nodded her head and looked at me.

"Mír, mír esto. Look, look at these," the woman gently spoke. And as she reached again into her altar, Madre Luna showed me her ritual tools, her sacred heart, and her secrets.

She pointed to a stone statue of an ancient Maya god and explained this tool was used to guide lost souls to the other realm. With their minds gone, thoughts became hazy and memories distant for these unfortunate few. No longer can these spirits even remember their names, much less where they live, much less what they are doing. The only thing these souls do is exist in a fog. But existence in a perpetual fog is not existence at all. It's a trap, for the fog keeps these spirits from the light. Moreover, these spirits refuse to believe they are dead, and consequently, they don't start looking for the light.

Madre Luna guides these lost souls as she clears hauntings from homes, jungle areas, and people. And people can be haunted just as easily as places. Madre Maya assists these souls to cross over. The statue helps, because once it is charged, it takes the form of a person who enters the dream fog and gently guides the disembodied soul into the light.

"Mír, mír." Madre Luna pointed to a fossil of an anteater paw placed low against the altar. This is another magical item and has a secret: it never came from a living creature. The anteater was never alive, for it exists only in the realm of spirit. After finding the paw print in the forest, Madre Luna called to the spirit of the anteater and befriended it. She then trained it to hunt and extract illness. To the Maya, illness can sometimes take the form of black spots or growths on a physical being's energetic field. The anteater uses its long tongue to catch and eat these black spots, and the person's health improves.

Since the anteater exists in the spirit world, it is not limited to working only in Madre Luna's presence. The anteater can travel anywhere in the world to catch and eat illnesses with its long tongue. And the anteater has a specialty: catching and eating diseases that affect pregnancy. Once directed and energized, the anteater travels to the expectant mother and flicks its long tongue into the womb, eating the illness and keeping baby and mother safe from disease.

"*Mas, mas,*" gently cooed the living saint as she pulled out other items from her altar. On the bare dirt floor, she placed a porcelain picture frame at our feet. The frame was empty, save for the flowing angels and gentle flowers on its border. Outside the frame, she placed a fork and spoon. This was also a secret item from a faraway time. This is how she found the moon.

As a young girl of seven, she had a dream to go to the forest and dig. Underneath a cedar tree, in the middle of a clearing, she found a porcelain frame surrounded by a knife and spoon, and in the center, a mystical glass orb she calls the moon. That presaged her life's work. Her mission would be to feed others with the beauty of her love, to nourish souls that have been emaciated by disease and sickness, to aid those that cannot care for themselves.

The frame is a recharging station for the glass orb. When the orb weakens or its energy decreases, the picture frame takes energy from the surrounding jungle and re-energizes the sphere. The fork and spoon symbolize the eating of illness, but there's no knife, for a knife would represent the violent cutting or tearing of disease from the body. The fork and spoon show how illnesses are gently taken away from the body so as not to cause further suffering.

Born in 1949, Doña Pancha is a natural intuitive healer. Never apprenticed to anyone, this elemental shaman gained spiritual insight and was taught by the glass orb through dreams. In her nighttime visions, the orb becomes as big as a person and speaks to her about healing, the upcoming week, the weather, and other phenomena. Eight years after beginning her journey, she questioned her work and her mission. At the age of fifteen, she was pressured by parents and church elders to get married and give up healing, so she immediately stopped tending to the infirm. But the spirit world had other plans. Within a week, she received an ultimatum.

In the middle of a church sermon, in front of all her family and friends, she stood up and then fell suddenly to the floor. Rendered unconscious for seven hours, she could not be woken by any means. Her parents thought she was in a coma, but she was in deep trance, having been taken to a realm of utter beauty and light and given a choice: continue her healing mission or permanently join the world of spirit. Thankfully, she chose to help us. Destined to spend untold hours ministering to the sick, healing their wounds and their souls, Madre Luna would spend the next forty years practicing shamanism.

But Doña Pancha is a different type of shaman. One of the aspects of shamanism is the ability to enter non-ordinary reality through altered states of consciousness. But Doña Pancha never has to enter an altered state of consciousness, because she exists in an altered state of consciousness. She never has to focus her mind on communicating with spirit, because she is more spirit than matter.

It's like a pro baseball player who never has to warm up, never has to practice, never has to rest, because they are a born ball-player. In other words, Madre Luna is not a woman that practices shamanism to contact the spirit world. She's a spirit that practices shamanic healing in the guise of a woman. Her mask of shamanism is not what gives her power; rather, her humble appearance belies her power as an elemental shaman.

Madre Luna is also blessed with tremendous mental faculties. Remember, altered states of consciousness are a hotline to the divine. To reach worlds of non-ordinary reality (or NOR), shamans go through a framework or process such as listening to drumbeats or deep meditation. This ensures two things: first, that the shaman is actually doing something. By following a pattern instead of simply imagining a journey, the shaman is initiating a process that has been perfected over thousands of years. Second, a framework insures the shaman's safety. This protocol protects the shaman so that the shaman's consciousness cannot enter NOR haphazardly and so that the denizens of the NOR worlds cannot affect the shaman's mind at will.

The universe is a mixture of good and bad, light and dark, just as Gary Gent said. And if a doorway is opened accidentally, without the proper framework and safety measures, then just as a shaman can go into the NOR, things from the NOR world can come out and play—and not everything in NOR is kind, gentle, and peaceful. Because of this, shamans that go too far or gaze too long into the rabbit hole can lose their connection with reality and become insane. Or worse, they become haunted by creatures from the NOR that have escaped and now plague the shaman.

To simultaneously exist in our physical reality and in an altered state of consciousness, a person has to be different by birth. One must be chosen and have the psychic ability and genetic predisposition for this type of work. If not, we can easily see the type of problems that would develop.

By nature, we are disconnected from source, or removed from God. And one of our primary missions on this planet is to reconnect with the Godlight and the all-loving, all-knowing mystical force of light in the universe. When we're in deep prayer, trance, or cavernous sleep, we reconnect with this enigmatic source energy for only moments at a time.

If we stay connected to non-ordinary reality, or non-linear reality, for longer periods, we risk dying or going insane. Not because our bodies and consciousness can't handle the Godlight, but because it's so beautiful and powerful that we desire to remain there always. And if we attempt to remain in the spiritual realm while we're still living, breathing organic creatures, we begin to lose our connection with waking reality. This happens because our minds can no longer shutter the doorway between our world and the other. Our minds cannot process the potentiality of simultaneously interacting, existing, and influencing two different planes of existence; the medical term for this condition is delusional psychosis. And then, not everyone can maintain the auric shield, prayer, and grace necessary to sustain the connection to Godlight. And a person who continually interacts with both realms also risks seeing the varied spiritual forces in the NOR.

Madre Luna can handle the mental strain and danger of existing in two worlds simultaneously because she was born that way. She's not human in the way you or I perceive; she's parahuman, beyond human. In our present evolutionary form of Homo sapiens, we don't have the mental capacity to exist in the two simultaneous realities of matter and energy. But Madre Luna naturally does this every day of her life.

FINALLY, MADRE LUNA pulled out her most powerful relic and placed it at my feet.

"*Mir, es la luna. Mi dice cuando tu ven.* See, it's the moon. It told me you were coming," softly spoke the ancient voice. "*Mir, tambien.*"

I held the glass orb entrusted to Madre Luna gently in my hands. It was an oracle, teacher, energy beacon, telephone to lost relatives, healing stone, protector, and guide. The orb also holds a bit of her essence, her gentle hands having used it for so long that it's attuned to her energy. The moon was left for her and no one else. With the orb, she can provide healings, conduct divination, pray to her ancient gods, and lead people to her. People like me.

We spoke for a few moments about her past, the tools, and her healing. I wanted to stay all day in her calming, soothing presence. But with the sick and ailing to attend to, Madre Luna asked if I would come another day when she had more time.

I wanted more answers; I had so many questions. I wanted to know her healing methods and the health of the planet. I needed to know about the Maya gods and our hopes for survival. And I desperately wanted the secret of 2012. I had all these questions and more, but I would have to wait a bit longer for the answers.

Gathering my belongings and notes, I stood and approached the ancient healer. Extending my hand and instinctively kissing her cheek, Chavez and I left. We would return to Cerro de Oro soon enough.


OUR THIRTY-MINUTE HIKE led us past farms and dirt roads, coffee trees and cattle, until we reached the town square. To the right was the cave we had passed earlier in the day.

"Wondrous things happen here. Come, take a look," said Chavez.

The entrance to the *cueva*, or cave, was not accessible from the street. To get there, we took a few steps up to reach a platform, then we crossed a home with a yard, and then we took more steps to the cave entrance. In Guatemala, it seems nothing with religious significance is at eye level. You must constantly climb, look up, or struggle through an expanse to reach divinity. The cave was no different. And in a short time, we were beholding the mystery and its beauty. As we stood at the opening, we faced a gigantic black mouth of shadow and shallows. For Mesoamerican cultures, caves represent something sacred and mysterious; they are doorways into other worlds.

"This is a special place. When the folds of the earth open, the Nahuales emerge!" Chavez boldly exclaimed. I saw the blocked cave for a moment. Then I closed my eyes and saw much more. The cave was a gate. A possibility.

"Look around. What do you see?" asked Chavez.

I scanned the cave and its walls. Its stones were huge megaliths that probably weighed twenty tons apiece if you could pull them out of the craggy temple. They had a smooth texture and powdery black sheen from an eon of soot and ash. The cave's surface was covered by countless layers of copal that had carbonized from over a thousand years of offerings. In the far back wall were offerings of flowers and candles. To our left and behind us was an altar with a blood groove, so that the earth would receive the sacred gift of blood from the living. And below us, in the earth, would be layer after layer of sediment. A thousand years of pot shards, bones, offerings, and sculpture—an archaeologist's dream.

Instinctively, I stood back to gain a better view. There was something important I had missed—something improbable. As I looked around, I began to make out shapes in the stone wall of the cave. Directly above us, near the right wall, was the head of a jaguar! Twelve feet up, the head and gaping jaw emerged from the stone. I could see the jaguar's eyes, teeth, and mane. I could make out the shape of its nose and its palate. I could even make out the dimples in its cheeks, formed by whiskers; amazing. This was a very special place.

But the cave was not finished with us yet, for to the left, about nine feet from the ground and opposite the jaguar, emerged the stone face of Maximón. Looking closely, I could make out its angular features, slit eyes, forceful mouth, and geometric jawline and cheekbones. I could also see its eyes looking right down at me.

"This is the cave of the Nahuales," declared Chavez. "It's called *Paq' alíb 'al*, or the Place of Revelation."

"Yes, I know," I replied. And as I stepped back further, I noticed something else. Directly above us and the cave, covering us like a giant frozen fireworks explosion, stood a tree, its roots reaching down into the cave and its fingers toward the heavens.

"No," I exclaimed, "this is not the cave of the Nahuales—this is the cave of the cosmos!" And after about five seconds of direct eye contact, or a short eternity, the surprised Maya nodded his head and looked down. I studied this place before, but I didn't locate it until now.

This was not just the Cave of the Jaguar, or the Cave of Maximón, or the Cave of the Maya, or even the Cave of Time. This was the one true Cosmic Cave, linking three worlds of existence. In other words, this was the absolute one true center of the Maya universe.

In Maya cosmology, a great emphasis is placed on caves, but an equal emphasis is placed on trees. A tree is a symbol for the cosmic order in the universe. If a cave is the opening to the underworld, then a tree is the structure that links the universal planes of existence. With its foundation deep into the earth and spires tied to the heavens, the cosmic tree links the gods, the planet, and the Maya underworld known as Xibalba—or, as a shaman would say, the tree connects the upper, middle, and lower worlds.

To the Maya, the Cosmic Tree represents the unification of the four cardinal directions at the axis mundi, or central point of the cosmos. As the axis mundi, the tree links the three realms. The branches represent a connection to higher spirituality, god, and the superconscious mind. In this upper realm, the gods are birds that land on the branches for brief moments of time to gift wisdom. The tree gains from this wisdom and grows. The trunk of the tree represents the middle world, our waking reality and the conscious mind. Human beings become the rings in the trunk that signify generations of life. The roots of the tree represent the lower world, with a connection to the subconscious mind, the shadow self, our ancestors, and the collective past. The roots provide stability and a link to origins. The Cosmic Tree is everything. It's a metaphor for the human machine. It's life, death, and rebirth. It's the face of God.

As I WALKED toward the opening of the cave, I bowed my head and said a silent prayer for the spirits of the Maya within. I then brought my hands together, honored the sacred ground, and gave thanks for being shown such a miracle. This entire journey had been miraculous. With the dreams of Madre Luna, Lake Atitlan, and the moon, I had been guided to this one singular and extraordinary moment in time. And after months of disbelief, self-doubt, and nonstop dreams, I was finally here. I gave the spirits my own humble and sweet words of thanks.

Walking out of the cave, I looked at Chavez and gave him a solemn glance. I would be in his debt for many a day. I thanked the Maya profusely for his time and faith. Together we walked forward, a son of the Maya and a son of the West, a Nahual bringing deep spiritual wisdom, warmth, and grace, and a Westerner bringing progress, joy, and hope. This is how the Conquest should have happened—not one culture subjugating another. Not one people enslaving another and throwing away thousands of years of spiritual wisdom. Not countless lakes of untold tears and suffering, followed by nighttime wails to the gods. Instead, two great traditions should have joined together to conquer ignorance, fear, and hatred. We can only dream of how history might have been different.

What other astronomical secrets might we have discovered from a people who had the capability to track and predict eclipses? What other concepts of space and time would we have gained from a society that developed the concept of zero, an idea never fathomed by the Greeks? What other methods of healing would we have learned from a culture that conquered the jungle, spoke to the gods, and raised stones to touch the sky?

We took the camioneta back to Santiago. Chavez stood at the front of the truck bed, while I held the frame rail on the right side. As the truck departed, we were flanked by trees and the lush greenery of mountain beards. I felt as if we were two knights returning triumphantly from a sacred quest. Riding back into the world of the real, having left the land of spirit, our chests were laden with arcane knowledge and ancient wisdom. Had I been on this road before? Had I once returned from a great distance, holding something sacred within my heart? I don't know. It all seemed familiar.

After reaching Santiago, I walked back to the pier with Chavez. Parting ways, I boarded a lancha for the return trip to Panajachel. The day had been successful. I had accomplished two important things: I had found the lady of the moon and deepened my connection to the spirit of the Maya. It had been an incredible day, and perhaps far too easy.

At this point, I should have realized that something was wrong; I should have figured out that something was amiss. The ancients don't give up secrets easily. In archaeology, our folklore is filled with tales of researchers and professors who went too far, knew too much, and came too close to unlocking the *verus secretu*, or true secrets, of ancient civilizations. These women and men were struck by lightning while standing atop stone temples, or died suddenly of mysterious deaths, or were forever lost to the jungle, only to become footnotes in their own textbooks. So, like a trusting Icarus, I began my ascent, sailing far too close to the sun.

The return ferry was slow. Upon reaching the pier, the small boat crawled and made a creaking sound as the fiberglass hull rubbed up against the weather-worn and rough-hewn timbers. As the captain turned off the engines and threw a rope to one of the boys on the landing, the undulating motion of the waves rocked the boat back and forth. Unable to gain a steady footing, I wildly grasped for the side of the boat, then the pier, to steady myself. Climbing onto the wooden planks, my sense of balance quickly returned to normal as the seasick swaying of waves gave way to the steadiness of wood and earth.

Walking further up the pier, I stepped onto the beach and turned eastward. The path led through sand dunes and retaining walls, up to the main boulevard of Panajachel. The walls further up, bordering the path, were covered with green moss. A slow rain began to descend upon the land as the sun began its journey underneath mountain peaks. I could see the individual puddles of rain form in the cracks of the cobblestone road. The wetness would grow until it filled the cracks, then it was channeled effortlessly down, down to the lake.

## CHAPTER 14
## Calm Before the Storm

———◀○▶———

THE NEXT DAY began with the finest Guatemalan breakfast I could ever imagine: golden-fried tortilla strips topped with egg, tomatoes, and salsa, with a side of delicious black beans and a glass of the freshest, tastiest orange juice. I spent the rest of the day walking to shops, admiring fine paintings, beadwork, beautiful textiles, and expertly carved stone and wood effigies. And was I bored. Where's the adventure? What happened to the excitement? There was still work to do.

Looking at my travel guides and notes, I decided I could easily return to Santiago on my own. Going alone wouldn't be so bad. Chavez wouldn't return for several days, as he had business in Guatemala City. Heck, I could hire another guide and overnight in the hotel. The jungle? Whatever. I was the master of the jungle and could easily handle myself in Santiago. And like a waft of ether, a false sense of security began to fill my thoughts, lulling my senses to sleep.

I had two vivid dreams that night. In one, I was nowhere to be seen. All that was left of me was my explorer's hat and notes, scattered on top of the waters of Lake Atitlan. There were no waves, no storm, just calm blue water. Where the heck was I? I hadn't planned on going swimming.

The other dream was much better. I was in the upstairs of a house, knocking on a door to see how someone was doing. In the hallway, a painting was on the wall, with the brightly colored, misshapen figures that could only be created through a child's love. Drawn with crayons, the composition spoke sweet words to my eye. A child's voice soon emerged through the door. "I'm OK, Daddy." Knowing our daughter was safe, I descended the stairs and saw my other love. Wearing jeans and a tan sweater, our eyes met once more. It was the young woman with the orange eyes . . .

I AWOKE THE next morning intent on discovering more about Santiago's cofradías with my remaining time in Guatemala. How did they revere Maximón? What types of relics did they guard? What's in the holy boxes? What were their secrets? These were all the noble intentions spinning about my head in the early dawn. Yet the murkiness of the afternoon lakeshore waters would belie the luminescent morning. And there was my mistake. Because instead of just waiting patiently for Chavez to return, instead of just being still, I decided to venture out on my own.

After crossing the lake to Santiago once more, I landed at the shore, but my arrival wasn't met with the usual greeting party of hopeful tour guides for the day. That seemed strange. Throughout the city, in fact, there was very little activity. The hustle and bustle I had seen on Friday

CALM BEFORE THE STORM

afternoon was gone. If Friday morning found Santiago asleep, today it was comatose. Walking to the top of the first small hill, next to a row of cinderblock buildings, I saw someone. It was a portly man wearing a straw cowboy hat, embroidered shirt, and white pants. I walked closer as he introduced himself. His name was Francisco, and he wanted to be my guide for the day. We talked about price for a few minutes, settling on a steep 180 quetzales. But I trusted in his government-issued ID that everything would be okay. Still, something seemed a bit off. He had seen me the previous day with Chavez. Had I known his watchful gaze had been tracking me, I would have been more careful with what I shared.

I briefly remembered my first day in Santiago, when my young guide and I were looking for Chavez. The city center was an ocean of vendors and buses, taxis, chickens, food, smells, and activity. Yet as soon as we began to ask questions, everything seemed to stop. All eyes were on us. It's like the moment you disturb an ant hill: the second before, each ant is moving busily on its way, in some sort of pattern. Then, just as you poke at the mound with a stick, for a split second, all the ants stop. And then—*whoom!*—the ants are alerted to your presence and rush off in a flurry of activity. That's exactly what it felt like with Francisco. I intuitively sensed something dangerous but couldn't pinpoint the source . . .

I pushed these thoughts out of my mind and turned my attention to the mission. The plan was to visit all of the cofradías. And if there was time, I also wanted to go back and visit Doña Pancha in Cerro de Oro. Did I mention I'm headstrong and impatient? We started by going to the cofradía of San Nicolas, or Saint Nicholas.

If you try to find cofradía houses on your own, you'll miss them. There are no signs, markings, or banners of any type directing you to the sacred space. On the outside, the cofradía quarters look exactly like normal block homes in Santiago. Gray, weather-worn, and guarded by the occasional stray dog, the house is quite plain. The only thing that gives away the magical site is the thick smell of copal incense. In Santiago, if there's copal burning, then there's almost certainly a cofradía nearby. And if someone is burning copal in a cofradía, rest assured the air is filled with spirit and magic.

The scene at this cofradía was very familiar. Walking inside, the altar stood to the left side of the room. The dirt floor had detritus of ash, litter, water, fire, and incense. A handwoven tablecloth covered the gray wood table serving as the altar. On top, a statue of a saint stood proudly, gazing at and greeting onlookers. Flowers were in vases, and white candles were lit to honor the gods.

One of the most important aspects to keep in mind when you are visiting a cofradía, or shamanic temple, is that all is not what it appears to be. It's almost as if you've stepped into an illusion, because the power objects are not glowing with energy or sparkling with life. Rather, it's just the opposite: it's like a spell of concealment has been cast throughout the room. The most powerful magical items are cloaked to non-native eyes. Instead, they appear as the most mundane objects in the sacred space.

To direct attention away from objects of power, the holy is made plain, the extraordinary is made common. Yes, that gnarled tree branch is really an ancient magical wand. Yes, the old felt hat on top of the table can make the wearer invisible, allowing his consciousness to travel unseen to other parts of the world. And yes, that old bit of twine is used to bind your enemies' hands, then string up their bodies and snap their necks. Not all items in the cofradías are used for benevolent ends.

Back at the altar, the saintlike statue of a small boy greeted and smiled at visitors. To his immediate left was a collection of thirteen rocks, each about the size and shape of a melon. Curiously, it seemed as if the rocks were looking at me. Each rock had eyes, some sort of nose, and a mouth. And each had some type of colorful head garment, like a scarf. And each scarf was tied crown-style, making the rocks look like a gathering of weathered Romani elders. My guide offered an explanation.

"You see, these are the sacred spirits of the forest. People come here when they want favors from the spirits," said Francisco.

"You mean these are the rock heads of the Maximón that have been used before on the statue?" I half-asked—perhaps more replied.

Francisco recoiled with utter disbelief. His eyes sent a cold chill through my body. At that point, I should have stopped. I should have just kept my mouth shut or ended the tour. But no, I was going to continue, and for the rest of the afternoon, I would explain exactly what each ritual item did and how it was used. It was as if Francisco was trying to guard the cofradía's secrets, merely providing a pedestrian and inaccurate tour for a tourist. Instead, I insisted on pulling away the wizard's curtain.

YOU SEE THAT old coat, the ordinary one that was being used in the cofradía of San Nicolas? It's really a magical cape. The shaman uses the cape to capture illnesses by heat. The shaman energizes the garment by praying over it and passing it near a fire to begin the heat exchange. As the patient sits near the fire and then dons the coat, the patient's body is heated, any illness is extruded and then captured by the coat's fibers. The wearer of the coat sweats out any impurities, spiritual or otherwise. And just like a vedic fire ceremony, or sweat lodge, the heating of the body irritates, dislodges, and removes any negativity cast upon the person.

Some of the cofradías were interesting. Some were bizarre. And some were garish, even for me. I think the most disturbing was the cofradía de San Juan de los Animales (animals), for suspended in the ceiling, along with the requisite streamers and phallus-shaped squash, were the remains of once-living cats, dogs, anteaters, mice, and other animals. They were desiccated but still very lifelike, and hung from the rafters like some sort of large-scale vampire mobiles, capable of swaying to and fro with a strong enough breeze. And they were all black! Not a single one of the mummified animals was white, or beige, or even cream-colored. We were told by the caretaker that shamans use the spirits of the dead animals to train or help locate living animals that are lost. The caretaker even said that after nighttime, he can hear the meows and howls of the cats and dogs, each one scratching and trying to escape from their sky harnesses. Now that I absolutely believe, one hundred percent. And he didn't need to show me video or photos to prove it, and I wasn't going to stick around and find out firsthand either.

As we visited the other cofradías, I followed the same pattern for the rest of the day—telling my guide what was happening and explaining precisely what the shamans were doing. By the end, Francisco's look of amazement turned to sheer annoyance. The most disturbing look came when I asked him why the cofradías didn't just keep the Maximón in one place and distribute the collected money to build schools and buy food for the poor. He didn't say anything. He just provided me an icy stare.

WHEN WE COMPLETED our tour, Francisco offered to take me to Cerro de Oro. His mood suddenly changed from somber to eager and overly friendly. Wisely, I refused. Something just wasn't right about this guide. What lurked behind his constant smile and pleasant veil? I then made it to the last lancha of the day.

The boat ride across Lake Atitlan was treacherous. The lancha, designed to hold twelve, was burdened with twenty. At the same time, a stormfront crossed the Lake of Dreams, bringing forth gale-force winds and quickly creating twelve-foot swells. I looked around the small tub. Twenty passengers and four life vests; the math wasn't good. I turned back to see the captain's steady hand on the boat's motor. I could see his clenched fist and the white of his knuckles as he struggled to keep the boat on course. The only way to make it over the swells was to cross each of the waves head-on. Any slight turn, any sudden movement or deviation, and the tub would turn sideways. Parallel to the wave, we didn't stand a chance, as the boat would quickly capsize. As the vessel started to fill with splashes of water, a young lady stood up on the boat's tail end. Throwing off the boat's balance for a second, the captain then yelled at her. For a moment, I thought it was all over. As the girl sat down, the captain quickly recovered.

I said a few prayers. With twenty passengers and four life vests amidst twelve-foot seas, God is never far.

# CHAPTER 15
## Heart of Compassion

———————◦O◦———————

SHAMANS RELY HEAVILY on spirit guides for assistance and protection. Communication with guides usually occurs when dreaming or in trance, as the thoughts of the conscious mind are lulled to sleep and replaced by symbols of the subconscious. These images of the collective unconscious can include tears, gold, hearts, ships, and animals; spirit guides will use these symbols to communicate messages. If a message is complex or urgent, the spirit guides will repeat the symbols again and again. Recalling my own dreams, I found the lake, the woman, and the village. But where were the caimans I dreamt of, the dangerous congregation lurking beneath my raft?

The next day, I took the lancha back to Santiago in the early morning. On the opposite shore, I quickly found Chavez, ready to deliver me into the comforting presence of Madre Luna. After the

———◦◦———

drive and immediately upon seeing her, I was overwhelmed with a great sense of serenity. Moreover, she carries an aura of deep compassion about her. It's the air of something ancient, totally altruistic, and uncommonly human. It's the feeling of being around someone who has forgone fame and glory for a greater calling. The energy of the two shamans I had worked with before was different. Cantu was more of a mystic; spending copious time in otherworldly realms and channeling gave him the air of a wizard. Gary the Spiritwalker was more of a warrior. Having seen the carnage of Vietnam, having grown up with discrimination, Gary knew how to fight and stand his ground. But Doña Pancha was different; she was a part of the earth. Her energy was that of the mother, of unconditional love and compassion. This was the softness and essence of the moon.

"*Mir. Mir la luna*," spoke the ancient sage. "The moon told me you were coming a long time ago. You are on a journey. Your job will be to write about what you see and tell others. You must always write what you see. At times, others will not believe you. At times, you will lose hope. But remember today. Remember that the spirits brought you here, and they will always guide you. This is your journey.

"There is a woman that waits for you. She is young. She is very sweet and kind. But she is also old. The two of you have been together before. She may be distant, but she is already visiting you. The two of you must believe. You must believe in one another.

"The world is in a difficult time. It is filled with suffering and despair. We must help others. We must heal those that are suffering and bring light to the world. This is your job, too. You must give people hope— hope for the planet.

"Help one another. Love one another. Always do things with a good heart, and the spirits will always protect you.

"The spirits I will show you today are of the moon, the sun, and the earth . . . the sea, the lake, and the mountains. Let us begin."

The first patient of the day was a colicky baby. Dressed in a hand woven bundle of cloth, the infant was struggling with some sort of pain, crying desperately. I stood in the corner of the room and took a seat as Madre Luna reached into her altar, a small shelf draped over with a soft blue fabric. Out of the veil emerged a small woodchip about the size of a communion wafer. She held the chip in her hands, said a prayer in wonderous Cachiquel, and then placed it in the baby's mouth.

After a few moments, the baby stopped crying. A few minutes more, and the baby opened its eyes. Bright, deep brown orbs glistened in the light. As the child sucked on the chip, for a moment, I could almost see him smiling. Madre Luna instructed the mother to let the baby suckle from the chip for two more days, then to give the child small sips of a special tea, a preparation of leaves and a honey-colored liquid.

The next patient was a woman from the capital. Hurt in an industrial accident, most of the flesh of her left arm had been sheared off; all that was left was remnants of skin and bone. Madre Luna's treatment was to help ease the woman's pain and reduce the scarring. Pulling out a few leaves from her shelf, she placed them into her mouth and gently chewed for a bit. After a few minutes, she took them out and mixed them with white gel from a native tree. Putting the salve on the wound, the patient breathed a sigh of relief as the pain was released to the gods of the jungle.

Leading the woman out of the treatment room, Madre Luna returned and looked directly at me.

"You have many questions. Let me answer some of them. People come from all over to see me. Some come from New York and California, and others from Texas." Of course, I had never told her that I was from Texas.

"The first thing you want to know is how I learned to heal," stated the sage.

"After I found the moon inside of the picture frame, the spirits of the forest began to speak to me. It was slow at first, but after some time, they began to teach me more and more. I use herbs from the forest, over 120 herbs. No one ever taught me. I learned from the spirits, and the moon.

"I heal with my hands, my heart. The spirits tell me how to prepare and what I must give my people. And since I started healing, I've never gotten sick," said Madre Luna.

I thought about the implications of what she was saying. Did she have some sort of natural immunity, some genetic predisposition against illness? Or was her energy so high that she was able to just throw off illnesses, like automatically washing hands after getting them dirty? And how could she not get sick after coming into contact with so many ill people?

"What do the spirits tell you about the people who come to see you? How do you know of their illnesses?" I asked.

"The moon will tell me about the people that come. The moon will tell me when someone is coming—it will tell me about that person. Many people come to see me. Not all are sick. Those that are not sick, I send away.

"I can also see into their thoughts. If someone is ill mentally, I can see that, and the moon will tell me. For injuries deep inside, I use the moon," noted the seer.

I'm not really sure what happened next, because I was looking outside, and when I turned to face her, she was holding the glass orb in her hand. But it was no longer a globe! The same glass sphere I had seen before was now shaped like an upside-down teardrop. Its jelly glass was leaking onto the floor, with the cone side dripping downwards.

"See, the moon told me you were coming, too," she continued.

I tried to regain my composure. "Where do you put the illnesses when you have removed them?" I asked. Most shamans see illness as either a physical growth or a small sphere of dark energy on a person's auric field that has to be removed and returned to the earth. Would Madre Luna do the same?

"When I remove illnesses, I place them in vegetables or in tortillas. The corn and tortillas will hold the sicknesses until I burn them at night. When these items are cooked, the diseases are neutralized and change form, disappearing into the air. As ash, the items are harmless," she said.

Once again, the ash! Some shamans avoid the ash after the fires have remedied the illnesses. Others, like Hindu swamis, will treat the ash as holy.

"And yes, I pull out physical objects," she continued. "I once pulled out a bullet from a colonel's arm. About twenty years ago, the soldiers came to my home. They had heard about me. They wanted to see what I was doing. They wanted to know if I was part of the *guerrillieros*, part of the war. I told the soldiers to send their colonel.

"The colonel came to see me. He sat down right in that chair," she pointed to the chair were Chavez was seated. "He asked me if I was a witch or if I was planning to kill him. I said no, I heal all those that come to see me. As I spoke to him, the orb told me there was something wrong with his shoulder. I asked him to remove his shirt and lie down.

"On his back, on his left side, below the bone, I saw a scar. He said he was shot in the back and still carried the bullet. I asked him to take deep breaths, and as he exhaled and loosened his muscles, I placed my mouth on the wound and pulled out the bullet. I then showed it to him.

"The colonel said it was a miracle. I said no, it was the Maya—the spirits of the moon, the sun, and the earth; the sea, the lake, and the mountains. After that, the colonel ordered the soldiers never to bother me again. And they never came back."

I was very much caught up in the moment, struggling to scribble notes while tons of ideas were racing through my mind. What other secrets did this amazing woman hold? The next question jumped from my lips.

"Where do illnesses come from? Why do people get sick?" I asked.

Doña Pancha looked down toward the moon orb for a few seconds. The globe was once again whole and placed gently on the ground, atop a blue and white cloth. Then she looked up.

"It is very important to understand that people do not ask for disease, people do not ask to get sick. Illness comes from two sources: from unsanitary conditions and from other people. This is how illness is spread. Many times, we are not careful with how we cook our food, wash our hands, or go to the bathroom. This is how we become sick. Other times, people bring illnesses from other lands. As people, we talk to others, we travel, and others come to see us. Disease will sometimes travel like this.

"No one asks to become sick or infirm. No one asks to become ill or have their bodies eaten by disease. This is very important, because it means that we must show compassion to those that are ill. We must not be fearful. We must not judge. We must show compassion.

"You look tired. Come back tomorrow. I will answer more of your questions," said Madre Luna.

And sure enough, I was drained. I'm not sure if it was the work, the altitude, or just the sheer weight of revelation. The episode of finally meeting someone who had come to me in dreams and inspired me to travel thousands of miles to solve riddles was exhausting. But there was someone else who kept coming to me in dreams—someone who inspired me to become a better person and, more importantly, gave me hope. This woman was a bit more distant yet also more familiar. Someone with dark hair and beautiful eyes.

"There is also a woman that waits for you," Madre Luna continued. "She sees you from a distance. She will become a part of your life very soon. The moon will help the both of you meet," the healer said.

That was the final message of the day. So, with my hat jumping from my left knee to my head, I gathered my notes and thanked Madre Luna. I slowly bowed to her and kissed her softly on the cheek. After giving my gratitude, I stepped outside and back into the world.

THE RIDE TO Santiago and lancha back to Panajachel went by quickly. I was deep in thought. I don't even think I ate dinner that night, I was so haunted by Madre Luna and her words. She possessed so much knowledge, yet so much humility. With her abilities, she could be living anywhere, making untold riches. Instead, she chose to heal the neediest, the poorest, the most helpless people. Simply amazing. And as I slept that night, I was shown her origin . . .

BIRTHED FROM A vulcan womb, what I perceived in Cerro de Oro with my eyes as a Maya woman was actually a reincarnated fire goddess. From the depths of the earth, shooting upwards toward the heavens, emerged deity. Her body a deep red, with veins of white fire emerging from her legs to her torso and then to her arms, she was pure spirit and energy! Madre Luna wasn't just a channel for the gods, she was a goddess in her own right. This is how she knows the future, has the ability to peer into human hearts, heals the sick, and talks continually to the spirit world. This was her true origin and form.

# CHAPTER 16
## Wisdom of Ancients

—◆O◆—

THE NEXT DAY began with Madre Luna treating a few more patients. I resumed my questions during her free moments, and I saved the most important question for last.

"Madre Luna, what messages do you have for us? What must we learn and practice?" I asked.

"This is what people must know. First, use your power for good, never evil, never to harm. Don't conjure ill thoughts against others. Don't speak ill of others. Thoughts and speech can be the same. Use your powers for good. Use your gifts for healing. Always conduct yourself by and with good thoughts.

"Next, pray every day to your deities. I pray to Jesus and Mary, and I also pray to the spirits of the moon, the sun, and the earth; the sea, the lake, and the mountains. Pray to your gods. Acknowledge them, honor them, remember them.

"Be thankful for what you have. Be thankful for even the smallest grain of rice or the tiniest piece of corn. Be thankful for the smallest crumb, the tiniest piece of clothing, the smallest of anything you have. The spirits are listening; show thanks for what you have.

"Honor the earth, the moon, the sun, and the natural surroundings; they all have spirits that protect us. These spirits comfort us, provide for us, and guide us. Show these spirits respect. Honor them as you would your mother and father. Show compassion for the planet. We are all children of the earth, the sun, the moon, and the stars. Honor the forces that brought you here.

"Don't judge others because they are ill or have a disease. Show these people compassion and mercy. They didn't ask to become ill. They didn't want to be crippled. They didn't ask to suffer. Disease just visited them. So show them compassion and understanding.

"The world needs more love—more love! We have so much hate and suffering in our lives. When we live with hate, we suffer. As we suffer, we bring in more hate. This continues on and on. We must learn to let go of hate, let go of suffering. Every person on this planet has difficulties. Don't be a source of hate. Show love. Increase love. Show love, and be loved.

"We must also share the things we have. There is more than enough food on the planet so that no one should be hungry. No child should be crying at nighttime because no food is in their bellies. No beggar should be without a meal, no lost person without a place to call home. No one should be digging their own graves. The earth has enough to provide for its children. We must share the things that we have. And we must share the goodness within our hearts.

"The spirits are always with us. The spirits are around us; they protect us, listen to us, and guide us. They listen to us. Honor the spirits. Listen to them. When we are sad, lonely, or think we are alone, we are not. The spirits of our ancestors and the natural forces are always around us.

"Stay on the path. Don't give up. Despite whatever obstacles you encounter, do not give up on your journey. Each of us is gifted with a destiny. You must use your gifts for the betterment of the world. As you are doing this, you are fulfilling your destiny. Whatever hardship or difficulty you encounter, never give up. Continue your destiny. Stay on the path."

Awestruck, I asked the next question. "Madre Luna, why is it important to work with the light?"

"You must always work with the light. The force of light is much stronger than the force of darkness—not as fast but always stronger. If you work with the forces of light, you will always be protected. Those that choose the other path, their lives are fraught with peril. Light is stable. Our universe emerged from the light. We are part of the light, and to the light we will return. But our universe also has darkness. The darkness is unstable. The darkness is fear. The darkness is suffering. When someone works with the darkness, hate and disarray are magnified. And the darkness returns to its source. Never work with the darkness, always with the light. Embrace light, embrace love. Embrace tenderness, and live with compassion! This is the last true magic."

"Madre Luna, what are we doing to our planet?" was my next question.

"Our planet is suffering. Our world is overwhelmed with greed, fear, and envy. Because of humankind's thoughts, our planet is being destroyed. People want to control the planet. They want to collect and hoard water, minerals, crops, food. Yet this is not correct, this is not the way. This only brings more suffering. Remember, the fattened pigs are the first to be eaten.

"The earth has plenty of resources for its children. We must share what we have, and we must not fear loss. If we don't fear loss, then no one will take more than they need. If everyone only takes what they need, then there is enough for all. If we continue to gather more than we need, then we head toward disaster."

"Madre Luna, what happened to the Maya? What happened to the civilization that tracked the moon, developed calendars, and built ancient cities? What happened to the great cities like Tikal?" I asked.

"My son, the Maya are not lost. They are right here—right in front of you. The Maya never disappeared. They are right here," she said as she pointed to herself and Chavez. "They are there," as she pointed toward the town square in Cerro de Oro. "They are over there," she said as she rose and pointed to Panajachel on the opposite side of the lake. "The Maya are all around you. We never left. We never disappeared. We might have left the cities, but we did not die."

"Madre Luna, why did the Maya leave the cities?" I asked.

"The cities were abandoned because the children of men forgot that they were really the children of the gods. Too many people were living in too many cities. Food became scarce. Crops failed. Disease spread. The Maya forgot how to live in harmony with the land. The Maya forgot how to honor the gods. The gods didn't want blood sacrifice; the gods wanted respect—respect for the earth, the moon, the stars. When the children of men forgot this, the gods became angry. And as the gods were angry, cities were destroyed. Famine spread. Disease devoured the Maya. Suffering filled the land. And all the while, the great kings kept killing one another, inflicting more and more suffering," the ancient seer said.

"What went wrong? What did we do?" I continued.

"The gods wanted reverence, but instead, man gave them despair. So the gods wanted to start again, but there were too many men to kill. And there were still priests and shamans who revered the spirits. Small in number, yes, but they were still there. So the gods did not desire humanity's destruction. Instead, the gods chose to give the Maya a lesson: 'Listen or be punished. Honor the earth or suffer. Respect the forces of nature or feel nature's wrath.' This was the lesson given to the Maya. This is a lesson for all of us."

And there it was. The Maya didn't disappear, they just moved back to the countryside after the cities were abandoned. And the cities were destroyed at the Maya's own hands. Overpopulation, pollution, deforestation, crop disease, and warfare were all human-made disasters that visited the Maya by their own hands. Is our modern age any different? Do we not pollute our planet as well and race toward our own destruction? The Maya didn't disappear. The civilization collapsed because of the way the Maya treated their home. Finally came the penultimate question, the one that had plagued me for months.

"Madre Luna, will the world end in 2012, as the calendar says?" I asked.

"What happens when your clock strikes twelve at midnight? What happens?" she asked me.

"Well, it's just a new day." I said.

"Exactly. *Es el mismo*. It's the same. The world is not ending at 2012. It's just the end of a cycle. It's just like the start of a new day.

"More people will become interested in healing the planet. Leaders from different nations will work together. The spirits of the Maya will speak to us more. But the world's not going to end," she said.


INTERESTING. IN OTHER words, 2012 is what we make of it. There is no upcoming catastrophe, no meteor shower, no tidal waves, no gateways opening into other worlds, no Pleiadian visitation, no events of epic and supernatural proportion. The year 2012 is simply what we make of it—a date that reflects our own beliefs.

If we decide, as a race or even as a people, that 2012 is a cosmic marker for increased awareness, a resurgence of dynamic spirituality, and a deeper connection with nature and the universe, then this date will become inspirational and superlative. However, if we decide 2012 is a date to fear, a time stamp for a catastrophe, and an alignment to bring about chaos and despair, then it will be those things as well. In other words, 2012 is created by our own realities and subconscious thoughts.

2012 is the ultimate inkblot test—nothing more, nothing less. By feeding into our own fears and dreams, we are actually programming the date of 2012 right now. December 23, 2012, is what we make of it. So do we see it as a time for prosperity and a new era of peace? Or do we fall once more to the illusion of industrial dreams and plastic greed?

"Madre Luna, what will eventually happen to the planet, to the people of maize?" I asked.

"We must change or be destroyed," she said as a cold shiver raced down my back. "We must learn to respect the planet and one another, or our time will come to an end."

I spent the rest of the day watching Madre Luna as she cured the infirm and tended to the sick. I saw her give out teas, place hands on wounds and elbows, and give hugs. After about forty patients, I stopped counting. It was so amazing to just watch this tender woman simply give the best of what she had: her sacred bundle and her heart.

At the end of the day, I was joyful. I had been gifted with the information I was looking for. I had met the healer, the lady of the moon with a blue face and black hair, the woman of the moon who used the moon as her orb. I was entrusted with her messages for humanity, and I was determined to share these with the world.

I returned to see Madre Luna just one more time. After spending a few days gathering my thoughts and journaling, she invited me to see a fire ceremony for the people of the earth. And as I bore witness, I had no idea that I would never see her again.

WE BEGAN IN the cosmic cave I had visited with Nicolas Chavez. Out of the shadows stepped the Vulcan goddess. Dressed in her finest ceremonial attire, she approached the cave with a staff in one hand and the hopes of a world in another. At her feet lay a sunburst of color and light: a fire mandala had been created. From light and lifeforce came energy. As Madre Luna tapped her staff three times on the cave floor, the doorway to the land of the ancients emerged.

"Hear me, Nahuales. Hear me, ancient Maya, lords of time and space! I am the Madre Luna, and I command you to open this door."

The thick copal incense rose up into the heavens and past the arms of the Cosmic Tree overlooking the cave. And as the resin and veins of the tree began to pulse, the tree came alive. Each leaf, each cell, each stomata gulped down the influx of energy. As the tree shuddered, its roots broke deep into the earth. Deeper and deeper in the core the roots went until the glory of the entire underworld was unleashed.

"Hear me, ancient ones, open this doorway between worlds. Show us the beauty of your kingdom. Forgive us for our transgressions upon the earth." The incense from the fire mandala first rose up in the shape of a circle, then grew larger still as it changed into a vortex and returned its noble fire to the stars.

The ground seals were extraordinary. The fire mandala was set up with a red candle in the center, representing the sacred blood in all living things. A white candle was in the north, representing health. A green candle was set toward the east, representing renewal. A blue candle was in the south, representing spirituality. And a yellow candle was in the west, representing godlight. Around the center candle were smaller candles parallel to the ground and arrayed in a heliacal formation. The smaller candles were blue and red, yellow and green, pink and brown, each candle representing the peoples of the earth. Atop the smaller candles was placed cinnamon to unite humanity. And atop the cinnamon was sugar and bits of chocolate to coax help from the gods, for just like humans, the gods favored sweetness and compassion.

This wasn't just a fire mandala, this was the a'j r'ij's table, her mesa for casting healing spells and rituals. And this wasn't just a mesa, this was the cosmos.

As her words reached the right tone, the right pitch, the right inflection, time stood still. The gate opened, and the elemental shaman connected with the forces of nature.

"Here me, great lords of time, forces of the unseen and unknown. We have committed great transgressions upon the earth. We ask for your forgiveness and your protection. Hear me, ancient ones. I come from the earth, and I speak for its people."

Her words became harmonic chords offered to the forces of nature. They changed from Cachiquel to a more ancient Nahuatl, then to another language more ancient still. And when the earth goddess spoke into the cave, the spirits of the cave reached toward her. Their energy emerged and leapt forward, at first as a trickle, then a few rays, then more and more, until the energy became a wild plasma stream cascading about the woman.

Gathering the energy, she reached up and out until finally, with her arms extended toward the heavens, the shaman radiated her energy to every living being. And at that moment, all creatures both grand and small were embraced by the goddess's light. Everything on the planet felt her love and energy. From the smallest insect to the largest whale, all of Earth's creatures were healed.

She then let out a breath and put her arms down as the doorway closed. Exhausted from the release, she collapsed to her knees, then the ground, as she let out a deep sigh.

It was done. The ceremony was finished, the prayer complete. More woman than goddess now, more human than deity, Madre Luna had finished her task. And why was she more human than goddess? What made her real, capable of feeling sadness and hope, despair and joy? Was it her ability to cry, her ability to love? It was her tears of love—it was her love that made her real. Her love and compassion for all of us. It was her love and her tears of compassion that made her the moon.

Slowly, the woman walked back to her home. Tomorrow would be another day of healing—another day of colicky babies, broken bones, infections, and tired muscles. Another day to guide, heal, and love the planet. But I would no longer be there to see . . .

SOMETHING HAPPENED THE next day. I found I was being followed by men from one of the cofradías. Apparently, they wanted to speak to me.

However, their speech was not to be carried by vowels or consonants. It was to be carried by guns and violence. Apparently, I had asked too much, saw too much, possibly knew too much. I could tell someone was following me.

I was now a danger to the men of the cofradías. I knew their secrets. I had endlessly babbled to Francisco. And Chavez had confided in me about one of the cofradías's most precious possessions: a second copy of the Maya Popol Vuh. A codex, or collection of spells and myths, drawn right at the time of the Spanish Conquest, this was a priceless relic that people would kill for. The brotherhoods no longer supported my search; behind their pleasant smiles stood the countless blades of caiman's teeth.

I also understood the power of the men who desperately sought control over the access and money given to the saint. The Maximón, or mam, was just another tool of religious control used by a few elites who became wealthy while the rest of the city languished in poverty. The true power of the mam had always been in the hearts of the Maya people. It was their intent that created the god in the first place. It was their hearts and songs that infused the statue with vital lifeforce. It was the hearts and thoughts of the people of maize that were truly powerful. Maximón was the heir apparent, but the true rulers were the believers and the faithful of the Maya.

This was the arcane knowledge I had gained in Santiago. Back at home base, someone tried to break into my room during the night. Against firearms or knives, I was defenseless. Fortunately, the lock, and my luck, held out.


I FLED GUATEMALA the next morning. Arranging quick transport, I was packed and out of my hotel room within ten minutes. Ten minutes more and I was on the road, wearing the disguise of a tourist. Fleeing my pursuers, I hastily made it to the airport. And two hours after leaving the hotel, I was on a plane bound for the States.

And so, like a triumphant Apollo or wily Odysseus, I sailed away into blue skies, having escaped the children of men and the Cyclops gaze, carrying my own sacred bundles—my notes, pictures, recordings, and, most importantly, my heart.

It was my heart that was filled with joy, because I had found what it searched for. I had met the Vulcan goddess, the Madre Luna who had visited me through dreams. I had recorded her messages about suffering, disease, the year 2012, and, most importantly, hope. I experienced her love and compassion. I saw her love back to health those that were ill. I saw her tears of love heal the sick and save the planet. I had found what I needed.

Or had I? What about the other woman in my dreams, the woman Madre Luna confirmed I would meet? Was I any closer to that elusive answer, her soft embrace, her simple warmth? I remembered what she had said about flowers—her favorite flowers were the blue ones, the ones with the small petals. But her dad once had given her orange flowers, and she loved those also.

When she was young, she loved to braid hair. Bits and pieces of our talks were all I remembered. Would it be enough to find her? And what would I say when we met?

I had obtained the secrets of water, but at nearly the cost of my life. Other travelers have gone missing in Santiago over the years, victims of bandits and gangs, but I made it out alive. It is the water that allows the tree to grow. Water, through tears of compassion, heals us. By loving others with this nonjudgmental compassion, we begin to expand our potential and stretch our limbs into higher consciousness. Water from tears grows our hearts. Water from tears heals the planet.

But did the journey to jungles of Central America bring me closer to the woman of my dreams, the one from my visions in the desert, the young woman with orange eyes and dark hair that I was destined to meet? Or would visions of her be forever fleeting, like the mists above Lake Atitlan?

# PART FOUR

*Air*

# CHAPTER 17

## Manchen Lopon: Vajrayana Buddhist Master

—◆—

THE ONLY COUNTRY in Asia to have never been conquered, Bhutan rests near the top of the mighty Himalayas. With its rugged terrain and fierce Dragon Kings, the small Buddhist nation was able to fight off armies of Mongols, Tibetans, and even the British Empire. With no railway, travel in this Buddhist realm is perilous and slow. Yet this didn't stop the most important Buddhist masters of the last two thousand years from crossing its mountain peaks and vast terrain. What is so compelling about Bhutan that called Pasdmasambhava, the most powerful Buddhist magician of our age, from Swat, or modern-day Pakistan? Why did realized masters such as Drukpa Kunley and Shabdrung Namgyal emerge from this isolated yet proud country? What secrets did the Dragon Kings and their mystical sect of Vajrayana Buddhism hold?

About three months later, the dreams started once more. I kept seeing a temple, or a fortress really, next to two streams of water. I remembered grey stone, vaulted ceilings, and a thin, snakelike dragon flying counterclockwise around the granite sentinel. Protecting the fortress, the dragon guarded what was inside. And something incredible was inside the temple, a box that speaks and monks who jealously guard it. The head of the order was a realized master, a high lama with messages for our planet.

I wasn't quite sure what to think of the dreams, so I began to draw. Buying colored pencils and paper, I drew sketches of the temple, pictures of the dragon, and outlines of the rooms. I wasn't brave enough to show anyone my work. I had learned the lesson of secrecy during my mishap in Guatemala when I blurted everything out to Francisco—and it almost cost me my life.

And what would I say? "Yes, these are drawings of a temple and a monk living inside who speaks to me in dreams. The ceilings are vaulted, the structure is made of grey stone, and there is a long, thin dragon that flies around at night and protects it." Right.

I also dreamt of soldiers with Kalashnikovs who were guarding something ancient, something hidden; a miraculous site too holy and too provocative to reveal. The temple and site were somehow connected.

And the dreams of the young woman kept coming. They were stronger, and her features were more distinct. The waking hours were most interesting of all. I would wake to the sound of an alarm clock buzzer. But then I would remember this wasn't possible, since I used a cell phone as an alarm. So I bought a buzzer alarm clock. And instead, I would wake up to songs from the 1970s. Once I even woke up to the sound of a VCR on rewind. That's interesting, considering there wasn't a VCR in the entire house! Other times, I could feel someone sleeping next to me—a thin shape, warm, with long hair, that would hold me close. It seemed as if our souls were synching at nighttime. Connecting across thousands of miles of time and space, we were drawing closer together, sharing energy.

I knew she was near. And perhaps I was close, too—close to the edge of sanity and reason.

Still, it seemed my mission was not yet complete. I needed to track down one last shaman. And a name kept floating in my head. It sounded vaguely familiar, yet I had never seen it on a map or nor read anything about it. The name was Bhutan. And so I began my search in earnest.

KNOWN AS DRUK Yul, or Land of the Thunder Dragon, Bhutan is the last remnant of pure Buddhist culture in the entire world. Other places have long since disappeared. Tibet fell to the empty, cold shell of Chinese Communist logic. Nepal is mostly Hindu and secular. But Bhutan is special. It is the home of a mysterious sect of Buddhism, one that may someday hold the answer to our collective salvation. The Buddhists call it Vajrayana, which means Diamond Vehicle or Diamond Thunderbolt. It is indestructible, like diamond, and all-powerful, like a bolt of lighting. But why was the temple important, and what would the Buddhist master tell us about our planet?

I started with the Internet, contacting guides, reading travel sites, applying for visas, looking at schedules. I had a feeling luck and timing would be important on this trip. After saying goodbye to a soulless job, I packed my gear once more, hugged my family goodbye, and boarded a plane. In Bangkok, I was nearly denied access to Bhutan because of a missing visa, but my luck prevailed again. Soon, I was in the air skirting the Himalayas and Mount Everest. A short time later, we landed in Paro.

With one of the largest valleys in Bhutan, Paro is home to the country's only airport. By air, there is one way in and one way out. There are also three land routes out of the country, complete with armed checkpoints—not quite the best way to leave if an escape was necessary. But I hoped my luck would hold out one more time.

The first lesson of Buddhism is reverence for every living being—every leaf, every flower, every animal, every blade of grass. Everything having the sacred lifeforce is to be respected, for every living thing has a soul. And just as we're reborn as people, we can easily be reborn as animals, plants, or trees. In this shared life journey, all living beings seek but two things: to escape suffering and to achieve happiness. It is in this quest, in this seemingly endless cycle of birth, death, and rebirth, that we seek escape from samsara, our mortal prison, which keeps us from ascending and becoming fully awakened beings of light.

Buddhists also believe that much of what happens in our lives is due to karma. Karma is the idea of action and reaction, that every action we make, every decision we take, resonates in eternity and ultimately affects us. That all choices eventually return to either help us or haunt us. And that nothing goes unnoticed on the path and practice of dharma, or the "do," known as the way of life. Did you open the door for that stranger who was struggling with boxes outside your building? Did you pick up that piece of trash in the park, the one that blew right past your feet? Did you make a call on Mother's Day and wish your mom well? Karma is all these things and more. As I kept thinking about karma, the reality of the airplane flight brought me back to earth.

After a high-performance landing with three severe banking turns and a razor-sharp descent, we arrived in the Paro Valley. The airport in Paro is amazing. More temple than facility, its two stories are painted with protective dragons and *garudas* (magical griffins) serving as its primary guard force. Buddhist symbols both inside and out served two goals: keeping the good luck in and frightening unwanted spirits away. Still, there were armed military police to meet us. I made a mental note of their weapons—Indian-issued short-barreled SLRs. Full automatics. A gift from a protective and wise tiger charged with holding back the hungry bear called China. I also took a closer look at the dragon paintings. The red and green scales of the *druk*, or dragon, contrasted sharply to its jagged white fangs. One can almost imagine the slim form compressing and tensing right before bellowing out a deadly breath of blue flame.

Outside the airport, a small, wiry Bhutanese man of about 120 pounds met me. With the grip of a lion, he shook my hand and said, "My name is Sonam. I'll be your guide." After walking to a small red four-door sedan, we loaded my gear and were off.

Sonam looked like a character from one of Rudyard Kipling's stories. With a thick, jet-black mane, tan skin, and focused eyes, he looked like a mountaineer or a legendary sherpa ready to adventure through the Himalayas. Today, we would make a short stop for tea and then drive to Thimphu, the capital city. And then the search would begin, visiting temples, talking to monks, and showing the drawings. I would try to unmask the riddle of the temple, the box, and the dragon. Who had called for me? And what were the messages?

AFTER ABOUT AN hour of dusty driving through the mountains, we ground our way to a dead halt. A road-widening project, financed by the government of India, was underway. Teams of workers broke rock with sledgehammers, moved rubble, and carved a new two-lane road through eons-old stone. I stepped out of the coach. I wasn't sure if it was the dust, heat, curvy road, or altitude, but within seconds, I was standing over the piles of freshly ground granite filler, violently throwing up. All I had in my stomach was water. And thankfully, after a moment, my belly was clear. I walked to the right side of the road and peered over the edge to see the clear blue-green waters of the adjoining river. Water from the roof of the world, washing away our sins. Water from the roof of the world, washing away our tears.

The effort to remove our accumulated karma and free ourselves from the suffering prison of samsara occurs along what Buddhists call the Wheel of Life. In the Wheel of Life, we embark along a journey. It is a path to enlightenment along three upper quadrants and three lower quadrants.

Buddhists feel that all of our acts during life, both good and bad, are measured at the time of our passing. Upon our death, at the judgment, the lord of death, named Yama, measures our actions on a set of scales. Good deeds, or merit, become white tablets and are placed on the left side of the scale. Bad deeds, or sins, become black tablets and are placed on the right. Arguing to and fro, pleading with the judge of the soul are the White God and Dark Demon. Each side asks—hopes—that their side of the scale will be heavier. When the scales are filled, the lot is cast, and the person is sent to either an upper or a lower realm.

The three upper realms consist of the God realm, the realm of humans, and the realm of demi-gods. The highest, or best place to be, is the God realm. There our souls lead a peaceful existence and are able to assist others in their transcendence of samsara. The second-best place to be reborn is the realm of humans. In this realm, we can work on our karma, heal the planet, be parents, and interact with other living beings. We're still faced with challenges, but we're also able to positively affect the lives of others, as well as our own. The last place in the upper realms is the realm of demi-gods. This is the haven of angels, both normal and fallen. The residents of this realm have miraculous powers, but the cost is constant warfare as groups battle for dominion and supremacy. This world is also a metaphor for a world without peace. It's a place of illusory superiority, as the constant struggle grinds down the victor until they are eventually replaced with another.

The three lower realms in the Wheel of Life are hell, the world of animals, and the land of hungry ghosts. Hell is the darkest, but even in this realm of utmost misery, souls can be redeemed through prayer. The world of animals is the next level, where humans are reborn as frogs, leopards, fish, elephants, and other creatures. This world is indeed a prison, where its denizens can understand what they see, but they cannot speak. Imagine knowing so much but never being able to communi-cate. Worse still, one can never find refuge, for animals are always prey of other predators, whether they run on four legs or walk on two. That's the world of animals.

The land of hungry ghosts isn't pleasant either. Here, humans are reborn as hungry phantoms with straw-thin throats and starved bellies. Condemned to constantly eat but never be full, hungry ghosts are ruled by their greed. Forced to wander the earth until they are redeemed, these spirits can see humans laugh and love. But they also experience deep regret, as they can never be held or feel love. Starved for emotional and physical nourishment, they wander earth until the hour they are released.

To escape the prison of samsara, we must take hold of three animal vices at the center of the Wheel of Life. The rooster, snake, and pig are the captors. To conquer and master the wheel, we must defeat the rooster, signifying greed; the snake, representing hate; and the pig, symbolizing ignorance. Only by taming our animal nature will transcendence be assured.

Quite simply, the three upper realms embody opportunity; specifically, the opportunity to transcend suffering. The three lower realms embody suffering and are the consequences of not heeding spiritual lessons.

BACK ON THE road, we leapfrogged small trucks and larger busses as we skirted the mountains above the river valley. Twisting and turning, the road seemed to have more curves than a troupe of Brazilian tango danc-ers. We passed many vehicles as we made our way to Thimphu. Some were small cars struggling up the ascents. Others were large dump trucks hauling stone and building materials. Larger still were busses holding countless travelers.

As we passed the road crews, I was taken aback by the sheer drudgery of their monumental task. Cutters chipped stone blocks from mountain walls. Teams of sledgehammer men broke the block into smaller boulders. Women loaded the boulder fragments upon their backs and carried the heavy bundles to other hammering areas. The stones were broken down further still to create roadfill about the size of marbles. The resultant pebbles were to be laid upon fresh ground, and then covered by asphalt to make a new road.

The Indian laborers were thousands of miles from the continent, away from their families and homes, working dawn till dusk. I was very humbled and felt quite small. I'm the one who complains about traffic jams in San Diego, running short of cream for my coffee, and not being able to get the latest cell phone or iPod. Yet my frustrations are trivial compared to those of the women and men building this road. While I was lost in thought, vehicles continued to pour down the highway.

A car, a large truck, and a bus. Lesser vehicle, greater vehicle, and diamond vehicle. Buddhism consists of three major lifepaths, or vehicles of virtue. The lesser vehicle is called Hinayana, the greater vehicle is named Mahayana, and the diamond vehicle is the Vajrayana, or Diamond Thunderbolt.

The first Buddhist lifepath—Hinayana, or the lesser vehicle—consists of personal mantras, individual meditation, and a strict diet. Hinayana asks, "How do I liberate myself?"

Mahayana, the next major type of Buddhism, is comprised of teaching mantras, profound compassion for all sentient beings, a belief in universal salvation, and a strict diet. Mahayana asks, "How do I liberate others?"

The last vehicle of virtue, the secret type of Buddhism that is only spoken of in reverent tones and on lonely nights in front of fires amongst the snow-swept Himalayas, is Vajrayana, or Diamond Thunderbolt. Vajrayana consists of powerful magic, a deep understanding of the universe, infinite meditation, and a manifestation of supernatural powers. The question Vajrayana asks is "How do I liberate the world?" Practioners of Vajrayana also study Mahayana, but the focus is on transcendance.

Fluids can be transformed to ambrosia—stories are told of monks who levitate; when these monks die, their bodies don't decay, and even when cremated, their bones remain white after hours of fire.

After three more hours, we arrived in the capital, Thimphu. The city is a mix of shops, four-story buildings, cows, hills, and cars. And amongst the curvy streets, markets of dried fish, and monolithic outer canyon walls, we would find rest.

MANCHEN LOPON

# CHAPTER 18
## Lost Amongst the Clouds

—◀○▶—

A GOLDEN BUDDHA FACED me as I checked into my hotel. The statue was encased in a tower behind the desk and seated in a lotus position. Infinitely meditating on the stars, the figure offered protection and peace. This was something I had not previously enjoyed in Guatemala. I wondered if the Buddha would accompany me in the Land of the Thunder Dragon, or if I would need to engineer another escape.

I was given room 311, which was a good omen. In numerology, three signifies the trinity, and eleven reminds us that we are never alone. Upon stowing my gear, I took a hot shower. Settling under the warm jets of water, I let tension effortlessly flow downward. Down, down, deeper and further to the bowels of the earth, I visualized a blue ray of light enveloping me, slowly scanning my body, and pushing out any remaining fears or anxiety. The light started at the top of my head and flowed effortlessly downward until all savage dreams were expelled at the soles of my feet. I left the shower, dried off, and took a nap. No strange visions. No dreams of being chased or fighting bandits. Not even a dream of the mysterious temple with a dragon. Just sleep.

I awoke in time to meet my guide, Sonam, for dinner. Downstairs waiting for me, he was dressed in the traditional *go,* or robe outfit, worn by Bhutanese men. The couture consists of several layers. The upper portion looks like a robe or Japanese *gi.* The bottom portion is wrapped around the legs so that the front is flat and the folds are in the back.

Inside the restaurant, we were attended to by no less than four waitstaff. With a proper British accent, the major-domo asked us after we were seated, "Gentlemen, would you care for some tea?" as he unfolded our napkins and placed them on our laps.

Our meal was pork medallions, carrots, fried fern leaves (yes, like the live ferns in your apartment), and crispy fried potatoes. The meal was surprisingly . . . unexpectedly . . . remarkably . . . bland. Gone were the exotic flavors of saffron and cinnamon, the deep, coarse tastes of curry and pepper, the light, sharp tastes of lime and lemongrass. Maybe I had spent too much time in Japan, where another exotic flavor was just a street away. Maybe I had spent too much time in the Far East—the land of ancient spices, daring flavors, and culinary minutiae. For whatever reason, the food here tasted homely. But that was to be short-lived.

After a few minutes, one of the waitstaff brought out a small serving plate with what looked like seven long green beans. Hema is what the Bhutanese call this particular type of chili; hemadatsi is the name of the dish when it is served with melted cheese. And it is a name I will never forget. Sonam began preparations to eat the hema: after sprinkling a small amount of salt on the upper edge of his plate, he gently picked up a hema chile, bit off the top portion, and dipped the remainder of the pod in the salt, only to repeat the process with another bite.

Easy enough; I'm a certified tough guy. I eat five jalapeños for breakfast each day, raw. A hema chile? Give me a break. I wasn't about to be outdone by this mountain man. I took hold of the hema pod confidently. Defiantly biting off the top of the chili with my incisors, I looked Sonam square in the eye as I dipped the rest of the chili in the salt. And in two further bites, I devoured the entire thing. Hot? Was it hot? Of course not. I didn't even taste it. Bring it on. I'm a former Marine, hiked the Grand Canyon, ran a marathon, trained with Green Berets, conquered the Guatemalan Highlands. I took another hema chili in my hand, dipped the entire outer portion in salt, put it in my mouth, and bit down. And for about two seconds, everything was fine.

Somewhere in the void, a young boy cried out in agony as the fire of a hundred thousand explosions erupted in his mouth. *"Nooooooooooooooooo!"* I silently yelled as my entire body shuddered. That damn Hema chili was so hot, I felt a heat wave begin in my solar plexus and radiate out of my mouth.

*"Nooooooooooooooooo!"* I was stunned. The subtle banality of the first chili lured me in for a devastating attack and quick kill. I couldn't even speak. Sonam was confused as I frantically made hand gestures, seemingly asking for water, until he recognized my hands pantomiming the rapid squeezing of a cow's udder, asking for one thing—milk! And as the waitstaff brought out a small amount of milk in a stainless-steel container used for cream and poured me a glass, I gulped the sweet fluid—only to discover it was steamed milk!

*"Yeeeeeooooowwwwccchhh!"* My mouth was on fire and my tongue was now scalded. The heat and pain eventually subsided, but I continued to feel the residual heat from the second chili on my tongue and palate for the rest of the meal. I will always respect that small green chili disguising itself as a long green been, waiting silently and patiently to take you out with one fell bite. Fellow traveler, beware the tongueslayer hema. You are warned.

When the meal was finished, I walked outside to gain my bearings. Darkness enveloped the surrounding hills. With no sodium lamps and cities on the edge of the horizon, the familiar copper glow of an urbanscape sky was absent. There were no stars to speak of, nor the bright suns seen from a ship in the middle of the ocean. Just darkness.

I walked along paths lined by buildings, seeing cars drive past, and people and dogs. There were no beggars, no homeless, no advertisements for the next this or the next that. There was no music blaring or sounds of bass thumping. There were no billboards, no blinking lights, or bright neon. I didn't even see a single advertisement for Coca-Cola. There was only peace. Peace and awe as I saw small storefronts selling dried beef, or freshly caught fish the size of a suitcases, or Yak cheese, or vegetables. But no ads. Is this what heaven is like—pure? I wondered.

I followed the path of city streets as it formed a series of long Zs through the town. And at the very end of the boulevard, I found a small, brightly lit shop of Buddhist religious articles. I walked in and saw sticks of incense, mantra books that looked like bundles of red bricks, and various golden deities adorning the shelves. Next to the Buddhist shop was a store of antiques. There I browsed the more exotic ware amongst the painted, gilded chests and ivory statues of Buddha. Three things caught my eye: a skullcap bowl, a Vajra scepter, and a bell. These are important tools in Bhutan; the latter set is the physical embodiment of the Diamond Vehicle, or Vajrayana.

It was a bit unnerving as I picked up and examined the skullcap bowl. The top portion of it was actually someone's skull. As I looked inside, I could see the bone growth marks form tight little lightning bolts as they converged in the concave hollow. On the outside, the base of the bowl was ornamented with silver, brass, and jasper, with inlays shaped like phases of the moon cradling the outer portion of the skull. Glued to the very bottom of the base was a deep red velvet cover. I didn't even look at the price.

It seemed too sacred and personal an item to buy. And I can't even imagine trying to get it past customs or the litany of explanations that might be offered to appease the inspectors.

"Yes, this is actually the upper portion of someone's skull, and I intend to use it for esoteric rituals and the advancement of planetary knowledge." Right. Or worse, if I didn't declare the item and then got busted. "Author nabbed for skullnapping, news at 11," the newsanchor would utter as she flashed her chemical smile.

Karmically, the consequence for buying this item might be heavy as well. By facilitating a market for someone else's remains, it might mean that one day the buyer's remains would likewise end up for sale.

The skullcap bowl serves two ends. One is clear, like quartz crystal on a sunny day. Another is hidden, occult yet vital. When used in a ceremony by Buddhist monks, the bowl's first purpose, the intuitive purpose, is to remind the monks that life is transitory. By holding the artifact, monks are reminded of the short time in which to practice dharma. And much like the legend of the wise Rom woman who keeps a skull near her morning table to show her that all beauty fades away, the skullcap bowl reminds us that our bodies are merely vessels. All physical beauty and strength eventually fades, and not even the most powerful can escape death. So, at the first level, the skullcap bowl is a tool of release, of letting go of attachment to one's body and physicality.

The second purpose of the skullcap bowl is to provide offerings to wrathful deities. The bowl functions as repository for water or food. The contents may be be changed to nectar, or an alchemical stew, to feed the gods. Other times, monks visualize placing their own negative thoughts and emotions into the bowls. The negativity is then eaten and absorbed by the wrathful deities to then be transformed and expelled into the universe as divine light. So, in turn, the wrathful deity is not the devourer of souls but the destroyer of inner negativity and evil.

It's a tool with a reverse meaning, a sacred object constructed out of sacrosanct human remains and used to facilitate life, renewal, and the perfection of human consciousness.

The next items I looked at were the vajra, or thunderbolt scepter, and the bell. The vajra is not shaped like a thunderbolt. When I visualize a thunderbolt, I think of the familiar stylized design—a thin-slanted line with a series of zigzags. Or I think of a thunderbolt in nature, which looks like a portion of thread removed from the center of a spiderweb, with blinding white flames and fingers sprouting forth. However, the end of a Buddhist vajra scepter actually looks like a crown, with four arcs of metal emerging from the base to rejoin at the top.

The bell is a normal bell, one you would hold in your hand, but it has a stylized handle. To use both the scepter and bell correctly, they must be held at the same time. The vajra is held in one's right hand and is spun; it symbolizes compassion and power. The bell is held in a person's left hand; it symbolizes voidness and the clear light of bliss. As the vajra is spun with the right hand and strikes the bell, a diamond thunderbolt of power and compassion is said to radiate forth. This sound, this ringing, is heard everywhere and embodies the clear light of bliss resonating in every sentient being.

Leaving the antique shop behind me, I headed back to the hotel with my thoughts turned to where I hoped tomorrow would take me. I had not shown them to Sonam or anyone else, but the drawings of my dreams were with me. I had brought them along to Bhutan and hoped that here I would find some answers. Tomorrow would be my first attempt.

THE NEXT DAY we loaded our gear and drove off into countryside of rolling hills. After about an hour, we came across a small village. On the outskirts of a small collection of farmhouses, we made our rest at a Bhutanese-style house. The homes in Bhutan are all built according to the same design. It's a two-story rectangular construction with corbelled windows. The roof is particularly interesting. The fascia near the roofline is colorful and fancy. It contains alternating and layered patterns of squares, flanges, pyramids, and arcs that are brightly painted with blues, reds, and oranges. With a slight slope, the corrugated roof actually sits about four feet off the top of the building. The resulting space between the top of the building and roof is used to dry and store hay. The exterior walls of most houses are painted white, with bright green dragons and blue garudas drawn on the wooden columns. Each druk and garuda bares white fangs or menacing beaks.

After off-loading the car, Sonam pointed to a distant structure on the other side of the valley, behind the house. Beyond the copse, past golden fields of wheat and a small stream, stood the hilltop temple to Drukpa Kunley.

Kunley lived in Bhutan in the fourteenth century and was known as the divine madman. One of the most famous Buddhist masters in history, Kunley wasn't mad or insane, but rather used humor to inspire his followers and spread teachings of the Buddha. Covering the countryside and lecturing using jokes, song, dance, and theater, Kunley was irreverent, whimsical, and successful. Often, we think of Buddhism as a somber, focused path on the road to enlightenment. However, similar to life, Buddhism teaches us lessons through comedy, joy, song, and laughter. It's not how the messages are being taught, but rather that the messages are being given. This is an overlooked yet important element in the evolution of Buddhist thought and philosophy.

The trail to the temple was gentle. I followed the slow, gradual slope to the bottom of the river valley, passing through fields of rice, grain, buckwheat, and cows. I saw a family of five using flails to thresh wheat and remove straw from bran. We were awash in waves and whitecaps amidst seas of gold. That morning, a forest fire started just east of Thimphu. The resultant haze in the air and sky gave a nostalgic quality to the fields and countryside. The atmosphere was Asia of about four hundred years ago—no cell phones, no power lines, no grid, no consumerism, and no programming. Just a small family completing an early summer harvest, with two travelers walking amongst golden dreams and skies of gray.

The final upward slope was steep but not too difficult. At the top of the small hill, we found a large prayer wheel. A prayer wheel is a tool Buddhists use to communicate with higher powers. It's a closed cylindrical drum suspended upright on its axis. It's usually painted with crimson red and other vibrant colors such as green, blue, and yellow. Surrounding the prayer wheel, near the top, is a mantra script painted in gold. Inside the cylinder are hundreds of thousands of slips of tiny paper, each holding a sacred prayer. When a prayer wheel is spun, all of the individual prayers on paper move around, sending their secret prayers to the cosmos.

Grasping one of the rings at the bottom edge of this seven-foot prayer wheel and giving it a good hard tug, I spun the ochre and gold cylinder of mystical hope, and the thousands of slips of paper inside twirled. And as the red vortex turned, countless wishes made their way toward heaven.

Closer toward the entrance, I could hear the faint monotone sound of monks chanting and singing mantras to focus their minds for meditation. A mantra is more than just prayer; it is a way of aligning one's soul.

In Bhutan, the most common mantra is *om mani padme hung*, which means through wisdom, compassion, and love, one can leave impurity to achieve enlightenment. Usually, the mantra is repeated until the teacher directs the disciples to stop or the monks sufficiently raise their vibration. However, there is a more powerful way to recite mantras: by experiencing them. To fully recite and feel the liberating effects of the mantra, the singer must visualize the syllables emerging from the body. As each syllable is recited, the individual sound pair in *om-ma-ni-pad-me-hung* emerges from a particular chakra in the body. If it's the first pair, then it emerges from the crown chakra and is white in color. As the sound is continued, the letter pair shoots forth from the body and is released from the top of a person's head. The letter pair then spins itself clockwise around the singer and is launched toward the center of the universe.

For example, when the syllable "om" is sung, the singer visualizes this letter pair emerging from the crown chakra. Since it is the first syllable in the mantra and corresponds to the crown chakra, the "om" script is white in color. The script emerges from the crown chakra, leaves the singer's body at the top of his head, then begins to spin around the singer. As the syllable spins faster, the singer feels the energy associated with that syllable and then, when the energy is sufficiently raised, the singer sends the syllable forth into space, toward the center of the universe. All along, the disciple is praying for the highest good of every living being. All along, the disciple is asking for forgiveness and to be shown the path to enlightenment. It's a very powerful way to meditate. Done correctly, the singer will feel a dizziness and disconnectedness from their bodies, as the direct effect of each syllable is experienced by their consciousness. This type of prolonged meditation will lead to greater focus, more lucid dreams, and an increase in extrasensory ability.

There were three small steps to the temple doorway. Walking up the steps, we passed a curtain, and to the left was a group of monks, numbering about twenty-five, with a lama, or learned master, on a thronelike chair. Two monks were also playing long trumpets on the left side of the lama. Opposite the group was an altar with a golden Buddha. The Buddha had four arms and was Avalokitasvara, or the bodhisattva of compassion. Bodhisattvas are enlightened beings that have chosen to be reincarnated so that they may help other beings reach nirvana. On the altar were fourteen copper bowls filled with water, lit incense sticks, ritual cakes, and a copper water pitcher with three peacock feathers sprouting from the top.

As Sonam bowed, then prostrated himself three times to the Buddha, I slowly bowed my head and body in a sign of deep reverence to the deity. After leaving offerings of ngultrum (Bhutanese currency), we were given water from the pitcher. The water was poured into the palm of our right hands. We each took a small sip of water and then placed the remainder on the back of our skulls, near the top portion of our necks.

The water is a blessing from the deity. The peacock feathers act to keep the water fresh, with their brightly colored eyes serving to ward off evil and energize the liquid.

We moved toward the far corner of the chamber, between the monks and the altar. As we sat down, the monks began to chant once again, and this time the two monks with the long trumpets began to play. A slow, radiating *pow-wow-wow-wow-wow* emerged from the thick vines. The sound is monotone, but it resonates, and if you listen, you can make out the pulses of sound generated by the trumpeter monks. And it has a structure. It sounded like one forced note, followed by ten pulsating notes, again and again. The trumpeter monks did this three times, then the other monks chanted. This continued for about fifteen minutes, until the master lama directed the monks to stop.

Suddenly, the graying elder looked directly at me and then toward Sonam. Uttering something in Bhutanese, the lama spoke to Sonam and then looked at me again. Something was happening. The lama knew I was there for a reason. Sonam turned his head toward me.

"He asked, 'What are you doing here?'" said Sonam.

"What do you mean? I don't understand," I replied. This time, Sonam rose to speak to the lama.

After uttering a few words to the master, Sonam looked at me again. "He says he can help if you tell him what you are looking for," replied Sonam.

The moment of truth was before me. Do I tell the lama about my drawings, explain to him about the images that pervaded my nighttime slumber, and have him think that I am halfway crazy? Or do I actually take out the drawings, show them to the lama, and in the process prove that I am totally crazy?

Better to be the star in a one-act play than have a nonspeaking role in a Broadway production. In other words, if you're going to do something, go all the way. Let it ride.

As I stood up and walked toward the lama, I reached in my note-book and pulled out my sketches. The paper was well-worn. I had folded and refolded them again and again, back and forth, each time wondering what the images meant. A spinning cross, gold in color. Ruins of a temple near a lake. A lama who meditates and uses a rainbow shield for protection. And a long, thin dragon that flies around a temple counter-clockwise.

I showed these to the lama and asked Sonam to translate. "These are in my dreams. They appear to me again and again. The lama is the keeper of a box that speaks. He lives a temple that is guarded by a flying dragon. Where can I find him?" I asked.

Sonam was in total shock; in his narrow eyes I saw two full moons. The lama looked up for a few seconds, then turned his head to look at me dead-on. "You must keep looking. You are close, closer than you've ever been. But you still must look."

Okay. That was cryptic. I waited for follow-up instructions, like "Head west. Look for the white rabbit. Follow the yellow brick road." But nothing more came. Instead, the lama signaled the monks to start chanting again. And soon enough, the trumpeters followed in song.

As we left the temple, I asked Sonam about the lama. "Wasn't he surprised?"

"Oh, no. He said he already knew you were coming," Sonam answered.

As we hiked out of the valley, back through fields of gold and amber, my eyes became transfixed on an abandoned farmhouse. It was built of mud, and half of it was collapsed. The roof was gone, as were most of the doors. Its sandy brown color was more akin to earth than building. And all that was left were bits and shadow of a once-proud home. But still, I couldn't keep my eyes off of it. The shape was familiar, as were the grooves on the wall and the way it stood upon the small hilltop with vistas of fields and crops. The road was recognizable as well, with the way it led to the bottom of the valley and gently curved around the farmhouse.

LOST AMONGST THE CLOUDS

Near the house would have been some drainage canals leading down to the river, routing water away from the surrounding hills. Animals like sheep or goats would have been tied in an area behind the structure. The front of the house was situated toward the road to greet any travelers that wandered by. Something about this place was so stunningly familiar, but I just couldn't remember what exactly it was . . .

Back in the car, we started our ascent again as we crossed the Black Mountain range. I could tell we were climbing by the changes in fauna, the decrease in temperature, and the popping of my ears. To travel from western to eastern Bhutan, you must go through two high mountain passes as you transverse the Black Mountains. As we increased altitude, we passed forests of giant ferns with fronds bigger than NBA basketball centers, and 100-foot waterfalls and broods of hanging vines. Further up the mountain, we saw ash and spruce trees, some still holding their orange leaves from the previous autumn. Higher still, we crossed alpine forests shrouded by fog, hiding juniper trees the size of ten-story buildings. I asked Sonam to stop in the forest of smoke and vapor, brume and cloud.

Emerging from the car, I felt enormously small—a snail amongst century-old sentinels. As I looked around, I noticed something peculiar: the color field of the previous forest layers was mysteriously absent. Everything was awash in black and gray, a gentle Sturm und Drang of dreariness. There were no red flowers, no white blossoms, no blue avians, not a single brushstroke of color in the entire landscape. Is this what an enchanted forest looks like? I looked around a bit further as my mind began to drift . . .

Just below the first wash next to the roadway was what appeared to be a small foot trail leading off into the distance. It was no wider than a squirrel and looked gently used with the occasional twig or branch. I wondered where would it lead . . . if you followed it for a few hours, would you come upon a magic stream, complete with faeries and a lady in the water? Or would you find a small wooden shack with graying planks furrowed by time, accompanied only by the sound of a *tat-tat* as the door is rustled to and fro by the breeze? Sonam soon broke the thought.

"Another bush break?" asked the guide. A bush break is a restroom break.

"Nah, just wanted to stop and take some pictures," I replied. "There's no flowers here," I stated, my tone being more akin to a question.

"Nope," said Sonam.

I waited for him to say something else, but he didn't finish the thought.

"Everything's gray and misty," I said, waiting again.

Nothing from Sonam.

If the forest was enchanted or haunted, Sonam wasn't about to tell me. And it probably wouldn't be a good idea to overnight here, either. Noted. Back to the road.

About five minutes further up the road, color once again began to fill our view. It first began with a single rhododendron with red flowers. Then there was a magnolia tree with white flowers. And then we were once again awash in emerald greens and forest greens, the colors of trees, the colors of life. But recollecting the enchanted forest, there wasn't a single drop of color in the entire panorama. And I knew there was something, or someone, just beyond the trail.

We soon came to the top of the mountain range and the first mountain pass. As the road turned into a Y, at its center was a large white stupa, or prayer mound. A stupa consists of a raised platform, built on top of other raised platforms, forming a layered structure that is topped by a dome and a spire. The dome usually holds a representation of a deity, such as a Buddha. The spire points to a crescent moon, then a single, mysterious star.

A stupa is many things. It's said to mark the area where ancient shamans subjugated demons, it's a location where great battles were fought, and it's a place to honor ancestors. In modern times, Bhutanese will appease deceased ancestors by placing their remains on the top ledges of the stupa. After a traditional cremation ceremony, a portion of the remaining ashes are baked into dome-shaped pods the size of small cups and are fixed atop the stupa so that the deceased's spirit can be honored.

Stupas are also said to be haunted. Most of the older Bhutanese won't go near the stupas during the day, let alone at night. Stupas are places where ancient magicians harnessed the forces of light and nature, to conquer the energies of fear and darkness. Bhutan is saturated with stupas and areas where evil spirits are said to be trapped and defeated. But were the evil spirits really vanquished? Farmers tell stories of offerings left for the spirits—sausage links and ritual cakes placed on the uppermost layers of the stupa, away from animals and packs of stray dogs. During the night, flashing lights would envelop the structure. And the next day, the offerings would be gone.

I took some pictures of the stupa and the prayer flags surrounding the outer perimeter of the mountain pass. Within a few minutes, and after a real bush break, we were gone. And as we traveled down the mountain, the scenery changed once more. I was awestruck to see the wide-open expanses of slowly rolling fields, acres and acres of pastoral green, the busy home of yaks, goats, and sheep. It was such a change from the forests and mists of gray. In the distance, I could see peaks of the snow-capped lesser Himalayas, figures of ice and granite standing for millennia. Further up the road, we encountered more trees of spruce and pine, and the second mountain pass. Ten more minutes, and we stopped at a guest house for tea and biscuits.

Afterward, we stopped at another stupa. Directly across from the prayer mound stood a raised platform of earth, with no less than three hundred prayer flag poles. Each pole held thirty flags, the cloth like leaves dancing with the wind. I walked toward the platform with a deep sense of awe. Amidst myriad prayers, I was filled with a great sense of harmony and serenity. The height of the poles was breathtaking, their splendor matched only by the age of the prayer flags: ancient. A throaty wind buffeted the flags throughout the forest of hope. And for a split second, I too was a prayer, floating effortlessly in the wind and expanse of time. All of my fears, all regrets, anything I wished I could change, was gone. My soul was simply a wish unto the cosmos.

Finishing my walk around the raised platform, I took some pictures and thanked Sonam. Jumping back in the vehicle, we drove for another two hours until we reached the next mountain pass.

I could not get the stupas out of my mind. Mysteriously, the modern object that the ancient stupas most closely resembled was a Saturn V rocket—with multiple stages, a crew compartment, a Buddha as an astronaut, and an escape tower that pointed toward the moon, then the sun, then a faraway star. So were the stupas crafted by monks dreaming about being astronauts? Or were the astronauts and designers of the Space Age rockets remembering that they were once Buddhist monks?

After crossing through a third set of monolithic gates, the winding road gave way to narrower straightaway. We were now in high alpine forests, traveling through fields of pine trees, grassy areas, and fences holding back goats and yaks—and yaks away from the potatoes. Houses became more and more common as we drove toward the Bumthang province. We passed government-funded buildings, agricultural substations, and schools all constructed in the same Bhutanese-style architecture. They were all two-story, square buildings, with special raised roofs to dry hay and feed, decorated with green dragons and a garuda's gaze. Each building was also ornamented with magical amulets, talismans, orbs, and brightly painted designs to ward off evil, none of which were used in the houses of Western Bhutan.

Near sunset, we arrived in Bumthang. We stopped at our accommodation for the evening, a lodging built in the traditional farmhouse design. Dinner was to be served an hour after we arrived, so I went to my room, unpacked my gear, and showered. The room had brushed concrete walls with large, dark timbers supporting the structure. The bathroom and shower were bare concrete, with just a toilet, a sink, and a showerhead in the same space.

Dinner was dried beef, cooked fern leaves, delicious potatoes, and hemadatsi, or hema chiles with cheese sauce. By now, I was used to the hema and could eat it regularly with every meal. But this batch was extremely hot. I couldn't swallow more than one bite of the local fire elemental disguised as a green bean. Sonam, who had been eating hema all his life, had exactly three bites and then called it quits. I could tell the hema had bested him, as his skin became flushed and beads of sweat appeared on his forehead. For dessert, we had a dish from India—spongy white rice treats dipped in a sugary glaze. And the dessert tasted exactly how a plain white sponge dipped in a sugar glaze would taste—pretty darn awful.

After dinner, the sun gently bedded down on the other side of the world as the eternal moon began its journey to scale mountain peaks and light valleys with its bluish gaze. Bumthang is more village than city, spread out in an elegant $T$ overlay. I walked both parts of the $T$, looking at shops selling dried fish, rice, buckwheat, beans, sugar, betel nut, and canned foods. Luxury goods such as electronics were nowhere to be seen. The hamlet seemed more akin to a faraway trading post than a bustling hub or marketplace. Still, I was able to find a cybercafé and surfed to my heart's content for about thirty minutes until the power went out. Outside, as I walked back to my hotel, I was escorted by a pack of wild, barking dogs. A small car quickly zoomed by and scattered my pursuers.

As I walked to the easternmost part of town, toward a bridge spanning the softly flowing river, I noticed the beauty of the valley held in the moon's contemplation. The soft, gentle mountain peaks became breasts in the far-off distance—the earth mother's body awash in a soft blue hue. As people slept, the land was draped in a delicate nightgown of lavender and mist.

The temperature dropped immediately once the sun went down. Twenty degrees of heat were lost to the nighttime sky. At 9 PM, I was back at the farmhouse. Thirty minutes later, I was fast asleep.

THAT NIGHT I did dream, but they were not the dreams I had hoped for. I was expecting more messages about my journey, more clues to the outcome of this final quest. Instead, I was greeted by a portly earth goddess. With dark skin, sackcloth-colored hair, and eyes of orange, she appeared powerful!

"My son, I have a woman for you to marry! But you must first drink these seven bowls of water and bow at my feet," demanded the mother.

"No, thank you," I replied.

"My student, I have this woman for you to marry, but you must drink this water and submit to me," said the ribald conjurer.

"I don't think so," I stammered.

"My servant, there is this woman you must marry. I will give you great power. But first, you must drink these seven bowls of water and kneel at my feet," said the Rubenesque sorceress.

"No thank you, your highness. I shall wait for the woman who is waiting for me," I finally said, forcefully, and then woke up.

I didn't come to Bhutan to marry a woman, either in the waking world or the world of spirit. And I certainly wasn't on a quest for power; power is what traps the sorcerer. This is the shaman's riddle. Nothing good ever comes from a quest for power. All I wanted to do was meet the monk who had called for me. And I hoped that by talking to him, I would be led closer to my dreams—the dark-haired lady of soft skin and a kind heart. Everything else was unimportant, and nothing else was important.

I had three dreams of the earth goddess that night. And I never saw her again, in dreams or otherwise. Still, why was she offering me power?

# CHAPTER 19
## Land of Myth and Dreams

—◀◉▶—

THE NEXT DAY, Sonam and I were in for a few surprises. After a hearty breakfast, we hopped in our transport and made our way to the northern edge of the valley. The road was mostly a straightaway, flanked by terraced trees of spruce and pine on our left and pastoral fields on the right.

Bhutan has only a few temples. But the places are steeped in legend and myth, honoring different Buddhas as well as temporal rulers. Our first stop was the Kurjey Lhakang, or the primary monastery to Padmasambhava. There are two major rulers in the two-thousand-year history of the Land of the Thunder Dragon. The first was a mystic, a magician who both summoned *dakinis*, or angels, and subdued demons, bringing spiritual tranquility to the land. He is known as the Padmasambhava, the Lotus-born Master, or more simply as Guru Rinpoche.

According to legend, Rinpoche, which means Precious One, arrived from Swat (now Pakistan) in the year AD 776. Capable of great magical powers—including levitation, flight, bilocation, mind control, and *verto tempestas*, or the ability the change the weather—Rinpoche repeatedly covered Tibet and Bhutan, gathering followers and gaining fame. Rinpoche brought Buddhism to Bhutan, usurping the widely practiced Bon, or Tibetan nature religion. In the Bumthang Valley, Rinpoche would face his most daunting challenge ever.

Summoned to the Bumthang Valley by the Royal Court, Guru Rinpoche was tasked to fight for the king's life and, by extension, the very existence of the populace as well. The king had offended a mountain deity by forgetting proper ritual and not bestowing offerings to appease the gods. In a fit of rage, the deity decided to steal a part of the king's soul as retribution for the ruler's lack of piety. The mountain deity transformed itself to a woman and approached the king in his bedchambers. Making love to the king, the deity was able to take a portion of the king's immortal essence as the king opened up his root chakra at the moment of ecstasy, dropping his defenses and internal protective magic. Afterward, the king was left in a stupor and was unable to make decisions or take his mind off the demon.

When the Bon shamans prayed to the mountains and begged the deity to return the king's soul, the deity became even more enraged and placed a curse upon the land and its inhabitants. Crops failed, the water from the mountain springs turned acidic, and skin ailments were visited on the people. Guru Rinpoche was then called to Bumthang. Upon arriving, he began to meditate in a local cave and spent more than two months trying to find an answer to end the plague and return the king's soul. During this time, Rinpoche was shown the secrets of life and death, he discovered how to call forth dakinis, or angels, and he also learned how to subjugate demons through tantra. Rinpoche's lifeforce grew so strong that his silhouette, in a meditating lotus position, was energetically carved into the granite cliff face.

Rinpoche had his answer. He gathered enough energy to transform his soul into eight unique, shimmering forms. The forms marched down from the mountain peak laughing, singing, cajoling, and making all types of noise and bedlam. When the forms reached the valley, they began to dance. So entrancing was the spectacle that all of the deities from the countryside arrived to see what was going on—that is, all but the vengeful mountain deity.

When the mountain god finally relented and came down from stone peaks, Rinpoche, who was still cloistered in the rock face, transformed once more into a garuda, or magical griffin, and flew down from the granite shelter. Rapidly swooping down to the valley, Rinpoche caught the mountain deity with his talons and squeezed the god's innards until the deity finally relented and agreed to release the king's soul. Once his soul was free, the king regained consciousness and was able to carry out the remainder of his rule. After conquering the mountain deity, Rinpoche also took the god's power for his own. And from that point on, Guru Rinpoche was a venerated hero with control over all the forest animals.

ARRIVING AT KURJEY Lhakang, we parked and walked to the temple's outer gates, where we encountered vendors setting up their wares for the day's sale. Necklaces of turquoise and red coral were interspersed with thighbone trumpets and antique vajras. Passing the gate, we were came upon not one but two large temples built into the mountain cliff face. The temple on the left was the newer construct, built by the current Queen Mother to house statues of golden Buddhas and a likeness of Guru Rinpoche. The temple on the right was a thousand years old, built to protect Rinpoche's blessed cave of meditation.

Removing our shoes and placing them on the floor, we took a set of stairs to the newer temple. Upon entering, we immediately saw a monk seated at a table, writing prayer requests for that day. As in other faiths, it is possible to make a donation and sponsor the day's prayers in honor of

a particular cause or person. I made an offering of ngultrum and silently
asked for knowledge and world peace.

Through another doorway, we came upon a second chamber with four
long rows of seated monks chanting the day's mantras. The monks were
seated opposite a brass-meshed screen, behind which was a golden statue
about thirty feet high with piercing red eyes and a thin mustache. This
was the legendary Guru Rinpoche, the subduer of the darkness, his fixed
eyes staring back at me.

To the left of the mesh barrier was a stairway leading down. Sonam
quickly brought me over, and we plunged into the darkness. After following a stygian wall for two turns and several steps, we ended up on a
lower level and were now behind the screen. I found myself at the base
of the statue of Guru Rinpoche, surrounded by eight Buddhas. Displayed in front of the statues was an altar with twenty-one bowls of fresh
water, brightly colored ritual cakes that looked like gigantic lollipops,
and flowers more akin to butterfly wings. Flanking the statues stood the
eight manifestations, or tantric forms, of Guru Rinpoche. The last form
depicted the Precious One subduing the mountain god and obtaining its
power.

Offerings were many and interspersed on the altar and base of the
statues. I saw slips of paper, coins, ngultrum, and rupees, signs of visitors
from distant lands asking for help. I took out some beautiful dragon dollars, or ngultrum, folded them lengthwise very neatly, and placed them
near the other offerings. There was a monk attending to the statues who
poured us some blessed water from the peacock-feathered pitcher. I
took a sip of the water that was poured into my right hand, then placed
the remaining liquid on my back. This time the fluid was orange in color
and tasted strangely metallic.

Sonam motioned me closer still as we walked behind the altar table,
right in front of the statues. I noticed even more offerings to Guru
Rinpoche: money, jewels, and other tightly folded bits of paper. But
there was something unnerving about the subterranean pit and prox-

imity to the deities. I think there should always be some sort of separation between us in the world of the living and those energies from the world of the gods. With our mortal eyes, we can never really be sure what we are seeing or touching. And without godsight as protection, I didn't want to inadvertently touch or make a connection with the wrong type of thing. I quickly followed Sonam to an ascending stairway, and we exited the temple.

Outside the structure, we crossed the platform to the other temple. Once inside, we were led into a large prayer room with four rows of seated monks. They were chanting at the direction of a lama seated on a chair throne. The throne was bathed in red with gold vajras. The chamber was made completely out of wood, with centuries-old pine as the floorboards and columns twice the width of telephone poles holding up the space. The columns and walls were painted deep red but were several shades lighter than the vibrant crimson of the monks' robes.

In the near and far side of the wall, encased behind glass, were no less than one thousand miniature golden Buddhas. Opposite the lama, behind glass, were golden statues of Guru Rinpoche, Shabdrung Ngawang Namgyal (the other great ruler of Bhutan), and Avalokitasvara, the bodhisattva of compassion. Directly behind the statue of Rinpoche was a small cave cut exactly in the shape of a meditating figure. This was the place where Guru Rinpoche had gathered his strength before he subdued the mountain god, magically burning his shape into the cave wall with the force of his will.

As the lama motioned for us come closer, we were quickly approached by a younger monk.

"My master asks if you would like to join us for tea," asked the young monk.

"Of course," I said. I looked at Sonam, whose eyes were once again as big as saucers. As we stepped closer to the lama, we made ready to receive his blessing. Bowing our heads, Sonam and I each received the gentle crack of a small whip on top of our skulls. Okay, that works for me. Strangely, I felt the thin leather tongue, but it didn't hurt at all.

We were led outside the main room into a smaller waiting area. A monk emerged with cups filled to the brim with toffee-colored milk tea. My mug had a picture of a hummingbird on it. I had to laugh: the hummingbird was one of the protector animals Gary, the Cherokee Spiritwalker, had given me after a soul retreival.

"Welcome to our monastery," the lama said as he entered. "Is there something you wanted to show me?"

I nodded my head. Here we go, *Twilight Zone* time again. I unfolded my artwork—drawings of dragons, temples, spinning crosses, and a tomb—and handed it to the learned master. The lama looked them over and fixed his gaze upon me.

"You must go to Punakha. You'll find something there."

And I waited . . . and waited . . . and that's all he said. After a few moments, he rose and took his leave. Punakha. A destination. Answers. Finally. As we left Kurjey Lhakang, Sonam and I were both silent. I don't know who was the more stunned, he or I.

Driving south and descending the river valley, we turned north after crossing the bridge in Bumthang. Our next stop was Tamshing Lhakhan, another temple to Guru Rinpoche and the Pema Lingpa sect of Buddhism. The structure was two-storied and located within a walled compound. We called to town and waited about thirty minutes for the caretaker to arrive. No monks lived at the temple, and I would soon find out why.

When he arrived, the caretaker greeted us and led us to the temple entrance. After unlocking heavy wooden doors, we were led inside. The first part of the temple was more akin to a theater, with an open area, a stage, and an upstairs gallery. Climbing up the narrow Tibetan-style stairs, we viewed the theater from above. The ceiling was low, no more than six feet high. As we walked around the upper gallery, I noticed the beautiful, centuries-old paintings of Buddha, various bodhisattvas, and the Wheel of Life on the ancient walls. There was such a sense of devotion in the paintings, the offerings to the Buddha so profound. The closest thing I could compare it to would be paintings found on the base of the Pyramid of the Sun in Teotihuacan. It's like the artists chose their immortality to come by the stroke of a brush.

Finishing the tour of the upper gallery, we returned to the first level and were guided to the main chamber. Past heavy wooden doors thicker than Manhattan telephone books was a singular statue of Guru Rinpoche. But this one was different. Instead of a menacing gaze cast downward, Rinpoche was looking upward with a pleasant expression, and with orange eyes! I crossed the threshold and immediately felt the power of the shrine. Stepping forward, I almost fell to the ground. Something powerful was here. Whenever close to supernaturally charged objects, I feel that immediate sense of vertigo. I felt it again in this shrine. I latched on to Sonam's arm and steadied myself with his sinewy frame.

Regaining my composure after a few seconds, I told Sonam that I must have slipped on something. With bowed heads, we both left offerings to the statue of Guru Rinpoche. Quickly walking behind the figure, I noticed the eight smaller golden statues of his manifestations. I didn't feel like waiting for the caretaker monk or Sonam to explain the statuary, so I quickly left the room. Outside the dynamic heart, I asked Sonam why the statue was different.

"This statue of Guru Rinpoche was made by the dakinis. That's why the guru was looking upwards, because the dakinis came from heaven, and Guru Rinpoche looked up at them as they left," Sonam replied.

We took leave of the caretaker and thanked him for the help. As we left the temple grounds, I asked why more monks didn't live at Tamshing Lhakhan.

Sonam replied, "Too powerful. Too many ghosts." I nodded. I believed that part of the legend. And I didn't need to come back at night for a follow-up tour. Thus far, this was one of the most powerful temples in all my travels. And so two adventurers drove off in a small red car toward another sacred site. Better still, two believers headed out once more into the land of mystics and eternal time.

THE NEXT TEMPLE we visited, Konchogsum Lhakhang, was much smaller but home to an important memento. During the 1500s, epic wars were waged between Tibetan and Bhutanese armies to gain control of certain precious relics, including remains of monks, statuary, prayer books, and treasure. The expeditions lasted years and cost hundreds of lives. As neither side was experienced in military campaigns, none was ever able to gain a decisive victory, which unduly prolonged the war. However, because of the mountainous terrain in Bhutan and strength of the *dzongs*, or fortress monasteries, the Bhutanese prevailed in almost all of the battles.

Walking up a small trail past numerous marijuana plants, we reached the small outer wall of the temple. Yes, the bud grows wild in Bhutan. But no one smokes it, and neither do I. I just made a mental note and hiked on.

After summoning the caretaker, we walked up a short flight of stairs to the temple doors. Inside, it took a few seconds for our eyes to adjust. On our right stood the main altar with seven bowls of clear water, a pitcher, and some offerings. Behind the altar was a golden statue depicting the god of compassion, Avalokitasvara. As we walked closer, to the left of the altar I noticed three-quarters of a large and ancient brass bell resting on the floor. I looked at Sonam, who then asked the caretaker.

"It's from Tibet. Look at the writing and design on the upper part. Trophy from the war," said Sonam.

Wow. I had always thought Buddhists were peaceful, living lives of quiet contemplation and study. But this wasn't always the case. Buddhism is a complex religion with different sects, kings, lords, and holy people. Hundreds of years ago, Buddhists waged fierce and bloody battles against their fellow monks and lamas. The relative peace and good relations between modern Buddhist sects is the result of diplomacy and a focus on shared goals rather than highlighting differences and acting on aggression. Maybe the Buddhists do have it right after all. It's an older religion, but one that doesn't fight amongst its faces as to which is the correct path to God. The two other widely practiced world religions, on the other hand, have yet to duplicate such lasting periods of international peace.

We walked behind the back of the altar and left another offering. I received holy water poured into my right palm and took a sip. This time the water tasted deep and refreshing. I also noticed a heavy floral scent from the fluid. I jotted some notes and then walked outside to the fresh air. Why was I called to Bhutan? What did the symbols in my drawings mean? Who was I looking for? More importantly, what would I find in Punakha? I took a sip from my water bottle and waited on the temple stairs until Sonam came out once again.

"Ready for lunch?" he asked.

"Sounds good. Where's the hema?" I replied.

After a quick meal, we were once again driving through the mountains, this time south, as we climbed the river valley's upper shelf. Thirty more minutes into the mountains, we arrived at Mebartsho, or the Burning Lake, one of the most sacred areas in Bhutan.

When Guru Rinpoche prepared for his death, he prophecied that other powerful lamas would return to take his place. He said these holy men would locate magical relics that Rinpoche had hidden in the countryside. Only those monks annointed and realized would be able to find these sacrosanct treasures. About eight hundred years after Rinpoche died, one such monk did arrive and located a *terma*, or a sacred text. The lama's name was Pema Lingpa.

THE LEGEND SAYS that when Pema Lingpa arrived from Tibet, he was both shunned and ignored. Others had claimed to be descendants of

Rinpoche, ready to fulfill Padmasambhava's prophecy, but none of the pretenders were able to gather the treasures. At nighttime, Pema Lingpa summoned all the elders of the Bumthang district. To show his abilities, Pema Lingpa said he would hike into the mountains, find a hidden lake, jump in the water with a lit lantern, and emerge with both a sacred text and the lantern still lit. Hearing such a preposterous claim, the elders laughed wildly. However, they agreed to follow Pema Lingpa so they could once again revile another imposter.

For hours, Pema Lingpa led the group through the mountains, past thickets and up tremendous slopes, in search of the lake. By trees, around hills, and through fields Pema Lingpa led the group of disbelieving elders. And when the group was about to give up, the sound of a flowing river began to fill their ears. "Now see and listen," he told them.

Running toward the sound of the water, Pema Lingpa jumped into a gorge while fully attired in his robes and carrying a burning lamp. The elders cautiously approached the edge of the cliff and looked into the water. At the bottom of the pool, they could make out faint colors and a shimmering light. Suddenly, with an enormous thunderclap, Pema Lingpa emerged from the water's surface at the bottom of the gorge and bounded to the exact spot from where he dove. In one hand, Pema Lingpa was holding a golden book, and in the other hand was the lit lantern. And there was not a single drop of water on the saint, except for the wetness in his hair. The elders quickly prostrated themselves at Pema Lingpa's feet.

Recognizing the saint's power and connection to Guru Rinpoche, the elders adopted Pema Lingpa's teachings. The hidden book Pema Lingpa brought forth would become one of the most important tantric texts of Buddhism. And since Pema Lingpa jumped into the water and emerged with the lit lantern, the place would forever be known as the Burning Lake.

The Burning Lake isn't a lake at all. Mirroring the story, it's a black pool at the bottom of a narrow but deep river gorge. The source of the flowing water is tightly channeled river rapids, and the water leaving the pool is turbulent. But the pool itself is very calm, the sign of a deep chasm with strong underwater currents. After parking the car and hiking a short distance, we reached Burning Lake and walked to the outcrop where Pema Lingpa jumped in. Unbeknownst to us, a group of monks from a distant monastery had already begun an important ceremony.

The group included Zuri Rinpoche and his followers. Zuri Rinpoche is a recognized reincarnation of a Tibetan holy lama. In his current manifestation, he is a youthful and energetic twenty-seven-year-old master. Accompanied by two elder lamas and a small monastic body, he was at the Burning Lake to bless a family from Hong Kong. The monks were beginning their beautiful and mysterious chants when we arrived.

To chant, monks will either use unbound mantra books about the size of bricks or recite mantras from memory. To achieve that deep and rich sound, monks use their diaphragms and resonate the sound from their tongue and jaw. The mantra essentially is a prayer, but a mantra is also a song, a tool for grounding, a way to connect with the ancestors, a path to gain merit, a hymn to ward off evil spirits, and a method to resonate and to connect with universal knowledge.

Deep sounds filled the chasm as the monks continued their hymn. On the farthest side of the ledge, overlooking the river, two monks began to break branches and snap twigs. Soon, the kindling was placed on pile, bits of paper were added, and a small fire was lit. As I looked around the ledge toward the monks, I also saw three tall bottles of beer perched on the rock and effervescing as foam overflowed.

The monks began a faster chant. Zuri Rinpoche walked toward the family seated upon the rocks and placed white scarves around the pilgrims' necks. I asked the closest monk about the ceremony, which was a blessing ritual. Rinpoche was asking for all negative feelings, thoughts, and sentiments to leave the family. In place of darkness, the precious master asked that the family be imbued with blessings and golden light. The chanting continued for another ten minutes. As fragrant smoke filled my lungs, I was overtaken by the beauty of the gathering. The elements of earth, water, fire, and air were being harnessed by a millennia-old tradition that practiced peace, preached harmony, and sought to convert no one.

Suddenly, Zuri Rinpoche assembled the monks and walked across a suspension bridge to the center rock formation overlooking Burning Lake. On both sides of the stone island was a sheer drop of thirty feet into rushing water. One slip on the rock, and death was most assured.

Zuri Rinpoche called for each of the family members to approach. First the father, then the mother, then the two children. With each one, as a soft rain began to fall, Rinpoche pulled the white scarves from their necks, placed them on his forehead, uttered a silent prayer, and cast the scarves into the water. Not one of the scarves floated away; rather, they sank to the bottom of the pool. Stranger still, I looked at the bottles of beer, open for at least thirty minutes by now, and they were still bubbling. I approached the bridge and crossed cautiously.

Finding dry spots on the slippery rock, I stood with the monks for a few minutes as they talked to Zuri Rinpoche about the ritual. Then, out of nowhere, we were enveloped by a swarm of bees.

"Quick, across the bridge!" said a monk.

"Where did they come from?" I asked as I found my footing and allowed the monks to cross first. No sooner had Zuri Rinpoche crossed the span than a large bee landed right on the tip of my nose. It was about the size of a Ping-Pong ball! And a split second thereafter, another one landed on the back of my head. More scared of the bees than the fall now, I managed to cross the rickety suspension bridge rather quickly. Back on the first outcrop of rock, I immediately tried to pull the bee off my nose, but it hung on. A monk quickly appeared and pulled it away with his fingers. And as he turned to outrun the swarm, I noticed no less than five bees stuck to his crimson robe. Quickly, I stopped him and batted the bees off with my hat. As soon as the last bee was gone, the buzzing stopped, and the swarm vanished. Within about two minutes, the melee was over: Monks 0, Bees 7.

We counted about seven stings among us, total. The monks said it was a very auspicious sign, the swarm of bees—something that had not happened in the fourteen years they had been visiting Burning Lake. Even more auspicious still was to be stung by a bee—good medicine, as the locals called it. But neither the bee on the tip of my nose nor the one on the back of my head had stung me. I did feel a bit of venom, though, as minutes later, I pulled my hand over my mane and wound up with a stinger in my thumb, a memento from a temporary passenger. Pulling the remnants of attached bee abdomen out, I had no choice but to squeeze the tube a bit and feel a quick tinge.

Near the car, I'm not sure if it was the bee venom, the sudden rush of adrenaline, or my lungs pumping at full capacity, but everything appeared brighter. The colors seemed more vivid, the sun cast a brighter shine of yellow on the trees, I could make out the individual shades of green on the leaves, and the rocks even had a strange orangeish glow. The colors were denser, and I felt somewhat different. I was reminded that Buddhists say we become overwhelmed by a great sense of peace the moment we die.

Dying is not a painful thing. Rather, at the moment of death, we feel a deep connection to the surrounding environment. Colors are brighter, sounds are stronger, a lightness fills the body. Within a few moments, we are surrounded by loved ones who have passed on. These kind souls, these familiar roots, hold our hands and walk us into the great light. Once we rejoin with the forces of universal consciousness and eternal compassion, our life events and karma are weighed, and we are sent back to the world to live another life. Most of our memories are wiped clean. We emerge at the moment of birth, a refreshed soul to live and walk, breathe and cry, learn and love upon the earth again.

Advanced spiritual masters are provided with an alternative. In the journey to the forces of the universe, their souls are rerouted, diverted from the pathway to great universal consciousness and instead injected into select births. Their memories, learned spirituality, and distinct personalities are left intact. These are indeed fortuitous births, for these high masters can quickly regain their lost footing and continue along the path to enlightenment.

After climbing in our car and looking for any stowaway bees, we drove northward. Coming down from the mountains, we were once again in the Bumthang river valley. Crossing rushing waters, we drove westward to the other side of the valley and followed the main road through the village. Turning northward, we followed the street until we came upon a smaller artery to the left. A few minutes up this path, and we were in view of the Jakar Dzong, or White Bird monastery fortress. This dzong had overlooked and protected the river valley for over four hundred years. Like most dzongs, Jakar is still in use. One-half of the fortress holds the monastic body, and the other half houses government offices. During the harsh winter months, the monastic body moves to Punakha. Yes, Punakha—the same place the monk from Kurjey Lhakang advised me to visit.

Crossing the outer gateway and bounding across huge stone blocks serving as the threshold, the space opened to a larger courtyard. Since the monastic body had not returned from Punaka, the inner ward was elegantly quiet but spiritually full. There was something about this dzong that was beautiful, humbling, and inspiring. In a few moments, I would know why.

"There are archer ports near here," said Sonam.

"Yeah, they're past those larger doors, two sets on each side." I replied. *Huh?*

I quickly walked to the doors, pulled them aside, and sure enough saw the arrow slits.

"Look, in the middle of the floor there's a . . ." Sonam's voice trailed.

"A channel, with removable stones so the water drains in the castle as the snow melts," I finished. Another correct answer.

"The monks live—" Sonam continued.

"Below ground, on the far side of the fortress. The soldiers were kept on the near side, so they could quickly emerge and join the battle," I replied.

At this point, Sonam's voice began to stammer.

"And look, there's a—" he began.

"Spinning golden cross on the railings, like the one in my dream," I completed the thought.

It was something magical. Before he could even begin the tour, I was explaining to Sonam the outlay and purpose of the castle. But I had never dreamt about this place. I've dreamed of ancient Rome, biblical Judea, and countless forests and numerous deserts. But I had never dreamt about this fortress. I just knew where everything was.

"We need to go to Punakha," I said. Sonam nodded. But it would have to wait until another day. We traveled back to the hotel and stowed our gear for the evening.

In anticipation for the trip to Punakha, I scribbled some notes and began to prepare my questions for the person I would meet. Everything pointed to that eventual outcome. But who was I to meet, and why was I called? After dinner, I walked back through town and hiked toward the river bank.

As the sun set, mists of heat rose from the mountains, fields, and grasses as the earth gave up her breath to nighttime's gaze. Soon, the mist was overwhelming, and I could only make out the blackness of granite peaks against a sky of lapis.

To Buddhists, the transition from life to death to life is not always instant. Souls also can become trapped in the mists of the bardo, which is similar to purgatory but more confining. At the moment of an unexpected or untimely death, the soul transitions to this foggy, in-between state and is unable to advance. As the soul cannot travel freely, it becomes encapsulated in this cell of thought and memory. To the soul, the bardo appears as someplace familiar: a home, the shore of a familiar lake, or a bedroom. But imagine being locked in your house and never being able to find a door that opens to the outside. This is the bardo—as soon as you try to walk or travel somewhere else, you are stopped by an unseen force.

To be released from the bardo, a soul must recite numerous prayers and atone for whatever transgressions were committed during life. Another method of escape is calling upon the spirits of ancestors for help. When summoned with humility, members of the soul's transited family arrive to take the soul and guide it by the hand to infinity. To those of us in the waking world, if we go to the house where the soul is trapped, the spirit essence might appear and sound as a ghost. The prisoner doesn't know they are trapped in the bardo because they don't realize they're dead. The spirit attempts to cling to that last vestige of familiarity. The soul doesn't want to let go, but it must. So if you ever find yourself in a mist that you cannot leave or discover that you are at home but cannot escape, pray, and pray fiercely, for you are dead and trapped in the bardo, but divine help is right around the corner.

THAT NIGHT I dreamt of a figure. A being emerged from the darkness of a decrepit temple. Wearing a red robe with gold embroidery, it had the body of a man but the head of a bull with five horns. Three horns were on the top of its head, two on its chin. Its appearance was alien, its voice metallic.

"My son, I can grant you great power if you wear this mask," said the being while it pointed to a deformed carmine-red mask on a wall.

"No, thank you," I replied.

"You can conduct miracles if you put on this mask," the creature extolled.

"No, thank you. I don't want power."

"You will become one of the most powerful sorcerers of this age. Put on the mask," it ordered.

"No, thank you. Go in peace."

I HAD NO less than four dreams that night about the creature with the mask. After each dream, I woke up, clasped my hands, and prayed to God that the being would never bother me again. The last dream was the most prophetic: Sonam and I were driving away in the car, driving far, far away from the Black Mountains and Bumthang Valley, as I kept saying, "No, thank you. I cannot wear the mask. Go in peace."

The creature was offering great power, but I've never sought power. All I want to do is help others.

In the early morning, we left Bumthang. And I'm in no rush to return.

# CHAPTER 20
## Abandoned Temples, Darker Ravens

———◆◇◆———

THE DRIVE BACK to Western Bhutan was extremely long. After retracing our route for seven hours, we arrived at the second mountain pass but this time headed south. If there was ever a time to have a helicopter at the ready, this was it. I would almost have given my left arm to have Marine Air on standby. A triple-engine CH-53 Super Stallion helicopter, fully loaded with twenty-six Marines and combat gear, doesn't even burp upon takeoff. Unfortunately, there are no regular heli-flights in Bhutan. They have to be called from India. And due to several high-profile crashes involving Indian army officers, the government of Bhutan now requires that all helicopters flying in the country's airspace have three engines. Marine Air, where are you?

Upon cresting another mountain, a new valley of patchwork fields came into view. Meadows and pastures of light greens and dark greens alternated with mists and clouds. Following the road, we edged our way deeper and deeper into the valley. From our vantage point, the emerald quilt stretched to infinity. Since the terrain was so similar, one could easily get lost if hiking. With no discernable terrain features, you seemingly walk forever and become lost in an outdoor labyrinth of mystic greens.

Just as the valley posed an enigma to the weary traveler, the Buddhists often talk about the riddle of attachment in the journey of life. But the riddle is actually quite simple. One of the fundamental tenets of Buddhism is releasing attachment. To be happier, we must release our attachment to things, outcomes, events, and people. But what does this mean? Why should anyone ever want to give up on a goal of being successful? Why should we not desire love in our lives? What is wrong with wishing for peace among our fellow human beings? Does letting go of attachment mean we should give up on everything we hold dear in life? Of course not.

Letting go of attachment is based on the understanding that to liberate yourself from suffering, you have to let go of the delusion that happiness comes from outside you rather than from within. All living beings want two things: to end their suffering and to find happiness. But in the daily waltz of life, in our journey down the hallways of samsara, we must make choices. We either choose things that take us toward our goals or away from our goals. We choose paths that fulfill our desires or lead away from our most desired wish. The key is to realize that happiness doesn't come from achieving a goal or wish; happiness comes from within.

Say we have a goal; for instance, buying a house or finding a new job. We then construct and build a virtual roadmap that leads us toward this goal. We take steps to achieve our goal—we search for the job, we perform well at the interview, we sign the contract and then land the job. And guess what? When we have the new job, or new whatever, we find one simple truth: that we're not happy. So then we start the cycle again. We look for the next thing that will bring us happiness. We believe that we now need a new car. So we start comparing cars and looking at prices, because the car is going to give us the happiness that the new job didn't. And the cycle continues—we keep looking for a lighthouse amidst the black ocean, swimming to each flash of light only to find it was just a momentary reflection of the moon.

To conquer attachment, we must understand that obtaining the next thing or doing the next thing will not make us happy. This means we let go of things, events, and goals as we realize that these things will not bring us happiness. If we are happy already, we will not be disappointed by an unexpected event or outcome. And that whatever we do, the most important things in life are to show compassion, express joy, and be kind. That's the riddle of attachment: that you gain so much more by giving up so very little.

We arrived at our accommodations in the Valley of the Black-Necked Crane, a location in Bhutan so remote that there isn't any electricity. And at 9 PM, the hotel's electrical generator shuts down, leaving guests to warm themselves with woodburning stoves. Since it was early after-noon, Sonam was able to arrange a visit to the local monastic school and the abandoned temple under repair. We called before we arrived at the Gangtey Shedra. There, a young monk in crimson robes greeted us and unlocked the gate. Crossing a barbed-wire fence and cresting another hill, the school came into view. I was taken aback by what I saw.

All around the building, all along the temple of light, were signs of decay. Blocks were strewn about the perimeter. Holes were eating dark-ness into white walls. Weeds were creeping along steps. Wood was strewn about like someone opened and threw a box of toothpicks across the ground. I was surprised.

Crossing an open doorway into the inner courtyard, the inside of the structure wasn't much better. Walking to the edge of the square, we were led by the monk to Tibetan-style stairs. After climbing, we were shown to a corner room and asked to sit. In a few minutes, the head of the monastic school appeared.

ABANDONED TEMPLES, DARKER RAVENS

The head monk was very gracious. After providing us with tea and grains, he talked to me for thirty minutes about life, Buddhism, monastic traditions, and reincarnation. I was struck by what he told me about the soul entering the body for the first time.

Upon conception, when a woman's ovum is touched by a man's sperm, a tremendous amount of light and energy is released. Although the reaction is infinitesimally small, it is very powerful. The red female seed meets with the white male seed, and at the same time the seeds are joined by the blue spiritual seed of the soul. The blue seed holds the gene of the soul. All three seeds combine to create a triad of lifeforce and vitality. This is the embodiment and manifestation of a new sentient being. The soul's connection here is a bit ethereal. The soul can speak to the mother through dreams, and it can learn. And the soul can still travel; it is not permanently fixed.

If, for some reason, the fetus dies before birth, the soul is not destroyed. Rather, the soul leaves and searches for a new embodiment, hopefully in a loving and caring human situation and family. The soul is eternal and can simply incarnate in another womb. So continues the cycle of karma and samsara, until enlightenment frees us from our prisons of flesh, bone, and suffering.

After thanking the monk and retracing our steps, we left the school. On the other side of the ridge, past two knolls, stood the abandoned Gangtey Goenpa Monastery, which was under renovation. With Indian labor gone for the afternoon, we drove past earth-moving equipment and timbers the size of telephone posts that were stacked like bundles of pencils. Driving across a land bridge, with twenty-foot drops on each side, we reached the outer walls of the compound. Once we parked, we walked to the temple entrance on the opposite side.

Crossing the perimeter doorway, we entered another type of temple. This was someplace different, someplace darker. Inside the inner ward, a massive three-story structure had been built whose size and scope rivaled that of any temple we had seen thus far. Built of stone and wood, the architecture was impressive. The building's character, solid. In front was a covered courtyard area leading to an antechamber. Above, I could make out the large windows on the skin and corners of the temple. At the uppermost corners of the roofline, the heads of four garudas appeared, menacing and fierce.

Approaching the structure, we were greeted by the calls of no less than twenty ravens. The raven is the bird of Bhutan and symbolizes dharmapala, wrathful deities sent to protect sentient beings. But to be jeered by the caws of so many ravens was unsettling. The temple had the feel of an abandoned ghost town, desolate and lonely. It just didn't feel right. Moreover, when we first walked in, I felt something radiating heat from the left side of the temple perimeter. I was actually flushed on the entire left side of my body. I turned to look and see if there was anything like fire or smoke, indicators of combustion and radiant energy, but there wasn't a thing. And I didn't want to ask Sonam about it.

We quickly took some photos and left. I felt nervous. Something just didn't feel right. And it actually felt like we were being watched. Besides stupas, most Bhutanese stay away from temples and dzongs at nighttime. The legends say the fortresses are haunted, and not just by the spirits of long-dead monks.

Thinking about it now, maybe the ravens were acting as dharmapala and protecting us or warning us—warning us about something in the temple.

## CHAPTER 21
### Hope for the Future

———◄O►———

THE NEXT DAY, we finally arrived at Punakha. Stopping at the confluence of the green Mo Chhu and the blue Pho Chhu rivers, we observed the mighty Punakha Dzong in the distance. Located along the riverbank where the female and male waters meet, the monastery fortress was built as the second of Shabdrung Namgyal's centers of government and power. In the skies, the smoke from a forest fire provided the sun an eerie veil of white. Looking toward the castle, I could see purple flowers on a thin line of trees surrounding the walls. A solitary monk emerged from the monolith to wash his clothes.

Approaching the gray stone dzong, the view only became more impressive. I could see multiple roofs of gold and red, rosettes holding magical symbols, the beaks of garudas outlined by the sky, and intricate designs of blue and gold painted upon window frames. This was my moment of truth. I had a feeling my quest would end here.

Parking along the far riverbank, we off-loaded and made our way across a suspension bridge to the temple entrance. A flood from the previous year had washed away the permanent span. As I stepped on the wooden planks, I could feel the bridge sway to and fro with my weight. Beneath us, the cool waters of the river created an updraft of air and joy. Reaching the other side, we came upon a small grove of trees, followed by a convocation of prayer flags. Toward the right, our progress was blocked by an outer wall.

Three monks were at the gate. One was seated, two were standing. Sonam approached the seated sage, and with a few words, we were past the walled gates. Further in and to the left, towering steps emerged leading to the barbican. The way was arduous and narrow, like the path to enlightenment. At the top of the staircase was another platform with two monks, a scribe, and elite guards with automatic weapons at the ready. After showing the scribe our permit, we were allowed inside.

Past the gatehouse, the space opened to a much larger bailey. Inside, two groups of young monks passed us, the eldest monk no more than twelve years old. We were enclosed by two-story curtain walls and outer balconies, each adorned with designs of green dragons and bright cobalt and red pearls. In the center of the courtyard stood a holy tree. With a trunk the size of semi-truck, it must have been at least three hundred years old. Farther still, past the tree, was another doorway into the upper bailey and keep.

Following the path, we emerged into the courtyard, with a tower to the right and the main temple straight ahead. The hair on my arms stood on end. I felt individual beads of sweat on the back of my neck. My mouth was dry, and my hands trembled. On the handrails outside the temple, I noticed the golden spinning crosses. The temple's outer structure also matched my drawings. *I was here!* This was the temple in my dreams.

Sonam went to the keep and notified the head of the monastic order that we'd arrived. We were about to meet the Manchen Lopon, the highest-ranking religious leader, second only to the head of the entire Buddhist order in Bhutan. The Lopons are high masters with specialties in Buddhist tradition, liturgy, lexicography, and logic, but only one is entrusted to safeguard the sacred remains of Shabdrung Namgyal, kept in a secret burial vault in Punakha Dzong. Was this the high master who had called for me?

We would need to wait. The Queen of Bhutan was ahead of us and inside with the Manchen Lopon. But there was plenty of time, so I decided to explore the main temple. Walking toward the structure and taking off my shoes, I entered the sacred space and holy doorway to eternity.

Inside, the view was something out of a film, with the way the light shone through the ancient expanse. As I walked along the room, I noticed the faint smells of sandalwood incense and ancient pine. I felt grains of sawdust and dirt beneath my feet on the smooth wooden floors, rubbed soft after centuries of use. A breeze of cool air rushed past me. Along the walls, lovingly painted with deep awe and respect, was the story of Buddha, Siddhartha Gautama. I followed the brush strokes. A prince by noble birth, Gautama gave up the royal lineage after seeing incredible suffering. His mission was simple: to wander life as an ascetic and achieve enlightenment so that he, in turn, could show others the path to glory and oneness with the cosmos. The tale of his journey was drawn here—the escape from his palace, the refusal of various offers of rulership, as well as his attempt at starvation to achieve enlightenment. Also painted was his acceptance of a gift from a young girl: milk and rice that saved his life and thus alleviated his suffering. Afterward came the moment of his eventual enlightenment to become Shakyamuni, the Buddha of our current age. Shakyamuni taught humanity about the four noble truths.

First, life is about suffering. From the moment we are born until the last breath escapes our lips, we encounter situations that are difficult and challenge our concepts of right and wrong, good and evil, justice and tyranny. How do we react? Do we fall after seeing the acts of the unjust, participate in the cycle of suffering, and thus give up our sacred path? Or do we continue along the Wheel of Life in an effort to escape samsara?

Second, suffering comes from attachment. The root cause of our suffering is ignorance or delusion, which leads to unnecessary attachment to things both worldly and not of this world. We suffer because we *want*—we desire things, houses, goods, control, success—and we believe that happiness comes when we obtain these objects of our desires. But this is wrong, for this type of happiness is illusory and fleeting. True happiness comes only from within.

Third, suffering can be ended. We only suffer because we choose to ignore the path to enlightenment. We choose to shut our eyes to the greater destiny for humanity. Our future is to be enlightened beings, and our future is to one day travel the stars. This is our shared dream: to succeed and triumph over suffering.

Fourth, transcendence comes from following the middle way, or a path of moderation. We must avoid the demons of self-indulgence and self-imposed hardship. We must liberate ourselves by practicing right worldview, motivations, speech, actions, livelihood, effort, mindfulness, and concentration.

Liberation is opposite to gluttony. And the path to liberation is not about guilt. We love to feel guilty. "Woe is me" we say as time is spent feeling bad about ourselves and our failures. But our karmic mission in life is not to feel guilty and thereby experience more suffering; our mission is to be joyful, so we may help others on the path to liberation. Most important of all, no one else can liberate you. You must liberate yourself.

I walked toward the main altar and came upon the most beautiful golden statues of the Shabdrung, Guru Rinpoche, and Shakyamuni I had ever seen. Seated in a lotus position, all were adorned with gems, and flowers, and banners. At their feet were rice cakes forming suns of red, yellow, and blue. By their hands, flowers shaped like translucent butterfly wings were gently cradled as wisps of burning incense vapor slowly made its way toward the top of the room. From the ceiling were banners, streamers, and windsocks with alternating vibrant shades of blue, green, violet, red, orange, and yellow. The scene was breathtaking.

I was in the holiest temple in the entire country—perhaps even the most sacred Buddhist temple in the entire planet. Alone and at peace, I finally came to my knees and bowed. I was so thankful for the journey, thankful for the experience. I was glad to be breathing after traveling the deserts of Arizona, the jungles of Guatemala, and the majestic Himalayas. Glad for so many things, I felt such a feeling of peace. It was something that I had desperately longed for, yet it had eluded me for decades. As I wandered outside in a pleasant stupor, I came upon Sonam.

"He's ready for us," he said.

I gathered my gear. And into the cosmos, into the keep, two pilgrims walked. We were led through a series of rooms, up a flight of narrow stairs, and through other chambers, to be eventually seated near a window. After a few minutes, a holy man emerged. Stocky and tanned, wearing glasses and a crimson and tangerine robe, the Manchen Lopon sat down before us. And the stars turned.

"You're a bit late. Were you to arrive last week?" asked the master.

"Yes, and I apologize. Problems with transport," I replied. I had never told Sonam, but I had pushed my trip back a week because I couldn't get a Druk Air flight to Bhutan in April. But the Lopon knew. Of course he knew. He was the one who had called for me.

"Master Lopon, what is the first lesson of Buddhism?" I asked.

"You already know this. We talked about this months ago. The first lesson is reverence for every living being."

And he was correct. I kept journals of my dreams. And two months ago, in my dreams, the monk had told me the first lesson of Buddhism—

reverence for every living being. We must be reverent toward all life—from butterflies to people, from amoebas to eagles, and from ants to fish—all living creatures. We must respect and care for all life forms, since all carry the divine breath, the essence of creation.

"Master, these are the drawings of my dreams," I said as I took out the sketches. I unfolded the paper depicting flying dragons, spinning crosses, castles, and praying monks.

The lama nodded his head as he pointed to the spinning-cross design in my drawings and along the temple walkways. It was also an exact match.

"The dragon is our protector deity. The tomb you drew holds the remains of the Shabdrung. Very good," the lama replied. The Buddhist master confirmed the information I had gleaned about Punakha Dzong during my dreams.

"What is your next question?" He wasn't even fazed.

"Do the Buddhist texts talk of planetary suffering—about a great catastrophe and the destruction of the earth?" I asked.

The Buddhist master leaned forward and looked right into me. "Yes. The ancient texts tell us that the earth and the entire universe is made up of four elements: earth, water, fire, and air. When the gods created the universe, they used these four elements to make the land, to make plants, and to make beings who walk on the land and care for the plants."

"You mean humans?" I asked.

"Yes," he replied. "And just as the gods used these elements to make the world, so are human beings using these elements to make new life—engineering to make new crops, breeding of new animals, creation of new bacteria, even talk of creating new human beings.

"But in the beginning, the gods were wise; the gods had wisdom and power. Yet humans only desire the power. So when we use the power without wisdom, then we are acting as ignorant gods—gods that kill and will be destroyed by their own creations.

"So the texts say when human beings begin to act as gods, the world will be in great turmoil. And only through wisdom will humans survive," the elder finished.

"Master, then what do the texts say about the outcome?" I asked.

"It's up to us. We hold the power. Do we act with compassion or do we act out of fear and greed?"

"So, Master Lopon, how do we follow the Buddhist path, the path to enlightenment?" I asked.

"To begin living as a Buddhist, to be in harmony with the cosmos, you must have a clear mind. Your mind must be clear. Your mind must be like cold, clean, fresh water. Free of debris. Free of falsehoods. Free of hate and anger. Your mind must be clean.

"Did you see the bowls of clear water in our temples? Those bowls are refilled every day, every morning, with clean and fresh water. That is how your mind must be: clear. It doesn't matter if you meditate in a cave for one hundred years or even a thousand years. Your meditation is a waste of time if you do not have a clear mind."

"Master, life can be painful. Life can be filled with loss. Why is there suffering in the world? Why is there both good and evil?" I asked. This question has plagued me for years.

"This is just the nature of the world. There must be good and evil, there must be a conflict, because in that conflict we are able to make choices.

"If someone commits a great transgression against you, if someone treats you with hate and anger, and hurts you, do you respond with more hate? Do you embrace the evil, reflect it, and thus magnify it, ultimately becoming a part of that which hurt you? Or do you instead embrace goodness and respond with love and compassion?

"This is why there must be good and evil in the universe—so we can make choices. And either we choose to follow the teachings of the Buddha and embrace the dharma in an effort to escape samsara, or we choose hate, greed, and anger, and descend into the madness of the lower realms. This is the ultimate truth."

I had never heard a clearer explanation. Everything that seemed contradictory was actually very simple.

"Master Lopon, how do we improve our karma?" I asked.

"Karma is everything. Everything we do affects our karma. Look at your clothes, your shoes. Did any living beings die or suffer so you could wear those clothes? Your dinner: when you eat dinner tonight, did any living beings suffer so you could eat? Your transport: when you flew over, did any living beings die so you could arrive? That's where karma is—in every decision you make, from the clothes you wear to what you eat. To improve your karma, be knowledgeable and wise about what you do."

"Master Lopon, what can we do to escape samsara?" I continued.

"It's hard. It's very hard. We must have a clear mind. Only with a clear mind can we find happiness in everyone and with all living beings. We must do good deeds, we must always be happy with one another, we must embrace peace and share this vision of a new world. The main thing to do is control your conscious mind. You must have a clear mind, and you must eliminate hate and anger.

"If we really live with a clear mind, it will be much easier to break the cycle. But the journey is still very difficult, for we must eliminate all the accumulated karma from the sum of all our previous lives. We must wash away all bad things. We must wash away all our sins. Only by eliminating all negativity can we break the cycle of death and rebirth. The main thing is to possess a clear mind."

"Master Lopon, how many times do we reincarnate on the earth?" I asked.

"Thousands of times. Thousands upon thousands of times. It doesn't matter. The number of times doesn't matter. Our lives are like matchsticks, thousands of them stacked from floor to ceiling. It's unimportant how many matchsticks there are. What is important is how bright the flame burned."

"Master Lopon, tell me about Vajrayana," I asked.

"Ahhhh, the reason you think you are here. You are not here to learn about Vajrayana. But I will tell you," said the lama. He was right. I also came to Bhutan to discover the secrets of Vajrayana Buddhism, the diamond vehicle that provides transcendance in one lifetime.

"Vajrayana is a very ancient form, a very special type of Buddhism practiced by only a handful of monks."

"Only a handful of monks—why so few?" I asked.

"Because of its power. Monks who are on the Vajrayana path have special abilities. They are able to do things you or I would call miraculous: the ability to change wine to nectar, to appear in two places at once, and to fly."

"Master Lopon, do *you* practice Vajrayana?" I asked. He didn't answer directly.

"The reason so few are taught Vajrayana is because of its power. We don't want to create a race of super-beings who hunger for power and control over humanity. That's why there are so few, because of its power.

"This is how the process begins," he continued. "We first select monks who can demonstrate advanced abilities."

"You mean psychic abilities?" I asked.

"Yes, but the purpose of Buddhism and meditation as part of Buddhism is not to increase psychic abilities. The purpose of Buddhism is to eliminate samsara. Vajrayana can do this in one lifetime.

"But to walk the path of Vajrayana, you must have some form of psychic ability. It is similar to a lightning rod. You must be able to attract the energy and use it correctly. The danger is that the energy can be used for evil as well as for good. This is why the students we select are those that have chosen the path of goodness, the road to Nirvana—a path in harmony with the energy of light, a street devoid of those who seek power."

"So the monks who practice Vajrayana can transcend samsara in one lifetime," I repeated.

"Yes, but the purpose of Vajrayana is not to transcend samsara and become one with the cosmos. The purpose is to create bodhisattvas," said the master.

"What do you mean, 'to create bodhisattvas'?" I asked. A bodhisattva is a saint who has transcended the cycle of life and death, the cycle of samsara, but has chosen to return to earth again to aid other sentient beings on the path to liberation and enlightenment.

"By creating bodhisattvas, we open the doors to universal transcendence. With a greater number of ascended beings who choose to remain in the earth realm and help others, the chances for transcendence increase tremendously—like many pools reflecting the sun."

"So, then Vajrayana is about planetary transcendence," I said.

"Yes, this is the ultimate goal of Vajrayana: to allow humanity to transcend. To cross the golden doorway in the cosmos and never return to the world of suffering."

"How will that be done? How is that possible?" I desperately wanted to know.

"Only when there are enough illuminated beings. Only when there are enough ascended masters will the doors open. Our earth waits for a song. When we sound the right chords at the right intensity with the right volume—*that* is when the doors will open. All around the planet, in lakes, rivers, streams, in caves behind waterfalls, trees, and in mountains, doorways to the other world will open. That is the promise of Vajrayana. That is the key to transcendence."

"Then, Master Lopon, what is the essence of Vajrayana? What is the most important thing for us to know?" I inquired.

"The most important thing is that to become a bodhisattva, we must act like bodhisattvas. We must act like bodhisattvas now! There is no separation. There is no wall between the future and now; it is an illusion, for all existence is occurring at the same time.

"Why must we to wait to become bodhisattvas before we radiate peace and compassion? Why do we delay showing our love until we ascend? We don't have to.

"Listen, the monks who practice Vajrayana become bodhisattvas because they act like bodhisattvas *now*. They talk like ascended beings, they think like ascended beings, they walk through life as an ascended being would. That is how they become enlightened, that is how they ascend. There is no separation. The concept of then is now."

That was profound. It took me a few moments to regain my composure and think about the next question.

"So, Master, what can we learn from Vajrayana if we're not monks or even if we're not Buddhists?" I asked.

"First off, you're correct. Not everyone can be a monk. If everyone was a monk, then there would be no monks. All have roles to play in the Wheel of Life. Our world needs bakers, politicians, kings, weavers, farmers, sailors, and shipbuilders.

"But the lesson of Vajrayana is useful for all. If you want to be an ascended being, if you want liberation from the cycle of samsara, then act like you're already liberated. Live with compassion. Show love and devotion to your fellow human beings. Act as if you are bodhisattva *today*. Why wait eons to show compassion? Why wait hundreds of thousands of years to show kindness to your fellow living beings? Do it now!" spoke the lama.

"Master, do you have any messages for the planet?" I asked.

"I do. The key to peace is having inner peace. And the key to peace is love.

"If world leaders are at war with themselves, then they will seek war with others. The opposite is peace. If our leaders are at peace with themselves, if they show compassion, then they will share that peace with the rest of the world instead of fighting one another and bringing the world into a nightmare.

"Keep your mind clear, like pure water. Meditate on this. Have clean thoughts, conduct clean deeds.

"The key is always love and compassion. This has not changed since the time of the first Buddha. That's how we heal our planet. Love and compassion for all sentient beings—the trees, the flowers, the fish, the animals, and all living things. Reverence for all living things; that is how we begin the path."

With that, our conversation was complete. I presented my offerings to the Manchen Lopon—gemstones of turquoise, red coral, fire opal, and tiger-eye from the other side of the world. I humbly bowed toward the aged master and walked out of Punakha Dzong forever . . .

I SPENT A few days more in Bhutan, visiting the National Archives, climbing to the Takstang fortress, and touring Thimphu. On the way back to the States, I sojourned a few extra days in Thailand, visiting the grand temples of Bangkok, slowly reintegrating myself into the Western world. The time was both precious and vital. I awoke strong and revived, ready to step out of the dream pool and back to the land of the living.

# Epilogue

WE LIVE ON a remarkable planet. A world of individuals that are blessed, gifted, and bestowed with paranatural prowess—abilities that transcend the boundaries of space and time, heal the incurably ill, and give the rest of us hope. These healers provide us hope that the universe is larger than we could ever imagine. Hope that spiritual forces can protect us and guide us. And hope that through our efforts and our collective dream, we can heal the planet.

These are the elemental shamans who harness the forces of nature every single day of their lives. The journey began with the fire element—mysterious shamans who cleanse and purify through heat and flame, but beware the ash. In the desert, we learned about the earth element with the help of a Cherokee Spiritwalker. We learned about dealing with our past so that we may be more alive and awake in the present. The Spiritwalker taught us to how heal our base, our roots and our subconscious, to provide strength for our spiritual journey.

In the jungles of Guatemala, we met a Maya a'j r'ij, who taught us about the water element. We ourselves grow by having compassion for those who are ill. By letting go of judgments, we see the infirm for who they really are: human beings who are still extraordinary and precious. Madre Luna taught us about healing so that we may heal others. Our tears of love help us to grow. With a healthy body and outlook, we can walk consciously upon the planet, showing reverence for all and sharing our love.

In the Himalayas, we met a Buddhist master who gave us the air element. One day there will be planetary transcendence, but in the meantime, we must remain on the earth and honor all living beings. We can also realize the effects of good karma instantly. The time of dharma is now! Salvation is at hand. We create the future of the planet by the palms of our hands and with the beauty of our thoughts. With compassion and purpose, we can touch the superconscious and the infinite mind of God. But we must remain grounded and purposeful in this world.

We are the shamanic tree, the beautiful cosmic tree of the elemental shamans. The elements link us to the secrets of the cosmos. It is in us that we find fire, earth, water, and air—the mysteries of creation. We are the tree—with feet that provide us the strength of the earth, our bodies and spirit that grow through the waters of compassion, and our hands and dreams that touch the nirvana of higher consciousness. By healing ourselves, others, and the planet, we connect to all levels of the infinite— the collective subconscious, our consciousness, and the superconscious mind of God. By using this wisdom, we can reach the ultimate expression of our destiny, the elemental secret of what it means to be human.

Two months ago, I spent some time with His Holiness, the 14th Dalai Lama of Tibet. He answered my questions, held my hand, and taught me that the true purpose of life is to show compassion. And India was amazing. The views of the Himalaya Range jutting toward the dawn-lit sky were breathtaking. It turns out that most of the answers are indeed within us. The study of Buddhism provides us the blueprint for consciousness and the limitless expanse of our human potential. The all-encompassing clear light of Buddha-mind is the connection with the thoughts of all living beings—the single focus of a conscious universe. But that is a story for another day.

I'm not sure what the next journey will bring or where I'll find the next series of great ones and learned souls. Where my travels will take me, I am unsure. But the dreams are starting again. I keep seeing dragonflies, a monument to a prince, and a riddle lost to time. There's also grassy mountain slopes hiding lost trails that lead to infinity.

And the dreams of the woman with orange eyes are much stronger now. Will I ever find her? I remember bits and pieces of our dreamtime together. Will it be enough? And will she remember me?

My gear is ready, my bags are packed. Now I'm just waiting for the next set of clues. A flight leaves somewhere tomorrow, and I just might be on it.

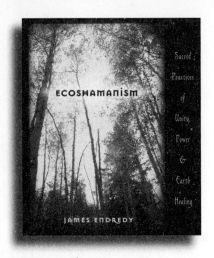

## Ecoshamanism

*Sacred Practices of Unity, Power and Earth Healing*

### James Endredy

In a society riddled with rampant consumerism and unsustainable technology, it's easy for everyone, including shamans, to lose touch with the natural world. James Endredy, who has learned from tribal shamans around the globe, presents a new philosophy of shamanic practice called ecological shamanism, or ecoshamanism. Designed to deliver well-being and spiritual harmony, ecoshamanism is the culmination of the visionary practices, rituals, and ceremonies that honor and support nature.

Exploring the holistic perspective of shamanism, Endredy encourages readers to establish a rewarding connection with sacred, life-giving forces using shamanic tools and practices. The author describes more than fifty authentic ecoshamanistic practices—including ceremonies, rituals, chanting, hunting, pilgrimage, and making instruments—that reinforce one's relationship with the natural world.

978-0-7387-0742-6, 360 pp., 7½ x 9⅛                    $19.95

## Beyond 2012

*A Shaman's Call to Personal Change and the*
*Transformation of Global Consciousness*

### James Endredy

War, catastrophic geologic events, Armageddon . . . The prophecies surrounding 2012—the end of the Mayan calendar—aren't pretty. James Endredy pierces the doom and gloom with hope and a positive, hopeful message for humankind.

For wisdom and guidance concerning this significant date, Endredy consults the "First Shamans," Tataiwari (Grandfather Fire) and Nakawe (Grandmother Growth). Recorded here is their fascinating dialog. They reveal how the evolution of human consciousness, sustaining the earth, and our personal happiness are all interconnected.

Discover what you can do to spur the transformation of human consciousness. See how connecting with our true selves, daily acts of compassion and love, focusing personal energy, and even gardening can make a difference. Endredy also shares shamanistic techniques to revive the health of our planet . . . and ourselves.

978-0-7387-1158-4, 240 pp, 7½ x 9⅛ $16.95

## The Sin Eater's Last Confessions

*Lost Traditions of Celtic Shamanism*

ROSS HEAVEN

Considered a madman in his English village, Adam Dilwyn Vaughan—a sin eater—was shunned by the same community who flocked to him for healing. This true tale records Ross Heaven's fascinating journey as the sin eater's apprentice, who is introduced to the lost art of sin eating and other Celtic shamanic traditions.

This spiritual memoir records the author's wondrous and moving experiences with the powerful energies of the natural world. He witnesses Adam removing negative energies from a patient, meets fairy folk, reads omens in nature, discovers his soul purpose through dreaming, goes on a vision quest in a sacred cave, and participates in a sin-eating ritual. Interlacing these remarkable events are Welsh legends and enlightening discussions that shed light on these mysterious practices and invite you to see the world through the eyes of a shaman.

Also included is a sin eater's workbook of the same shamanic exercises and techniques practiced by Adam.

978-0-7387-1356-4, 288 pp, 5 x 7 $16.95

---

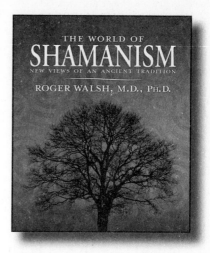

## The World of Shamanism
### *New Views of an Ancient Tradition*
### ROGER WALSH, M. D., PH.D.

After decades of being demonized by clergy, diagnosed by psychiatrist, and dismissed by academics, shamanism is thriving. So, what is fueling the West's new fascination with shamanism?

You'll find the answer and more in this objective exploration of shamanism and its place in contemporary life. Dr. Roger Walsh leaves no stone unturned as he examines shamanistic traditions throughout history, and how they intersect with modern psychology and metaphysical studies.

Are shamans enlightened or psychotic? Decide for yourself as Dr. Walsh unveils the life and mind of this revered figure. Delve into shamanic practices—healing, altered states of consciousness, journeying, channeling, vision quests—and discover if, how, and why they actually work. This cross-cultural, all-encompassing perspective will help you understand shamanism—its impact throughout history and its significance today.

978-0-7387-0575-0, 336 pp, 7½ x 9⅛                    $18.95

# By Oak, Ash & Thorn

*Modern Celtic Shamanism*

## D. J. CONWAY

Many spiritual seekers are interested in shamanism because it is a spiritual path that can be followed in conjunction with any religion or other spiritual belief without conflict. Shamanism has not only been practiced by Native American and African cultures—for centuries, it was practiced by the Europeans, including the Celts.

*By Oak, Ash & Thorn* presents a workable, modern form of Celtic shamanism that will help anyone raise his or her spiritual awareness. Here, in simple, practical terms, you will learn to follow specific exercises and apply techniques that will develop your spiritual awareness and ties with the natural world: shape-shifting, divination by the Celtic Ogham alphabet, Celtic shamanic tools, traveling to and using magic in the three realms of the Celtic otherworlds, empowering the self, journeying through meditation, and more.

Shamanism begins as a personal revelation and inner healing, then evolves into a striving to bring balance and healing into the Earth itself. This book will ensure that Celtic shamanism will take its place among the spiritual practices that help us lead fuller lives.

978-1-5671-8166-1, 320 pp., 6 x 9, illus.　　　　　$16.95

---

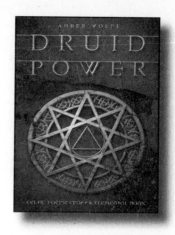

## Druid Power
### *Celtic Faerie Craft & Elemental Magic*
### AMBER WOLFE

### (FORMERLY TITLED ELEMENTAL POWER)

Gain greater personal awareness and increased magical power through the magic of Druidic tradition. Druid Power provides groundbreaking methods for self-transformation based on principles and practices of the Celtic Faerie Craft. By teaching spiritual development in the Celtic and Faerie Way, Amber Wolfe blends ancient Celtic ideas with modern psychology.

Readers learn how to reconnect with the natural world through traditional ceremonies, guided imagery, breath work, and other shamanic techniques. Packed with powerful rituals, historical references, and valuable techniques for spiritual growth, Druid Power is an invaluable resource for new journeyers or advanced Celticists.

978-0-7387-0588-0 288 pp., 6 x 9, illus.　　　　　$15.95

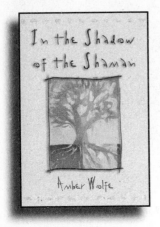

## In the Shadow of the Shaman

*Connecting with Self, Nature & Spirit*

AMBER WOLFE

Presented in what the author calls a "cookbook shamanism" style, this book shares recipes, ingredients, and methods of preparation for experiencing some very ancient wisdoms: of Native American and Wiccan traditions, as well as contributions from other philosophies of nature as they are used in the shamanic way. Wheels, the circle, totems, shields, directions, divinations, spells, care of sacred tools, and meditations are all discussed. Wolfe encourages us to feel confident and free to use her methods to cook up something new, completely on our own. This blending of ancient formulas and personal methods represents what Ms. Wolfe calls Aquarian Shamanism.

*In the Shadow of the Shaman* is designed to communicate in the most practical, direct ways possible, so that the wisdom and the energy may be shared for the benefits of all. Whatever your system or tradition, you will find this to be a valuable book, a resource, a friend, a gentle guide, and support on your journey. Dancing in the shadow of the shaman, you will find new dimensions of Spirit.

978-0-8754-2888-8, 384 pp., 6 x 9, illus.                    $16.95

---

To order, call 1-877-NEW-WRLD
*Prices subject to change without notice*
ORDER AT LLEWELLYN.COM 24 HOURS A DAY, 7 DAYS A WEEK!

## The Mystic Foundation
*Understanding & Exploring the Magical Universe*

### CHRISTOPHER PENCZAK

The sheer number of mystical traditions in the world can be overwhelming to seekers new to the metaphysical world. Summing up the universal truths underlying many mystic institutions, *The Mystic Foundation* is an initial step toward understanding the wisdom of each.

This nondogmatic primer outlines the mystical teachings of Paganism, Christianity, Islam, and other spiritualities spanning Eastern and Western traditions. Penczak transforms complex subjects and ideas—such as the powers of creation, life forces, elements, the world beyond, spirit entities, sacred space and time, magic, and metaphysical skills—into easy-to-understand concepts. Each chapter features exercises—including meditation, aura cleansing, chakra balancing, and psychic travel—to help seekers "go within" and ground themselves in a variety of mystic beliefs. By the end of the book, readers will have a solid foundation in mysticism for choosing a path of their own.

978-0-7387-0979-6, 336 pp., 7½ x 9⅛          $15.95

## To Write to the Author

If you wish to contact the author or would like more information about this book, please write to the author in care of Llewellyn Worldwide and we will forward your request. Both the author and publisher appreciate hearing from you and learning of your enjoyment of this book and how it has helped you. Llewellyn Worldwide cannot guarantee that every letter written to the author can be answered, but all will be forwarded. Please write to:

Omar W. Rosales
c/o Llewellyn Worldwide
2143 Wooddale Drive, Dept. 978-0-7387-1501-8
Woodbury, Minnesota 55125-2989
Please enclose a self-addressed stamped envelope for reply,
or $1.00 to cover costs. If outside U.S.A., enclose
international postal reply coupon.

Many of Llewellyn's authors have websites with additional information and resources. For more information, please visit our website at http://www.llewellyn.com.